STUDIES IN PHILOSOPHY

XXII

HORACE BUSHNELL'S THEORY OF LANGUAGE

In the Context of Other Nineteenth-Century Philosophies of Language

by

DONALD A. CROSBY
Colorado State University

1975
MOUTON
THE HAGUE · PARIS

ISBN: 90 279 3044 9

Printed in The Netherlands by Mouton & Co., The Hague

To Jack and Mary Lou

ACKNOWLEDGEMENT

Publication of this book has been assisted by a grant from Colorado State University, through its Faculty Improvement Committee.

PREFACE

Horace Bushnell was a New England Congregational minister who lived from 1802 to 1876, serving for most of his life as pastor of the North Church in Hartford, Connecticut. He was a prolific writer as well as a noted preacher, and he made a decisive impact on the theological thinking of his time. In 1849 he published a work called *God in Christ*, which George Hammar has correctly characterized as marking the opening of the liberal era in American Trinitarian theology.[1] This liberal era or the period of the "new theology", as it has often been termed, enjoyed a long life, stretching from 1849 down to about the end of the second decade of the present century. With Bushnell as its hinge, it was the successor of the so-called "New England theology", which had taken its rise in the time of Jonathan Edwards and had as its last great defender Edwards Amasa Park of Andover Theological Seminary.[2]

God in Christ consisted of three discourses on theological themes which Bushnell had delivered in somewhat different form before theological schools at Andover, Harvard, and Yale, in the year preceding the book's publication. Introducing the volume, however, was something new: a writing entitled "A Preliminary Dissertation on Language". Mary Bushnell Cheney, daughter of Bushnell and his first biographer, has emphatically stated that the theory of language set forth here "*is the key to Horace Bushnell*, to the whole scheme of his thought, to that peculiar manner of

[1] George Hammar, *Christian Realism in Contemporary American Theology* (Uppsala, Sweden, 1940), 127.
[2] Park retired from Andover in 1881, having taught there for a period of forty-five years.

expression which marked his individuality, — in a word, to the man".[3] Bushnell's own words bear out this assessment of the importance of his language theory to the rest of his thinking, for he stated in *God in Christ* that there was "an intimate, or interior connection ... between all these 'Discourses', and the views of language presented in this 'Preliminary Dissertation'". And he went on to request "that this 'Dissertation' may receive a little more attention than is ordinarily given to Introductions. For, if these views of language have been historically introductory to me, it is hardly possible that others will enter fully into my positions without any introduction at all."[4] One of the purposes of this study is to demonstrate in detail the "intimate, or interior connection" of which Bushnell spoke. To delve into his theory of language is to do far more than cast an incidental sidelight upon the man. It is to probe very close to the heart of his thinking. And given his recognized importance as the inaugurator of a new trend of thought in the theology of New England, demonstration of this fact alone would be ample justification for a study of the type that is here offered.

But there are other justifications. One is that the language theory itself is a masterful synthesis of a number of important cultural currents in nineteenth century America. When these are brought out, as I have attempted to do, Bushnell's rank as a contributor to the development of American culture is considerably enhanced. For instance, Bushnell saw in the burgeoning linguistic science implications for theological thinking no less sweeping than those discerned in the Darwinian science by the theologians of the next generation. His language theory appropriated leading elements in the Transcendentalist protest and served a function in Trinitarian New England similar to that served by Emerson and his sympathizers in Unitarian Boston. It reflected the strong romantic sentiment which welled up in so many ways in nineteenth-century America, and it mirrored the great European romantic movement.

---

[3]   Mary B. Cheney, *Life and Letters of Horace Bushnell* (New York: Charles Scribner's Sons, 1903), 203.
[4]   Horace Bushnell, *God in Christ* (New York: Charles Scribner's Sons 1903), 102.

It caught up some of the themes of the greatest of the continental theologians of the period, Friedrich Schleiermacher. It captured the embryonic ecumenical spirit of the benevolent enterprises that were bringing so many laymen and clergymen of different denominations into cooperative labor at a time when most of the theologians of those denominations were scarcely on speaking terms. It lifted into the clear light of day a symbolic consciousness which, though powerful, had lain submerged in the era of the Puritans under an anti-symbolic theory of discourse and which continued to be repressed in the New England of Bushnell's time by a prevailing view of language owing its impetus to Locke and the Scottish Common Sense philosophers. From the standpoint of cultural history alone, then, the theory of language put forward by Bushnell is eminently worthy of our attention.

A third justification is simply that the theory of language is stimulating and provocative in its own right. And this is particularly true in our time, where the problem of language in its relation to thought — especially poetic, religious, and metaphysical thought — has been so much discussed. The reader can judge for himself whether Bushnell has anything fresh or different to offer. But certainly he was ahead of his own time and foreshadowed much of what is now being said in defense of the truth value and meaningfulness of "non-scientific" ways of speaking.

The content of the chapters of this book may be very briefly characterized. Chapter One is an exposition, with little critical response at that point on the part of the writer, of Bushnell's language views, as these were developed in several of his works. This chapter also cites most of the writings of other men Bushnell explicitly made reference to in his works on language. Chapters Two and Three are attempts to place Bushnell's theory of language in the context of other discussions, most of them American, of the origin and development of language and of the relation of language to thought. Chapter Four brings out the connection between Bushnell's language theory and a new stress upon the poetic quality of the Bible, on the one hand, and also upon eloquence as the ideal form of language, on the other. Considerable space is also devoted in this chapter to a discussion of the affinities in viewpoint between Bushnell and another language theorist of the nineteenth century whose work has gained considerable notice of late, namely, Alexander Bryan Johnson. Chapter Five probes into the background of thinking implicit in Bushnell's metaphysics of nature, a fundamental element in his language theory. Attention is given here principally to the American Transcendentalists and to the Puritans and Jonathan Edwards. Chapter Six exhibits the use to which Bushnell put his language theory as a theological method, showing in a detailed way how it enabled him to explore and deal with the doctrine of the Trinity. By way of contrast the chapter also includes a discussion of Andrews Norton's attacks on Trinitarian theology and Nathaniel W. Taylor's defense of it, insofar as both of these were rooted in the prevailing conception of language. The final chapter is an inquiry into a number of criticisms which were leveled against Bushnell's language theory in the religious periodicals at mid-century, using these as a point of reference from which to explicate further some of the theory's implications and to come to some conclusions on its enduring worth. The chapter closes with a very brief excursus into the question of the role actually played by the language theory itself in the reorienting of theological thought which took place in New England after Bushnell.

Let me conclude this preface by expressing my indebtedness to Joseph Blau, who first suggested this topic to me and has given invaluable aid along the way, and also to Robert Handy and James A. Martin, who have stimulated me greatly by their suggestions and criticisms. I wish also to thank an earlier teacher of mine, Loefferts Loetscher, who first awoke in me a keen interest in nineteenth century American thought. Cheerfully taking the risk of banality, I also want to express my deep-felt gratitude to my wife Charlotte, who has made sacrifices innumerable in order for me to bring this project to completion.

D.A.C.

CONTENTS

I

THE THEORY OF LANGUAGE

> We can never come into a settled consent in the
> truth, until we better understand the nature,
> capacities and incapacities of language, as a
> vehicle of truth.
>
> *God in Christ* (1849)

Horace Bushnell gave sustained treatment to his theory of language
in three published writings. The first was a "Preliminary Dissertation on the Nature of Language as Related to Thought and Spirit",
which occupied fully one-third of the length of his most controversial book, *God in Christ* (1849). The second was a defense and
expansion at some points of the conceptions laid down in the
"Preliminary Dissertation". This constituted the opening chapter of
Christ in Theology (1851) and bore the heading "Language and
Doctrine". The third writing devoted to the language theme was an
essay entitled "Our Gospel a Gift to the Imagination", first
published in the *Hours at Home* magazine in 1869, and later in-
corporated into the posthumously published volume, *Building Eras
in Religion* (1881). The purpose of the present chapter is to give a
unified presentation of Bushnell's language theory as it was developed in these three writings. An analysis of the background of
thought out of which the theory arose, an appraisal of its significance for its times, and an estimate of its enduring value are
matters which have been reserved for discussion in later chapters.

1. THE ORIGIN OF LANGUAGE

Many early language theorists, guided as much by apologetic as by linguistic concerns, had sought in language a proof of the original unity of the human race, trying to trace behind existing languages the original primitive tongue which, as it was commonly believed, had been directly given by God to Adam in Eden.[1] Bushnell denied the feasibility of this attempt on several grounds. For one thing, he felt that its advocates, in trying to support the biblical account, actually tended to deny it. For the Scriptures taught, not that God had himself pronounced the words of language to Adam or framed them into grammar, but only that he had given him an *instinct* for language, leaving him and his progeny with the task of developing it for themselves. Moreover, no matter how the first language came into being, the Tower of Babel story made it clear that *that* language was in existence no longer; hence the futility of any attempt to prove the original unity of the human race on the basis of existing languages.

For another thing, the linguistic evidence of the day seemed to weigh heavily against any hope of arriving at a single tongue behind the diverse ones of the world. The few common terms found sprinkled through several languages were overbalanced, Bushnell thought, by the innumerable diverse ones, and the latter argued more conclusively for originally distinct languages than the former could for a single primitive one. And although the philologists had succeeded in pointing to certain definite groupings of languages, such as the Indo-Germanic group, it was unlikely in the highest degree that they would ever succeed in showing a common original behind such completely dissimilar tongues as, say, the Chinese, the American aboriginal, and the Indo-Germanic. In the researches of men like Johann Adelung and Wilhelm von Humboldt, Bushnell thought he saw a definite trend among the students of language toward a position in which the original diversity of languages would be recognized and the quest for an underlying unity abandoned.

But the most important reason for Bushnell's objection to the theory of a divinely-taught original language was the conviction that it implied false conclusions concerning the nature and capacities of language as an instrument of thought. "To understand the

---

[1]   See below, Chapter II.

precise power of words, or the true theory of their power, without some reference to their origin, will be difficult or impossible; for it is, in fact, the mode of their origin that reveals their power."[2] It will soon become apparent why he thought this was so.

Bushnell believed that after the dispersion of Babel separate small families or circles had been thrown back upon their linguistic instincts, each to develop a language in its own way. How, then, would they have proceeded? It was his hypothesis that they would have to have begun by attaching sounds to objects and actions in the physical world. Some words would no doubt be arrived at onomatopoetically, but the great majority would have to have been determined arbitrarily, or, at least, by causes so hidden or remote as to defy analysis. In time a string of nouns or a noun-language[3] would have been built up. Up to this point even animals are capable of language, for they can learn, even if on a much smaller scale than men, how to associate names or sounds with physical things.

But the distinctive and remarkable thing about human language is its provision of names for the interior sentiments and thoughts of the mind. How could this capacity have been developed? Bushnell's reply was that it could only have been developed through the mediation of objects and actions in the sensible world. A system of intellectual discourse had to be generated out of the names for such objects and actions already contained in the noun-language. The whole process had already been suggested by the gestures and

---

[2] Bushnell, *God in Christ* (New York: Charles Scribner's Sons, 1903), 13.

[3] Bushnell held "that verbs are originally mere names of acts, or phenomena of action, not distinguished from what are called nouns, or names of things, until use settles them into place in propositions or forms of affirmation. A *shine* and a *run* are names of appearances, just as a *sun* and a *river* are names of appearances. And when these names are strung together, in the use, the *sun* and the *shine*, the *river* and the *run*, the idea of subject and predicate becomes associated, and the grammatical relation of subject and predicate is developed as a law of speech between them." In another place he stated that "verbs, prior to the formation of grammar, are only the nouns or names of actions." (*God in Christ*, 27-28; 20). The names of actions, then, could not qualify for the designation "verb" until they stood in a predicate relation to a subject, that is, until a basic law of grammar had been developed. Prior to that time verbs were only "nouns" in the etymological sense of that term, i.e. they "named" actions (*noun* from Latin *nomen*).

expressions by which men without a language would first try to communicate their thoughts and emotions, for when the name of the physical action had been determined, it could serve also as a sign for the inner state. By the same "simple force of nature" the whole interior world came to be symbolized and figured by the system of physical names, now elevated to the plane of metaphor.

Bushnell was certain that this hypothesis concerning the origin of language was indicated by the etymological and grammatical evidence. The most abstract words could be found to have physical images inherent in their roots. Though the philologists had not always been able to trace out the physical base of a word, they had no doubt that it was there. Adjectives and adverbs were formed out of original nouns, as were prepositions and conjunctions.[4] Inflections are simply spatial relationships transferred into the intellectual realm. As documentation for this last point Bushnell cited an article by Josiah Gibbs, the Yale orientalist and philologist who had been his teacher, in which Gibbs had tried to show that the four cases of nouns represent the *where*, the *whence*, the *whither*, and the *by* or *through what place* of predicates.[5] Just as the etymological bases of words are in space, so they are declined into grammar under the relations of space. Only time and usage could have produced a complete grammar, and language could therefore roughly be said to have evolved through the three stages of development of physical terms, development of intellectual terms, and development of grammar. However, Bushnell qualified this last statement by saying that the relations of some things in space are such as to suggest embryonic laws of grammar even as they are noticed and named, and a rudimentary tendency toward grammar must also have been present in the very first efforts toward speech.

---

[4] "Thus a *warm*, that is, a sensation of warmth, being always spoken of in connection with some object in which the warmth resides, will become an appendant word, or ad-jective. Adverbs will be formed out of original nouns or names of things in a similar way." The preposition *through* and the noun *door* could be shown to have the same root. Horne Tooke and other philologists had traced the conjunction *and* to the imperative mood of *add*, or *an-add* contracted (*God in Christ*, 26-27).

[5] J. Gibbs, "Historical and Critical View of Cases in the Indo-European Languages", *The Christian Spectator*, 9 (1837), 109-134; 415-434.

The rest of Bushnell's theory of language consisted of implications which he drew from this account of its origin. The first implication, to which we must now turn, was metaphysical in character, and on it depended, as Bushnell thought, the very possibility of language as we know it.

2. THE LOGOS IN NATURE OR THE ANALOGY BETWEEN MATTER AND MIND

The fact that a vocabulary and grammar derived from man's experience in the outer world could be so easily suited to the uses of his mental life intrigued and fascinated Bushnell. Unlike most other language theorists, he refused to take this fact for granted and insisted that it lays open a momentous metaphysical principle. "On the one hand, is form; on the other, is the formless. The first represents, and is somehow fellow to, the other; how, we cannot discover."[6] Mystified though he was, Bushnell yet reasoned that there must be some "hidden analogy" which makes this possible. The metaphysical principle that seemed to be thus required was that there is a "logos" in the outer world which answers to the logos or internal reason of thinking beings. Nature is

a vast menstruum of thought and intelligence. There is a logos in the forms of things by which they are prepared to serve as types of images of what is inmost in our souls; and then there is a logos also of construction in the relations of space, the position, qualities, connections and predicates of things, by which they are framed into grammar. In one word, the outer world, which envelopes our being, is itself language, the power of all language .... And if the outer world is the vast dictionary and grammar of thought we speak of, then it is also itself an organ throughout of Intelligence.[7]

This Intelligence moulded into the forms of nature is nothing other than the Intelligence of God, and the logos, or analogical property in things, is woven into them by the Divine Logos "who is in the world".[8] But perhaps because this latter way of putting the

---

6   Bushnell, *God in Christ*, 43.
7   Bushnell, *God in Christ*, 30.
8   Bushnell, *God in Christ*, 43.

matter seemed to smack too much of pantheism,[9] Bushnell in his later work *Christ in Theology* tended to trace the analogic property in nature from the fact of its creation by God.

if the creation of the world be issued from God, it must represent the mind by which it is conceived, and must, in all its particular forms or objects, reveal those archetypes of thought in God which shaped them in their birth. I can not but suspect that there is an eternal and necessary connection between the *forms* God has wrought into things, — thus into language, — and the contents, on the one hand, of his own mind, and the principles, on the other, of all created mind.[10]

Bushnell's allusions to Plato and the Egyptian Hermes show that the Platonism of these statements was not merely unconscious with him, and it is notable that other writers he cited in this connection, Swedenborg, Origen, Kepler, and the English naturalist and divine who authored one of the famous Bridgewater Treatises, William Kirby,[11] were all profoundly influenced by the Platonic philosophy.

Bushnell was emphatic in declaring that such a metaphysical principle required that there be nothing accidental or arbitrary about the fitness of particular natural images to express particular thoughts or sentiments. He observed that

there is always some reason in every form or image made use of, why it should be used; some analogic property or quality which we feel in-

---

[9] Critics of *God in Christ* were quick to accuse Bushnell of being a pantheist. Cf. for example, C. A. Goodrich's first article entitled "What Does Dr. Bushnell Mean?" *The New York Evangelist*, 20, 13 (Mar. 29, 1849), 49; and Enoch Pond's *Review of Dr. Bushnell's 'God in Christ'* (Bangor, Maine: B. F. Duren, 1849), 22.

[10] Bushnell, *Christ in Theology* (Hartford: Brown and Parsons, 1851), 36, 31. In this second formulation of his Logos Concept Bushnell reflects the influence of a masterful article written in defense of his views by a licentiate for the ministry from his own church, Henry M. Goodwin. In this article a lengthy section was devoted to a discussion of the relation of language to nature. Henry M. Goodwin, "Thoughts, Words, and Things", *Bibliotheca Sacra*, 6 (1849), 271-300.

[11] Bushnell, *Christ in Theology*, 37-38. Kirby's work was entitled *On the Power, Wisdom and Goodness of God, as Manifested in the Creation of Animals and in their History, Habits, and Instincts*, 2 vols. (London: William Pickering, 1835). Bushnell quoted from II, 524. Kirby's Platonism was imbibed at least in part from the Cambridge Platonist Henry More. See II, 254-255.

stinctively, but which wholly transcends speculative inquiry. If there is no lineal straightness in rectitude, no linear crookedness or divarication in sin, taken as an internal state, still it is the instinct of our nature to feel some sense of correspondence between these images and the states they represent.[12]

Thus John Locke, despite the admitted close affinities of his views on language with those of Bushnell, had erred at a vital point in declaring that the significance of words is given "by a perfectly arbitrary imposition",[13] for this seemed to imply that there is no analogy whatever between the images in words and the thoughts they come to represent. And the German scholar, Friedrich Schlegel, while correctly grounding words in the creative Logos, had unfortunately adhered to a "very transcendental theory" in which the vocal sounds themselves, and not simply the types or bases of words, were thought to be the key to the idea of the innermost being of a creature or thing.[14] Finally, Frederick Rauch, the late President of Marshall College, in his textbook on psychology, had grounded the possibility of language on an "identity" of reason and nature, rather than on the *analogy* between them, thus failing to perceive that the terms of spirit and intellect come under a wholly different law, with regard both to their origin and interpretation, from the terms of sense.[15] Bushnell expressed great amazement that no writer on language, in fact, seemed to have caught the significance of this distinction, especially as it related to matters of moral and religious inquiry and the task of theology.

His conception of the analogy of intellect in nature led Bushnell to the expectation that an advance in mental and religious truth

[12] Bushnell, *God in Christ*, 42.
[13] See Locke's *Essay Concerning Human Understanding*, ed. Alexander Fraser (New York: Dover Publications, 1959), Vol. II, 12.
[14] Bushnell quoted from Schlegel's Third Lecture in the series on the *Philosophy of Language (Philosophie der Sprache)*, delivered in Dresden in 1828-29. This work appeared in English translation in 1847: *The Philosophy of Language in a Course of Lectures*, by Frederick von Schlegel, trans. A. J. W. Morrison (London: Henry G. Bohn). The English in which Bushnell quotes the passage found on p. 397 of the Morrison translation does not match that translation, however, and I have been unable to discover the means by which he gained access to Schlegel's thought.
[15] See F. A. Rauch, *Psychology* (New York: M. W. Dodd, 1844), 256.

beyond the current "multifarious industry of debate and system-making" would be linked at least in part to the advance of the physical sciences. While admitting that he could see this matter "but dimly" and could only "faintly express, or indicate" it, he asserted:

physical science, leading the way, setting outward things in their true proportions, opening up their true contents, revealing their genesis and final causes and laws, and weaving all into the unity of a real universe, will so perfect our knowledges and conceptions of them, that we can use them, in the second department of language, with more exactness ... language will be as much more full and intelligent, as it has more of God's intelligence, in the system of nature, imparted to its symbols. For undoubtedly, the whole universe of nature is a perfect analogon of the whole universe of thought or spirit. Therefore, as nature becomes truly a universe only through science revealing its universal laws, the true universe of thought and spirit cannot sooner be conceived.[16]

Bushnell's language theory was founded on the conviction that physical objects, in their laws of relationship, furnished the ground for the symbolism of intellectual discourse, with its grammar and propositional logic, and it was only reasonable for him to surmise that increased penetration and insight into the one would give new power and precision to the other. Thus, the commonplace observation that on account of the impact of science "it is not the same world to think in, that it was",[17] had its explanation for him not simply in the idea that science gives new orientations to the mind, but even more fundamentally in the belief that scientific advance sharpens the mind's tool, language. This belief, in its turn, was founded on the premise of an "inner light of divine thought"[18] in the objects and laws of nature.

Bushnell's observations on this point bring to mind a remark made about him by a man whom he deeply influenced, Theodore Munger: "It is pathetic to think of him as standing on the borderland of evolution but not entering it. Few would have so fully grasped its central meaning, and so clearly traced it to its divine

16   Bushnell, *God in Christ*, 78-79.
17   Bushnell, *God in Christ*, 79.
18   Bushnell, *Christ in Theology*, 38.

conclusion."[19] Still, the sweeping changes introduced into the language of philosophers and theologians by the evolutionary science in the late nineteenth and twentieth centuries bears out at least in part the idea that Bushnell had labored to express. For terms once entirely "physical" in their import were adapted to the whole range of metaphysical, ethical, and epistemological inquiry.

It was not in the nature of Bushnell, however, to spin theories about the future and forget the needs of the present. The languages of the future, by aid of an advancing science, might well be "much more full and intelligent" than the ones then at hand. But men had to make the best use of what they had, and there was room for worlds of improvement in the comprehension of the theologians of New England of the principles of the language they already possessed.[20]

3. THE DIALECTIC OF FORM AND THE FORMLESS

Given what Bushnell called the "two-departmental" character of language, the one department descriptive of objects and relations in space, and the other department applicable to the inner states of the intellect, how should their relationship to one another be conceived? It was in failing to answer or even to pose this question that Bushnell felt that other theories of language had proved inadequate, and it was here also that he felt that theologians had committed some of their most characteristic mistakes.

He declared, to begin with, that it was important to recognize that not even in the physical department of language can words exactly represent particular things. Whether one were Nominalist or Realist, he would have to acknowledge that words name only

---

[19] Theodore Munger, *Horace Bushnell* (Boston, Houghton, Mifflin and Company, 1889), 344.
[20] In fact, he criticized such prominent divines as Richard Baxter and Nathaniel W. Taylor for dwelling on the language problem only to the extent of drawing wistful comparisons between the imperfections of our present sensibly oriented language and the perfect spiritual language we could expect to have in heaven. *Christ in Theology*, 25-30.

genera, never individuals.[21] To be even more precise, they represent only certain groupings of sensations. As a discerning philosoper of language, Alexander Johnson, had shown, this fact provides opportunity for serious mistakes and fallacies even in reference to matters purely physical.[22]

But at least the objects referred to in the first department of language possessed the definiteness of form, while "Thoughts, ideas, mental states, we cannot suppose to have any geometric form, any color, dimensions, or sensible qualities whatever".[23] Thus, given a word which already refers only imprecisely to a physical form to be applied to the formless states and ideas of the mind, its inexactitude of signification in the second stage of its use is bound to be considerably increased. Add to this the fact that in its intellectual signification it can name only a *genus* of thoughts and sentiments while it will be continually applied to *particular* states or conceptions of the mind, and it would seem no wonder that men fall so easily into disputes that are at bottom only verbal.

The problem was compounded even further by what Bushnell took to be a seductive tendency in words to impute the forms inherent in their roots to the formless truths they were intended to convey.[24] On the much debated question of whether any thought at all is possible without language he affirmed: "The truth-feeling power of the soul may have truth present immediately to it, or may directly intuit truth, without symbols or representations of lan-

---

[21] Bushnell wrote "only of genera, not of individuals or *species*" (my italics), but certainly words can stand for species of things. Moreover, there are words which can stand for particular things, namely, proper nouns, though even these can be applied separately to a number of individuals.

[22] Johnson's *Treatise on Language, or the Relations of Words to Things* was published in 1836. A new edition of this classic has been edited by David Rynin and was published by the University of California Press in 1947 and 1959. Johnson hammered at this point throughout his work.

[23] Bushnell, *God in Christ*, 41.

[24] Charles Feidelson alleges that "when Bushnell refers to the 'formlessness' of truth, he seems to mean a universal potentiality of form". *Symbolism and American Literature* (Chicago: University of Chicago Press, 1953), 153. But while he did hold that truth can clothe itself in an infinite variety of forms, I think he means more simply that truth, like thought, is formless in the sense of having no "geometric form ... or sensible qualities whatever", *God in Christ*, 41.

guage."[25] But as soon as the thinker moved beyond intuition he was compelled to make use of form. The moment the soul would think discursively, or represent to another any subject of thought, that subject must be clothed in forms that are only signs or analogies, and not equivalents of the truth. Even definitions and the most abstract modes of terminology will be true only in a sense more or less visibly formal and analogical.[26]

Even if a word were utilized whose original form was lost or un-known, there would be the instinctive need to give it some kind of form or outward representation, in order to endow it with meaning. There was the factor, moreover, of what Bushnell called the "latent presence" of the original forms or roots in words which stood by them with a stubborn persistence, regulating their significance within certain limits even in the hands of those totally ignorant of etymologies.[27]

This presence of form in all words was but another proof of the ambiguity and inaccuracy of language. For while on the one hand the form guarded the meaning of terms and provided an indis-pensable clue to their sense,[28] it was on the other hand an element in them which continually threatened to distort their meanings. The incautious thinker could be beguiled by the form in his words into forgetting that the terms of sense and those of intellect come under a wholly different law of interpretation. By failing to master the subtle art of continually separating "between the husks of the forms and the pure truths of thought presented in them", a thinker

---

[25] Bushnell, *Christ in Theology*, 15.

[26] Bushnell, *Christ in Theology*, 15.

[27] To illustrate this point Bushnell declared: "The Latin word *gressus* ... is one that originally describes the measured tread of dignity, in distinction from the trudge of a clown, or footpad. Hence the word *congress*, can never after, even at the distance of thousands [sic] of years, be applied to the *meeting* or *coming together* of outlaws, jockeys, or low persons of any description. It can only be used to denote assemblages of grave and elevated personages, such as councillors, men of science, ambassadors, potentates." *God in Christ*, 51.

[28] Bushnell contended that, despite the seductions of the form element in words, a "wonderful light" is shed upon them, in most cases, "by the simple opening of their etymologies". He insisted that even the most diverse meanings of a given word could be found "to have a clear historic reference to its radical type, and to grow out from it, by a perfectly natural process", *God in Christ*, 54-55.

could fall to the level of "a mere logician ... spinning his deductions out of the form of the word".[29] Thus in discussing a great question like human liberty he would be

> overpowered by the terms and predicates of language; which being mostly derived from the physical world, are charged, to the same extent, with a mechanical significance. And then we shall have a sophism ... all a mere outward practice ... on words and propositions, in which, as they contain a form of cause and effect in their own nature, it is easily made out that human liberty is the liberty of a scale-beam, turned by the heavier weights. Meantime, the question is only a question of consciousness, one in which the simple decision of consciousness is final; — to which, argument, whether good or bad, can really add nothing, from which nothing take.[30]

Given this inexactitude in language and the recognition that "the words, whose ambiguity is most frequently overlooked, and is productive of the greatest amount of confusion of thought and fallacy, are among the *commonest*, and are those whose meaning the generality consider there is least room to doubt,"[31] how could a hopeless skepticism regarding the adequacies of language as the instrument of thought be avoided?

Bushnell was certain that it could never be avoided along the path generally proposed. It was commonly assumed that semantic precision could be achieved by a careful process of abstracting and defining the meanings of words and that the norm of proper reasoning is the employment of terms thus settled in their significance in logical operations perfectly analogous to algebra.[32] But if

---

[29] Bushnell, *God in Christ*, 49-50. By "logican" Bushnell meant one who employs a method of reasoning in which the abstractness, univocity, and precision of deduction to be found in mathematics are the constant ideal.

[30] Bushnell, *God in Christ*, 62-63.

[31] Bushnell quoted this remark from Richard Whatley's *Elements of Logic*, a book which went through numerous editions both in England and in America. Whatley devoted an appendix to an examination of a little more than forty words "which are peculiarly liable to be used ambiguously". The remark Bushnell quoted can be found on page 262 of the 1834 American edition, published by William Jackson in New York.

[32] This assumption, the germ of modern symbolic logic, can be found in a whole host of writers after Leibniz and Locke. But to cite a prominent example, it was expressed in exactly the above form in Dugald Stewart's *Elements of the Philosophy of the Human Mind*. See the edition published by William Fessenden

nothing else where gotten from his theory of language Bushnell wanted it clearly understood that all words in the second department of language, no matter what their history of usage or the care devoted to their definition, could have only a figurative or metaphorical significance. They could effectively suggest or point to a meaning, but they could never perfectly designate or define it.

... there needs to be a careful revision of the distinction between literal and figurative language. I have virtually denied this distinction as commonly held, insisting that we have no properly literal language, save in reference to matters of the outward physical state. When we come into the world of mind or spirit, words get their significance, as I have insisted, under conditions of analogy, and never stand as a direct and absolute notation for thought.[33]

Mathematicians, on the other hand, had no bothersome tropes to contend with. One mathematician could literally *force* another to accept a truth, because the mathematical terms used between them, signifying as they did exact quantities and relations, could have a perfectly determinate sense. Hence, it was entirely futile to hold up the mathematical mode as a model for verbal reasoning.

It was not Bushnell's intention to deny the usefulness or even the inevitability of definitions but only to point out that

being commonly drawn in the most abstract language possible, they are supposed to have absolute meanings clear of form and figure .... And then, after the definitions have been accepted as absolute, how many deductions, spun out of the mere forms of the words or sentences, will be taken as the veritable sons and daughters of the truth defined.[34]

Bushnell took as an instance of this fallacy the attempt by a philosopher of the Scottish School, Thomas Brown, to define the perfectly clear and intuitively given idea of cause and effect[35] with the words "antecedent" and "consequent". Far from having "absolute

in Brattleborough, Vermont, 1808, 160-162. This book, along with the writings of other representatives of the Scottish Common Sense philosophy, was used widely in American colleges during the 19th century.
33 Bushnell, *Christ in Theology*, 40.
34 Bushnell, *Christ in Theology*, 51-52.
35 Bushnell viewed the idea of causation in Kantian terms, as is made clear from his calling it a "first idea, or we might even say, category of the mind", *God in Christ*, 66.

meanings clear of form and figure", these two terms merely conjured up the figure of before and after, leaving an unresolved ambiguity between the spatial and temporal senses of that figure, and did not begin to penetrate the inward conception of causation.[36] Brown had compounded his "very insipid blunder" by making his definition "a law to his thinking", drawing out through an entire book deductions from the mere outward form of his words.[37] So little did such ruling definitions serve the cause of clear thinking that Bushnell could hold it as a general rule that "the language that is most palpably figurative is generally more determinate and clear, and ... far less frequently misunderstood than that of abstractive propositions".[38]

In addition to pointing out the difficulties and dangers involved in definitions, Bushnell sought to expose the limitations of the logical method by asserting that "no turn of logical deduction can prove anything, by itself, not previously known by inspection or insight".[39] When logical reasoning *appeared* to multiply truths it was only because the conclusions were not contained in the premises, making them invalidly derived anyway. Furthermore, logic was grounded in the grammatical structure of language. And since that was derived from the relationships in nature it could apply to truth and spirit only in an analogical sense. Logical method, like

---

[36] Brown's definition ran as follows: "We give the name of *cause* to the object which we believe to be the invariable antecedent of a particular change; we give the name of *effect*, reciprocally to that invariable consequent; and the relation itself, when considered abstractly, we denominate *power* in the object that is the invariable antcedent, — *susceptibility* in the object that exhibits, in its change, the invariable consequent." *Inquiry into the Relation of Cause and Effect* (Edinburgh: Archibald Constable and Company, 1818), 15-16. The work was first published in 1803.

[37] Bushnell, *God in Christ*, 65-67.

[38] Bushnell, *Christ in Theology*, 42.

[39] Bushnell, *God in Christ*, 58. Locke had argued this point, declaring that "in every step reason makes in demonstrative knowledge, there is an intuitive knowledge of that agreement or disagreement it seeks with the next intermediate idea which it uses as a proof". He had also stated that on intuition "depends all the certainty and evidence of our knowledge." Locke, *Essay* II, 177; 180-181. Fraser notes that Locke's intuitive intelligence, under the guise of "common sense", became afterwards the characteristic of Thomas Reid's account of human experience.

words, imputed form to what is out of form and threatened to distort truths that could be apprehended in their purity only by intuition.

To sum it up, the error of the logician, for Bushnell, was not absolute, as though logic had no place in human thought and experience, but one of degree.[40] The logician was too naive, too ignorant of the limitations of his terminology and method. He tried to polish into transparency a medium that was fated by its very nature to remain translucent. He sought to imprison in mere words a truth that could be grasped only by "a power of poetic insight".[41]

Having shown that logic held no solution for the problem of the inadequacies of language, Bushnell had now to propose one of his own. And he was confident that his positive suggestions could "open a wider heaven of truth than ... all mere formulas and abstractions could possibly contain".[42] He observed that logicians were always intent on achieving consistency in their systems. But they fell thereby into the trap of presenting only half-truths, because the consistency they endeavored to attain always turned out to be a mere consistency of form. They seized upon certain dominant propositions and tried to bring all else into consistency with them, expunging from their systems those expressions whose formal aspects could not be accommodated to the forms of the dominant ones. In this way one logician would achieve his own "thimble measure" of consistency and another his, neither dreaming that perhaps it would take many such thimbles to fill up the truth.[43]

As over against this method of logical construction, so productive of bitter and needless quarrels, it seemed quite clear to Bushnell that the truth could best be attained and expressed and the deficiencies of language most effectively mended when the forms of representation were boldly multiplied, rather than restricted.

Thus, as form battles form, and one form neutralizes another, all the insufficiencies of words are filled out, the contrarieties liquidated, and the

[40] I am indebted to Feidelson for this point. *Symbolism*, 155.
[41] Bushnell, *God in Christ*, 58.
[42] Bushnell, *Christ in Theology*, 32.
[43] Bushnell, *Christ in Theology*, 54-55.

mind settles into a full and just apprehension of the pure spiritual truth. Accordingly, we never come so near to a truly well rounded view of any truth, as when it is offered paradoxically ...[44]

The poets had always known this and had allowed no hobgoblin of foolish consistency to hamper their proliferation of symbols. John Eckermann had noted of Goethe's remarks on poetry that, while they had at first the appearance of mutual contradiction, the contradictions were only facetings of the True, guiding the reader by their convergence to a perception of truth in its organic nature. But a comprehensive power and insight were required for grasping the priority of the whole which brought each partial and particular statement into its proper place.[45] The piling up of figures not only gave language force and vividness but better enabled it to discharge its proper function of holding up images or hints before the mind of another to put him on generating or discovering within himself the thought intended.[46] If inconsistency was the price to be paid for this way of using language, it could be regarded as a positive good, for it served to reveal that truth resides not in the forms of words and grammar but in the concreteness of intuition and feeling.

Thus for Bushnell poetry, instead of logic, set the standard for the right use of language, for the poets were far more aware than the logicians of the actual conditions and limitations under which language must function. They saw clearly that

mind and truth, obliged to clothe themselves under the laws of space and sensation, are taking, continually, new shapes or dresses — coming forth poetically, mystically, allegorically, dialectically, fluxing through definitions, symbols, changes of subject and object, yet remaining still the same...[47]

Because of their deep insight into the comprehensive character of

---

[44] Bushnell, *God in Christ*, 55.
[45] Bushnell quoted from Eckermann's preface to his *Conversations of Goethe* published in Germany in 1836. John Oxenford translated the three volume edition of this work in 1850, but he mentions in his preface that he had made use of an earlier American translation of the first two volumes. Bushnell had probably read the work in this translation. The quotation from Eckermann can be found on p. viii of the 1879 edition of the Oxenford translation (London: George Bell and Sons).
[46] Bushnell, *God in Christ*, 46.
[47] Bushnell, *God in Christ*, 49-50.

truth and the necessity of approaching it from many sides and in many modes of expression, it could unequivocally be stated that poets "are the true metaphysicians, and if there be any complete science of man to come, they must bring it".[48]

It is necessary for us at this point to take account of two critical statements made by Feidelson with regard to Bushnell's theory of language, for the issue they raise is crucial to a full understanding of his point of view. Feidelson has argued that the account Bushnell gave of the metaphysical status of language was not wholly consistent. He was anxious to treat form as realistic, but at the same time he was under the influence of "theological prejudices" which made him unwilling to connect too closely mind, nature, and truth. Thus, while his theory of the *logos* was unitive, his idea of the analogy of nature and mind was divisive.[49] Then on the relations between reason, poetry, and truth, Bushnell's remarks were ambiguous. For when contrasting logical and poetical apprehension he held that logic is external, and poetry internal, to truth. But the implication of his theory of analogy was that *all* words are external to truth.[50] In answer to these criticisms we can note that, while Bushnell did contend for an eternal and necessary connection between the forms wrought into things by God and the contents of his own mind and the principles of all minds,[51] this connection could only be conceived analogically. For that is the only way in which something "out of form" can be connected with form. The logos in nature meant for Bushnell simply its capacity to represent mind and spirit, a capacity which the analogical or metaphorical power of the sensible images in words seemed to presuppose. To speak of the analogical properties of nature and the logos in nature would be, in the parlance of Bushnell, to speak of the same thing. There is, in fact, something both unitive and divisive in either term: unitive, because the possibility of analogy between matter and mind connects them, divisive, because that connection can never be anything more than analogical or approximate. And with

---

[48]   Bushnell, *God in Christ*, 73.
[49]   Feidelson, *Symbolism*, 312.
[50]   Feidelson, *Symbolism*, 314-315.
[51]   See the second quotation on page 20 above.

regard to the relation of logic and poetry, Bushnell's point would seem to have been simply that poetic expressions come closer to the formless truth because in them the formal (and hence inadequate) characteristics of language are so much in evidence. Poetry points clearly beyond itself to a fluidity of meaning which eludes its forms, while logic gives the false illusion of freezing the truth in cold abstractions. Poetry comes closer to the concrete and organic character of life, while logic leads men away from life into abstract worlds of their own making.

4. THE ORGANIC APPROACH TO LANGUAGE

Bushnell did not mean to suggest, of course, that all thinkers should become poets. But he did think that they needed to acquire an organic conception of language that could parallel the organic character of truth and life. Only in this way could they hope to handle intellectual problems with perception or to enter intelligently into the thought of a man, a book, or a philosophical or theological system. It seemed manifestly absurd to Bushnell to reason of man, life, self-active being, God, and religion under conditions of cause and effect, space and time, and the atomic relations of inorganic matter.[52] Want of an organic perspective had gotten theologians, for example, into the futile position of battling endlessly about

whether faith is before repentance, or repentance before faith; whether one or the other is before love, or love before them both; whether justification is before sanctification, and the like. We seem to suppose that a soul can be taken to pieces, or have its exercises parted and put under laws of time, so that we can see them go, in regular clockwork order. Whereas, being *alive* in God when it is truly united to Him, its right exercises, being functions of life, are of course mutual conditions one of another.[53]

An organic approach to language would also make it clear that, when one came to discuss with a man some of his statements or to

---

[52] Bushnell, *God in Christ*, 62.
[53] Bushnell, *God in Christ*, 63.

read them in a book, his own individuality would act as an organic principle, giving to his language the stamp of his total outlook and experience. "Life is organic; and if there be life in his work, it will be found not in some noun or verb he uses, but in the organic whole of his creations."[54]

... every individual mind generates to itself, unconsciously, a certain general form, or whole sphere of thought; which whole, by a necessary law of the mind, called reason (ratio), exerts a latent power over all the ratios of meaning, or relative forces of words, by which they are made to fall into their places, in the sphere or whole to which they are subordinate.[55]

In light of this fact, the mode of criticism generally practiced in New England deserved no better name, thought Bushnell, than that of "vulture talent". For it specialized in picking to pieces particular words and phrases of a man, priding itself in the discovery when they could be brought into an appearance of contradiction. It had none of that patience and sympathy required to reproduce in one's own mind the total point of view of another, to confront him in the organic structure of his thought. It satisfied itself with mere first impressions, not pausing to cross-examine the symbols used to see how one serves to interpret, qualify, and correct another. The outcome of such a method of criticism and approach to language could only be that the greater the thinker inquired into, the greater would be the disrepute into which he could be brought. For it was precisely the characteristic of the great thinker that he was many-sided, endeavoring to embrace all the complementary aspects of truth by coming at it from many directions. It required no profound and searching logic to isolate at many points in the language of such a writer formal contradictions. He had more than half way done that work himself by daring to use language in a comprehensive way, allowing outward repugnances to stand in order that an overall unity of truth might be brought into the reader's ken.

Similarly, a philosophical or theological system would impart an organic context to specific words and expressions essential to their

[54] Bushnell, *God in Christ*, 85.
[55] Bushnell, *Christ in Theology*, 46-47.

right interpretation. If a man brought up in New England orthodoxy were to ask of a Unitarian, "What is your religion?" he would find that such familiar and apparently determinate terms as "right", "truth", "sin", "love", "faith", "hope", and "duty" had been brought into an entirely new atmosphere of meaning. The conclusion from this was evident:

There is a form-element in every system of thought or doctrine, which assimilates all the words employed, insinuating into them, or imposing upon them, a character partly from itself; much as food is changed in form, when the *nisus formativus* of a living body imposes its own chemistry and requires it to fill and support its own type of growth and structure.[56]

It was in terms of this organic conception of language that Bushnell came at the Bible, creeds, and the central doctrines of Christian theology. He asserted that there was probably no more contradictory book in the world than the Gospel of John, "and that, for the very reason that it contains more and loftier truths than any other".[57] Because of the "inconsistencies" which ran throughout the Bible (a sign of its true greatness), it had to be read as a whole.

And when we are in that whole, we shall have no dozen propositions of our own in which to give it forth; neither will it be a whole which we can set before the world, standing on one leg, in a perfectly definite shape, clear of all mystery; but it will be such a whole as requires a whole universe of rite, symbol, incarnation, historic breathings, and poetic fires, to give it expression, — in a word, just what it now has.[58]

Bushnell concluded that the Scriptures gave little encouragement to the hope for a "scientific" theology forced into the procrustean bed of logic.[59]

As for creeds, they could be regarded only as "proximate representations", of more value for the time of their formulation than for later ages, and yet, when taken all together, important for illumining various facets of the truth. They should not, in any case, be regarded as laws over belief but more as badges of consent

---

[56] Bushnell, *Christ in Theology*, 46.
[57] Bushnell, *God in Christ*, 56-57.
[58] Bushnell, *God in Christ*, 71.
[59] Bushnell, *God in Christ*, 77.

and good understanding. With charming abandon Bushnell could say:

So far from suffering even the least consciousness of constraint, or oppression, under any creed, I have been readier to accept as great a number as fell my way; for when they are subjected to the deepest chemistry of thought, that which descends to the point of relationship between the form of the truth and its interior formless nature, they become, thereupon, so elastic and run so freely into each other, that one seldom need have any difficulty in accepting as many as are offered him.[60]

This sentence alone was enough to stir up a hive of controversy among the theologians of New England! Commenting upon it later Bushnell explained that he had not intended to offer any disrespect to creeds or church articles. He recognized their usefulness as a kind of banner under which individual communities come together. But he deplored their role as instruments of schism, "tearing us away from the body of Christ, in just the same degree as they condense and straiten our unity with each other, in the smaller circles to which we belong".[61] Thus, despite the ring of exaggeration, even irresponsibility,[62] in his statement, we can perhaps recognize in it a kind of "organic" truthfulness. For it has Bushnell's own liberality and ecumenicity of spirit imparted to it, and it doubtless served as a needed counterweight to the dogmatic divisiveness of New England theology at the middle of the nineteenth century.

Finally, with respect to the central doctrines, Bushnell noted that it had been customary among the theologians of New England to dissect these doctrines into abstract propositions, overlay the abstractions with logical inferences from their forms, and to build these inferences into schemes and systems.[63] But to subject such bold and comprehensive symbols as the Trinity, the Nature of Christ, and the Atonement to the "stern, iron-limbed speculative

[60] Bushnell, God in Christ, 82.
[61] Bushnell, Christ in Theology, 67.
[62] The charge of irresponsibility for the statement was leveled at Bushnell by Charles Hodge, among others. See his review of God in Christ in the Princeton Review, n.s. XXI (1849), 266.
[63] Bushnell, Christ in Theology, 22.

logic of ... New England theology"[64] was like trying to capture the import of a great poem or tragedy in abstract propositional prose.

The principal difficulty we have with language now is, that it will not put into the theoretic understanding what the imagination only can receive, and will not open to the head what the heart only can interpret. It is a great trouble with us that we can not put the whole scheme of redemption, which God could execute only by the volume of expression contained in the life and death of his incarnate Son, into a theologic formula or article of ten words. It is as if, being unable to compress the whole tragic force of Lear into some one sentence of Edgar's gibberish, we lose our patience, and cry upon the poverty of language and conception in the poem.[65]

But it was in fact an immense advantage that language was limited in the way described, for this made the need for faith and spiritual discernment in the user of theological symbolism all the more evident. Mere natural judgment of opinion could not hope to comprehend truths "glassed in images and forms, to be responsibly interpreted, with a delicate reverence, and a spirit waiting for the discovery of God".[66]

Bushnell accordingly called for a "nicer apprehension" of these doctrines as symbols, to be received in their wholeness by the aesthetic or imaginative consciousness of the believer. In this way the studies of the theologian could be drawn much closer to the practical and concrete life of religion, and it could even be expected that vindictive doctrinal warfare would give way to a modest and patient charity.[67]

It was his organic conception of religious language which had led Bushnell to lay almost exclusive stress on what he termed the "expressive" character and function of such doctrines as the Trinity, the Nature of Christ, and the Atonement. Of the Trinity he would only say that the three persons were given "for the sake of their external expression, not for the internal investigation of their contents".[68] And he had gone on to adopt a modalistic or "instru-

---

[64] Bushnell, *God in Christ*, 96.
[65] Bushnell, *Christ in Theology*, 33.
[66] Bushnell, *Christ in Theology*, 67.
[67] Bushnell, *God in Christ*, 92-94.
[68] Bushnell, *God in Christ*, 175.

mental" conception of the Trinity, where the emphasis lay upon God as he is revealed to man, not upon God as he may be in his essence. On the question of the Nature of Christ he said:

I look upon him only in the external way; for he comes to be viewed externally in what may be expressed through him, and not in any other way. As to any metaphysical or speculative difficulties involved in the union of the divine and the human, I dismiss them all, by observing that Christ is not here for the sake of something accomplished in his metaphysical or psychological interior, but for that which appears and is outwardly signified in his life ... Regarding Christ in this exterior, and as it were, esthetic way, he is that Holy Thing in which my God is brought to me ....[69]

And in place of the scheme of penal substitution, where the Atonement was explained as a transaction required to satisfy the justice of God, Bushnell laid stress on its effects in the life of man, holding that its significance depended not on any kind of literal altar ceremony in Christ's death but

artistically speaking, on the expressive power of the fact that the Incarnate Word, appearing in humanity, and having a ministry for the reconciliation of men to God, even goes to such a pitch of devotion, as to yield up his life to it, and allow the blood of his Mysterious Person to redden our polluted earth![70]

The expressive power of Christ's mission and sacrifice had as its end "the reconciliation of our race to God; or, what is the same, the moral renovation of their character".[71]

Bushnell was anxious, nonetheless, to complement the subjective emphasis of his organic approach to doctrinal symbolism with an objective aspect. And it was here that he introduced a conception of revelation which also rested squarely on his theory of language. To that conception we can now turn.

5. LANGUAGE AND REVELATION

One of the most significant applications Bushnell made of his

---

[69] Bushnell, *God in Christ*, 163.
[70] Bushnell, *God in Christ*, 236.
[71] Bushnell, *God in Christ*, 242.

theory of language was the idea that the Bible was nothing else than a description of a conscious process whereby God had prepared a special "language" out of the matrix of history in order to communicate himself to mankind.[72] The thesis was that just as physical images were necessary in ordinary language to represent data of thought and spirit, so it had been necessary for God to evolve out of the experience of the human race through time new types of words and images which would have at first a merely physical or external usage but could then be taken up as objective forms wrought into the Jewish mind and thence into the mind of the world, forms which would be vehicles for the presentation of the highest order of spiritual truths.

Of course, the creation itself could serve as a reservoir of metaphors through which many important spiritual truths could be transmitted. We have already seen how nature, for Bushnell, had been created in such a way that it was the analogue of thought, both divine and human. Therefore,

if God is to be himself revealed, he has already thrown out symbols for it, filling the creation full of them, and these will all be played into metaphor. The day will be his image,[73] the sea, the great rock's shadow, the earthquake, the dew, the fatherhood care of the child, and the raven and the feeble folk of the cronies — all that the creation is and contains, in all depths and heights and latitudes of space, — everything expresses God by some image that is fit, as far as it goes …. Metaphor on metaphor crowds the earth and the skies, bearing each a face that envisages the Eternal Mind, whose word or wording forth it is to be.[74]

---

[72]   Bushnell made this idea the subject of an address on "Revelation" delivered at Andover, Massachusetts, in September, 1839. See Mary B. Cheney, *Life and Letters of Horace Bushnell* (New York: Charles Scribner's Sons, 1903), 88-89.

[73]   Bushnell deplored the "grubbing literalism" that could not perceive that the "days" of Genesis 1 were only metaphors. "Was there over a case for metaphor more easily discernible beforehand?" "Our Gospel a Gift to the Imagination" (in *Building Eras in Religion*, New York: Charles Scribner's Sons, 1903), 258. It is a pity that he was so little heeded on this point by those whose scriptural literalism caused them to fly in the face of the accumulating evidence of paleontology and geology in the nineteenth century.

[74]   Bushnell no doubt felt that his conviction concerning the analogic structure of nature was reinforced by the appropriateness of natural images to describe deep spiritual truths which he found in the Bible. The quotation is from *Building Eras*, 258-259.

But nature, fertile seedbed of metaphor though it was, could not adequately convey by its forms the fulness of divine truth. So God had turned also to history. He had taken the Jews to himself, making their whole history a "Providential metaphor" of his kingly rule and redemptive concern for mankind, "leading them on and about by his discipline, and raising light and shade as between them and the world-kingdoms of the false gods about them, to set himself in relief as the true Lord of all".[75] He had also instituted among the Jews the ritual sacrifice, whose one great object was to prepare images fit to symbolize the significance of Christ when he came. The ministry and death of Jesus could never have been conceived in terms of atonement, sacrifice, and cleansing had the mind of man not first been "Judaized" in the stock images of Hebrew religious history.[76] Finally, following the same law of expression by outward fact and image, God had sent his Son as the crown of the revelatory "language". And nothing so "comprehensively adequate" could be said about Christ as to call him "the metaphor of God; God's last metaphor."[77]

In stressing the organic, symbolic, or expressive character of Christian doctrinal language, therefore, Bushnell was at the same time seeking to give it an objective basis and avoid the charge of mere subjectivism by showing that the images of that language were build up from external or public history. While Christianity had dismissed the outward rites and objectivities of Judaism, it had nonetheless erected them into "inward objectivities". This was why it could never be said to have displaced Judaism but only to have fulfilled it. "Thus, instead of a religion before the eyes, we now have one set up in language before the mind's eye, one that is almost as intensely objective as the other, only that is mentally so, or as addressed to thought."[78] It had been no mere "rhetorical accident" that the images of the Old Testament had figured so prominently in the language of the apostles and evangelists of the New Testa-

---

[75] *Building Eras*, 259.
[76] *Building Eras*, 262-263.
[77] *Building Eras*, 259.
[78] Bushnell, *God in Christ*, 249.

ment, for God himself had "prepared for such a result, by a deliberate, previous arrangement".[79]

In answer, then, to those who wanted to rid Christianity of its "Hebraisms" in order to bring it into consonance with modern ways of thinking and speaking, Bushnell could only say:

> But suppose it should happen to be true that the all-wise God made Hebrews partly for this very thing, to bring figures into speech that Greeks and Saxons had not; that he might give to the world the perfectly transcendent, supernatural matter of a grace that reaches high enough to cover and compose the relations of men to his government, a grace of reconciliation. Call the words 'old clothes' then of the Hebrews, putting what contempt we may upon them, still they are such types and metaphors of God's mercy as he has been able to prepare, and Christ is in them as in 'glorious apparel'.[80]

It was right at this point that Bushnell felt the Unitarians deserved sharp criticism. For while he could sympathize with their protest against scholastic and dogmatic forms of orthodoxy, as being of a piece with his own protest, he believed that they had gone about their attempted reform in the worst possible way. For they had only carried the logical methods which had made for the orthodox stagnation to their farthest point, emasculating the Faith of so much of its essential symbolism that the "tonic energy" of the gospel had been completely lost.[81] Their almost total lack of the "nice apprehension" of biblical symbolism in its organic structure and aesthetic character had made foreign and unintelligible the very language by which God had chosen to manifest himself to mankind.

Bushnell believed that the Unitarians had brought prevailing theological method to its inevitable dead end. And if a new thoroughfare was to be opened up for theology, it would have to be by a better understanding of "the nature, capacities and incapacities of language, as a vehicle of truth".[82] A sound theological method depended at almost every point on a sound theory of language.

---

[79] Bushnell, *God in Christ*, 258.
[80] Bushnell, *Building Eras in Religion*, 262-263.
[81] Bushnell, *God in Christ*, 99.
[82] Bushnell, *God in Christ*, 40.

6. THE THEORY OF LANGUAGE AND THEOLOGICAL METHOD

It was the inherent limitation of all second-departmental language, according to Bushnell, which had made it inevitable that the revelatory language should have been couched in images and metaphors built up out of a long history. For language in its second department could never conduct its meanings directly to the "notional understanding".[83] It could only suggest or approximately convey those meanings, and it could do this best by a multiplication of figures which, in spite of their formal contradictions, could stimulate the imagination of the hearer and set him on generating within himself the intended meanings. The more transcendent the truths to be communicated, the more nearly poetic would be the language employed. Anyone could observe that

a free, great soul, when it is charged with thoughts so high, and fresh beholdings in such vigor of life, that it cannot find how to express itself otherwise, does it by images and metaphors in flame that somehow body the meaning to imaginative apprehension.[84]

It could not be otherwise with the soaring truths of religion; hence the fact that religion had "a natural and profound alliance with poetry".[85] Religious truths had both to be received as "a gift to the imagination"[86] and to be handled imaginatively by theologians who wished to give them systematic expression. To treat them in any other than a symbolic way, to attempt to convert them into abstract propositional language, the language of the "notional understanding" instead of the imagination, would only be to distort their significance and to quench their flame.

Bushnell knew that there would be many who would charge that

---

[83]   The exception to this was, as we have seen, mathematical language, where a precise equation between term and meaning was possible. By "notional understanding" Bushnell apparently meant something like Samuel Taylor Coleridge's "notional Reason", or speculative reason, to be contrasted with practical reason. But Coleridge, following Kant, also contrasted Reason and Understanding. See below, p. 104.

[84]   Bushnell, *Building Eras*, 265-266.

[85]   Bushnell, *God in Christ*, 74.

[86]   The title of Bushnell's essay of 1869 was anticipated in *Christ in Theology* in 1851, where the Scriptures were spoken of as a "gift" offering "God and his mystery to the spiritual heart to be spiritually discerned", 66-67.

by reducing biblical and theological language to symbolism he had deprived religious truth of its "solidity", leaving nothing definite and fixed "to be the base-work of a firm-set, staunchly effective gospel".[87] But he thought that the trouble with such people was that they had never stopped to reflect on the expressive power of symbols. Far from wanting solidity, they were "food-full" of inspiration and meaning. What was true of one set of acknowledged biblical symbols, the parables of Jesus, was true of all great symbols: "We turn them a thousand ways in our interpretations ... but we revere them none the less firmly, that they are rich enough to satisfy this liberty."[88] Symbols had a many-splendored and enduring quality which not all the "one-figure" propositions ever contrived could begin to exhaust. As practical proof of this solid quality in symbols Bushnell noted the fact that while some "scientific" definitions of religious truths seemed serviceable to the preacher in his pulpit at first, they soon grew thin as he tried to use them week by week, and it was not long before he was forced to give them body and breadth by calling in once again the whole wealth of imagery and figure from which they had been distilled.[89] And as for the general run of abstract propositions formulated by theologians to "define" great religious truths, Bushnell slyly conceded that they had a kind of "solidity", the rigor-mortis solidity of death:

Lively, full, fresh, free as [the religious truths] were, the definitions commonly cut off their wings and reduce them to mere pebbles of significance. Before they were plants alive and in flower, now the flowers are gone, the juices dried and the skeleton parts packed away and classified in the dry herbarium called theology.[90]

Appealing to the imagination, pointing beyond themselves, and making no pretense to an exact signification, "the poetic forms of utterance are closer to the fires of religion within us, more adequate

[87] Bushnell, *Building Eras*, 281.
[88] Bushnell, *Building Eras*, 283.
[89] Bushnell, *Building Eras*, 281-282.
[90] Bushnell, *Building Eras*, 274. Although he did not acknowledge the fact, Bushnell borrowed the image from Edwards Parks' article, "The Theology of the Intellect and That of the Feelings", itself a response to Bushnell's theology. *Bibliotheca Sacra* VII (1850), 533-569. See 558-559.

revelations of consciousness, because they reveal it in flame".[91] These inner fires of feeling which could be adequately expressed only by symbolism and poetry and could themselves find expression only in that form, Bushnell held to be the fruit of faith. Hence he could go so far at one point as virtually to equate faith, feeling, and imagination.[92] And he could hold it as the "first and fundamental principle" of theological method that Christian doctrine "disallows the test of mere natural judgment or opinion, and refers all truth to its final adjudication before the final court of faith and spiritual discernment".[93] It was in fact a basic conviction with him that theology is predicated upon and is an explication of vital religious experience or consciousness. As a way of putting this point Bushnell stated that theology presupposes "divinity", which he defined as

interpretation made by experience — a knowledge had of God, through the medium of consciousness, and resembling a knowledge we get of ourselves in the same manner; ... it is not a doctrine or system of doctrine but a living State, the Life of God in the soul of man. Of course, it is an open state, and not a confined or closed state, a condition of germinative force and ever extending growth.[94]

At the same time, and this was the objective basis for the subjective experience, in Bushnell's view, theology "rests upon the Scripture body of fact, because, in that, the divine is bodied and expressed, and offered to experience ...".[95] Accordingly, all catechisms and confessions should adhere as closely as possible to the "simple historic matter of the gospel".[96]

Bushnell had found what he considered to be an able exposition of the relation between theology and the religious consciousness in a writing by the German church historian, Richard Rothe.[97] Rothe had declared that theology is the speculative or logical ex-

[91] Bushnell, *Christ in Theology*, 87.
[92] Bushnell, *God in Christ*, 110-111. Bushnell called for an acceptance of "these great truths of trinity and atonement as realities addressed to faith: or, what is not far different, to feeling and imaginative reason ...".
[93] Bushnell, *Christ in Theology*, 13.
[94] Bushnell, *Christ in Theology*, 83.
[95] Bushnell, *Christ in Theology*, 84.
[96] Bushnell, *Christ in Theology*, 78.
[97] Bushnell encountered Rothe in J. D. Morell's *Philosophy of Religion* (New York: D. Appleton and Company, 1849), where most of the Introduction to the

position of the Christian consciousness, considered as containing the divine, just as philosophy is the exposition of the natural and personal self-consciousness. But he had omitted two considerations of fundamental importance. In the first place, he had failed to point up the inadequacies and pitfalls of all *logical* exposition, as they are grounded in the limitations of language. Only a recognition of the metaphorical or symbolical character of all language of the second department and especially of religious language could prevent the theologian from attributing to religious consciousness notions that had actually been derived only from the forms of his words. And in the second place, Rothe had not adequately differentiated between the natural and the religious consciousness, in the sense of pointing out that the latter

is no constant quantity; that it fluctuates with the fidelity of the man and the spiritual temperament of his life; that it is always a mixed and never a pure state, mixed with lies, sensualities, and all manner of undivinities, and these so cunningly inserted as not to reveal their presence ...[98]

The infirmity of language and the infirmity of man's own religious life were thus two warning signals which the theologian ignored at his peril.

Given these two infirmities, Bushnell dismissed as "childish"the notion that what was needed to organize or consolidate the Church was a sound system of speculative theology. God did not rely on the puny theological systems of men to organize and keep up his Church for him. He himself was the organizing power of the Church as he incarnated himself in its consciousness and life, and the soundest doctrine for that purpose that man could furnish would, in God's view, be the doctrine of the heart.[99] Thus Bushnell could insist that "the grand test of orthodoxy is in what the heart receives, not in what the head thinks ...".[100]

---

former's *Theologische Ethik* (3 vols., 1845-1848) appeared in translation (340-359). Both Rothe and Morell were deeply influenced by Schleiermacher, with whom Bushnell also found himself in close accord, as the statements above indicate.

[98] Bushnell, *Christ in Theology*, 86.
[99] Bushnell, *Christ in Theology*, 79, 89.
[100] Bushnell, *Christ in Theology*, 77.

Still, Bushnell did not deny that theological systematizations were both necessary and valuable for the life of the Church. He recognized for one thing that such systems could make religious truths more intelligible.

It is easy ... to see that the instinct of system and a certain actual determination toward it are, in one view, necessary conditions of insight and true interpretation. We are forbidden thus to stop in the letter, and receive as truth a medley, or mere catalogue of symbols uninterpreted. We are required to observe and reduce their antagonisms, and, in order to do this, to penetrate their forms, and find the unity of truth in which they coalesce.[101]

Of course, extreme caution had to be exercised to avoid "setting one symbol, or class of symbols, above the others, and reducing these to system under the former, taken as being the literal truth; in which case they are virtually disallowed and rejected".[102] When it was borne in mind, however that these systems were only general rules of thumb or "pocket systems of the infinite," they could be of positive value in exposing the very limitations of theological language as it attempted to express religious truth. As a matter of fact, it was not so much the systems in their finished forms that were important, as the endeavor after system. For while "possibly another system, differently shaped and colored, may temple as much of God's truth" as one's own, yet the sheer effort at systematizing served to draw the discipline toward a closer coherency and compactness of thought. Thus Bushnell could flatly affirm that "No person will ever become ... a good and sufficient teacher or preacher of the gospel, without a strong theologic discipline".[103]

7. CONCLUSION

Horace Bushnell, confronted with what he considered to be the stagnation, confusion, and hopeless antagonisms of the theology of his time, had cast about for the underlying cause. And he had

---

[101] Bushnell, *Christ in Theology*, 81.
[102] Bushnell, *Christ in Theology*, 81.
[103] Bushnell, *Christ in Theology*, 80-81.

become convinced that the real problem lay not so much in the actual positions taken as in the almost universal failure among theologians to take account of the symbolic character of religious terminology, together with the inappropriateness of the logical methods by which that terminology was handled. More fundamentally, the whole difficulty lay in a misapprehension of the true nature of language.

Not realizing that all language relating to facts of the mind and spirit is only figurative or metaphorical, theologians had gone on the assumption that language could be made adequate to take the precise measure of religion. But their efforts to achieve more refined logical methods and more precise abstract definitions had caused them unwittingly to fasten on the physical forms in words and to set mere thimble-measures of formal consistency over against the organic whole in which the symbols of revelation interlocked. In the process they had not only completely missed the point; they had also deprived religion of its encompassing warmth and life, leaving behind them the strewn battlefields of needless divisive controversy.

Theologians needed to realize that language is not the reality of religion, nor can it ever hope to capture that reality. In place of theological discussions that revolved wholly about definitions and logical distinctions there was needed among religious thinkers an artistic or imaginative sense for words, the vision that sees symbols for what they really are: mere shadows pointing beyond themselves to the light by which they are cast. In the case of the doctrinal symbols of Christianity that light was the religious consciousness and experience in which the living God himself is incarnate. The new departure that Bushnell called for in theology can best be summed up in his own words:

Let us only take the attitude of reception; let us cease from our foolish endeavor to make universes of truth for God out of a few words and images that we have speculated into wise sentences; and then turning to his own living forms of expression, brought forth in Scripture and the world of Providence, set ourselves before them as interpreters and learners, with an imagination that is open, and a living and believing heart; we shall then begin to feel that there is abundance of language here, and that, too, which is abundantly significant.[104]

[104] Bushnell, *Christ in Theology*, 34.

II

THE ORIGIN OF LANGUAGE

> ... language is not a dead mechanism, but a living
> organic growth, springing directly out of the life of
> thought, partaking of its vitality and pervaded and
> organized by its spirit.
>
> Henry M. Goodwin, "Thoughts,
> Words and Things" (1849)

The purpose of this chapter and the next one is to set forth views
on the origin of language and its relation to thought which were
contained in a number of works written up to about the middle of
the nineteenth century in this country and abroad and to relate
them to the theory of language put forward by Bushnell. These works
have been selected with a broader aim than that of tracing direct
influences on Bushnell's thought, though that remains a major
consideration. The aim is to bring before the reader studies on the
theme of language which seem important for this monograph for
one or more of the following reasons: (1) Bushnell encountered
them at first hand; (2) they were influential in America or representative of views influential here; (3) they were the product of
nineteenth century American thinkers and are therefore significant
as a background against which Bushnell's own language theory can
be brought into historical as well as intellectual perspective.

In the present chapter we shall be occupied with the question of
the origin of language. We have seen how Bushnell linked his conception of the powers and limitations of language to a specific
theory of the mode of its origin. The conclusions to which he came
on this latter subject presupposed a background of discussion which
began in earnest about a hundred years prior to the publication of

God in Christ but had roots stretching back as far as the Cratylus of Plato. During this century of discussion a great variety of individual theories were propounded to account for the rise of language, but they can be grouped into the three main categories of mechanical invention, divine gift, and organic development.

The Cratylus had set the scene for this discussion by raising the question of whether names are the natural expressions of the inner essence of things or whether "all is convention and habit of the users". If the former, so the dialogue suggested, then objects were somehow imitated in letter and syllables by the early framers of language, or else recourse had to be had to belief in divine origin, that is, it had to be said that "the gods gave the first names and therefore they are right". Closely connected with these questions was the problem of to what extent language and thought are separable.[1]

1. LANGUAGE AS A MECHANICAL INVENTION

Proponents of this theory assumed that thought is anterior to language and independent of it. After a period of social life in which gestures, grunts, and grimaces sufficed quite well for communication, ideas had multiplied to the extent that it was found necessary to invent artificial signs, the meanings of which were determined by mutual consent. Language was thus a product, and not a prerequisite, of social life.[2]

According to advocates of the theory, there were several reasons why the inventors of language came to fix upon vocal sounds as the material out of which a system of communication could best be contrived. For one thing, gestures, though an obvious alternative, were found to be inadequate to express the range of thoughts of

---

[1] Plato, Cratylus, 390; 425-427; 437-438. Quotations are from the Jowett translation.
[2] Rousseau, in his essay *Sur les causes de l'inégalité parmi les homes, et sur l'origine des sociétés* (1754), had left unresolved the question of whether language presupposes society or society, language. The problem occasioned much debate.

which men are capable.[3] For another, half articulate and inde-
scribable cries are the instinctive way in which man expresses pain
or passion. Then there is the fact that so many things in nature emit
characteristic sounds which can be readily imitated by the voice.[4]
But interjection and onomatopoeia could only suggest the feasibility of vocal sounds as the stuff of language to its first framers and
could constitute only its crude beginnings. The bulk of words
would have to be derived either through arbitrary differentiation
and adaptation of words already established by those two means
or by agreeing upon entirely new sounds as the signs of still unexpressed ideas.

Many, however, were not satisfied with the assumption that the
great majority of words are merely arbitrary or conventional. They
surmised that there must have been some reason why certain words
were associated with certain meanings. They therefore extended the

[3] A distinction was customarily made between natural and conventional forms
of language, the former including gestures, facial expressions, and interjections,
and the latter being language as it had been developed by the art and contrivance
of human reason. Hugh Blair and others pointed out that though gestures would
seem to be inferior to words as a medium of expression, the art of pantomime
had reached such a peak of perfection in Rome that the famed pantomimist
Roscius was actually pitted against Cicero in a contest to determine whether
gestures or words could more effectively communicate thought. Observations of
this sort were almost invariably coupled with laments on the lack of eloquent
gesticulation in the oratory of the day. Blair, *Lectures on Rhetoric and Belles
Lettres* (Philadelphia: James Kay, Jr., and Brother, n.d.), 64-65. The work was
first published in 1783. David Fosdick, Jr., devoted nearly a fourth of an article
on "Language" in the *Biblical Repository* to a sketch of the history of pantomime. 1st s. X (1837), 203-208.

[4] Max Müller tabbed the theory that all roots are imitations of natural sounds
the "bow-wow" theory, and the notion that they are involuntary interjections,
the "pooh-pooh" theory. He himself favored a third theory for the origin of
roots which he attributed to the German philologist, K. W. L. Heyse. The
theory affirmed that everything in nature has its distinctive vibration or "ring",
and that man, at the time of the origin of humanity, possessed the capacity to
give to each conception as it thrilled through his brain an instinctive phonetic
expression or "ring". The theory was aptly called the "ding-dong" theory. See
Müller, *The Science of Language* (New York: Charles Scribner's Sons, 1891), I,
494-529. The book was based on lectures delivered in 1861 and 1863. See also
William D. Whitney, *Language and the Study of Language* (New York: Charles
Scribner and Company, 1869), 427; and John O. Means, "Recent Theories on
the Origin of Language", *Bibliotheca Sacra* XXVII (1870), 166-171; for
American criticism of the "ding-dong" theory.

imitative principle, saying that not only the sounds of objects in nature but also their *qualities* were somehow imitated in words. Charles de Brosses thought that throughout all languages there can be traced radical letters and syllables expressive of the most distinctive qualities of things. Thus *st* signifies stability or rest; *fl* denotes fluency; *r* a rapid motion; and *c*, cavity or hollowness.[5] He was followed in this assumption by a host of writers. Thus by 1839 Josiah Gibbs could announce that the

natural significance of sounds, although it has hitherto been exhibited imperfectly, and only in distant surmises, is now beginning to be regarded as one of the deepest and most important doctrines in philology. It is considered as an established fact, that any articulate sound has in itself a specific import. For in order to explain the existence of language, it is not enough that man has the organs of speech, that he has sensations of ideas, and that he has a desire to communicate them to others; but it is also necessary that sounds should have a natural adaptedness to express the particular sensations and ideas.[6]

Setting himself to the staggering task of identifying the meanings which generally accompany each of the vowels and consonants in English as well as the corresponding sounds in other languages, Gibbs did at least confess that, for the most part, it was "a matter of feeling".[7]

As a typical instance of how such investigations were made to bear on the invention of language there was this passage in a book by Benjamin F. Taylor, in which the author pictured for his readers how primitive man could have arrived at language upon the extended principle of imitation.

The waterfall, is suggested to him, and a sound involuntarily escapes his lips; it may be *dash* or *roar*, but whatever it is, it is an imitation, and by

[5] Charles de Brosses, *Traite de la Formation Mécanique des Langues* (1765). Cited by Blair, *Lectures*, 61 note.
[6] Josiah Gibbs, "On the Natural Significancy of Articulate Sounds", *Biblical Repository*, 2nd s. II (1839), 167.
[7] J. Gibbs, "On the Natural Significancy". Attempts of similar proportions were routinely made by philologists of the period. For example, one writer sought to show that one-fourth of the roots of the Hebrew language can be derived from three basic extensions of the hieroglyphic meaning of the letter *caph*. "Illustrations of the Elementary Principles of the Structure of Language", *Princeton Review*, 1st s. III (1827), 519-535.

the assistance of gesture, is understood by his companion; the image of the cascade glows anew upon *his* mental tablet, and thus mind communes with mind, and thought awakens thought. Soon, other objects attract his attention; perhaps the qualities, perhaps the movements of bodies. Is it agitation? Sway, swing, swerve, sweep, express it. Is it gentle descent? Then slide, slip, sling, or other words of similar sound, escape his lips. Is the forest tree prostrated by the blast, or rived by the lightning stroke? Crash and flash may express them both. If it acts more dully, the more obtuse sounds crush, brush, gush, are natural imitations. The liquid L, flows like the objects to which it is applied. The gutteral C, is hollow as the cave it designates, or the croak and the caw that it imitates. The sound st, is *st*rong, *st*able, and *st*ubborn, as the objects to which it is applied.[8]

If Taylor seemed unconscious of the fact that he was having the inventors of language speak *English*, it was because comparative linguistics was in its infancy. Its significance was not fully felt, its rigorous scientific demands not yet perceived. This was especially true in America. What Max Müller said about the too facile identification of onomatopoetic roots applies as well to specula-tions like those of Taylor. Most of them "vanish as soon as we trace our words back to Anglo-Saxon and Gothic, or compare them with their cognates in Greek, Latin, or Sanscrit".[9] But not all writers on language went as far as Taylor and Gibbs in trying to trace the "natural significancy" of sounds. Hugh Blair, though he recognized the suggestiveness of the idea, yet went on to observe that it "can, upon any system, affect only a small part of the fabric of language; the connexion between words and ideas may, in general, be considered as arbitrary and conventional, owing to the agreement of men among themselves; the clear proof of which is, that different nations have different languages ...".[10] David Fosdick went perhaps too far in the opposite direction from Taylor and Gibbs when he declared: "The existence of so many different languages proves that there is *no* natural connexion between the

[8]   Benjamin J. Taylor, *The Attractions of Language* (Hamilton, N.Y.: Atwood and Griggs, 1843), 175. Taylor wrote this book as a young teacher, to awaken youths to the "attractions" of language as a field of study. In the preface he promised a subsequent volume on the subject, but the promise was not fulfilled. He was best known in America as a poet.
[9]   Müller, *The Science of Language* I, 506.
[10]   Blair, *Lectures*, 58.

signs and the thing signified; it is merely arbitrary".[11] But it was a needed corrective. From England George Smith spoke wisely when he suggested that the significance of certain sounds seems inevitable and natural to us only because we are so accustomed to the language in which they have that significance, and that to a foreigner many such examples as those usually cited would fail to convey any adequate conception of the things they describe.[12] Finally, while it is true that "a system of initial and final *root-forming morphemes*, of vague signification" can be detected in English, such as [gl-] 'unmoving light': *glow, glare, gloat, gloom (gleam, gloam-ing, glimm-er), glint;* [fl-] 'moving light': flash, flare, flame, flick-er, flimm-er; [-awns] 'quick movement': *bounce, jounce, pounce, trounce;* etc.,[13] this says nothing about the primeval origins of language. As Leonard Bloomfield reminds us, "roots ... are merely units of partial resemblance between words. Our analysis guarantees nothing about earlier stages of the language we are analyzing".[14]

It is to Bushnell's credit, then, that in working out his own hypothesis concerning the origin of language he placed no stock in such ideas but held to the conviction that "all theories about the representative nature of names, taken as sounds, would seem to be idle, in the last degree".[15] This is all the more remarkable in that Josiah Gibbs, his former teacher who no doubt influenced him considerably in his language views, adhered so firmly to the notion that there is a "natural significancy" in verbal sounds. In rejecting this view, Bushnell also took note of and repudiated a theory which enjoyed considerable vogue in Europe and was held in America by F. A. Rauch. This was the famous "ding-dong" theory, summarized by Rauch as follows: "Words are either more or less correct, more or less happy imitations of the sounds that are peculiar to the phenomena indicated by them, and as everything

---

[11] Fosdick, "Language", 202 (Italics mine).
[12] George Smith, *The Origin and Progress of Language* (New York: Lane and Scott, 1849), 57.
[13] Leonard Bloomfield, *Language* (London: George Allen and Unwin, 1935), 244-245.
[14] Bloomfield, *Language*, 240 note.
[15] Bushnell, *God in Christ*, 35. Bushnell did not deny onomatopoetic origin to some words, though. See above, p. 17.

expresses its nature by single sounds, according to which man names it, man in his language expresses the true Being of all that exists."[16]

The problem for Bushnell was not how sounds came to be associated with things in nature; that could be attributed mostly to convention. Men could easily come to an agreement on common designations for objects which could be seen and pointed to or apprehended by the other senses. The problem came in trying to explain the origin of names for states and operations of the mind and heart. It was not enough to say that they were once merely physical in meaning and had somehow been transposed into the mental sphere. The recognition of the "two-departmental" character of language was not novel with Bushnell. He himself pointed out that Locke had made much of the recognition that words "which stand for things that fall not under our senses ... have had their first rise from sensible ideas".[17] Hugh Blair had observed of the first framers of speech that

as the objects with which they were most conversant, were the sensible material objects around them, names would be given to those objects long before words were invented for signifying the dispositions of the mind, or any sort of moral and intellectual ideas. Hence, the early language of men being entirely made up of words descriptive of sensible objects, it became of necessity extremely metaphorical. — For, to signify any desire or passion, or any art or feeling of the mind, they had no precise expression which was appropriated to that purpose, but were under a necessity of painting the emotion or passion which they felt, by allusion to those sensible objects which had most relation to it, and which could render it, in some sort, visible to others.[18]

And he had gone on to make a point about the preposition *in* that was very close to Bushnell's view that grammar, as well as words, is built on spatial analogies. Of the nature of the analogy, however, he could say only that it was "fancied".[19] William S. Cardell, the American author of a book on language published in 1825, stated at the outset of his treatise that the position assumed as its founda-

[16]   Rauch, *Psychology*, 262. See footnote 4 of the present chapter
[17]   Locke, *Essay*, II, 5.
[18]   Blair, *Lectures*, 66.
[19]   Blair, *Lectures*, 150.

tion was "that whatever may be the origin of our ideas, there is no possibility of constructing elementary language, to transmit them from one person to another, but by reference to sensible objects, consentiently known. This is a leading principle, to which our general train of reasoning will refer, and which, suitably attended to, will explain many of the mysteries of speech".[20] He commented also that "Mental *actions* follow the analogy of *corporeal things*, and will be most properly explained under the head of figurative language. The reader, in attending to this investigation, will be led to consider the great point of union between *physical* and *intellectual* philosophy ...."[21] Applying these observations to the words of language and its grammar, he attacked such assumptions as that articles and auxiliary verbs are meaningless and merely subsidiary when taken alone, showing that these have definite etymologies and had once stood as perfectly meaningful words designating some sensible object or act. The principle also showed that prefixes, terminations, or modifying words grew from subsequently compounding and refining elementary sensible terms. They were not an original part of language. Another American, Rowland G. Hazard, remarked in his *Essay on Language* that

for the advantage of communicating our thoughts we are indebted to the material world. For no one can look directly into the mind of another, or know his thoughts and feelings, except as they are manifested in material action, or described by analogy to some external object, of which both have a common perception. Language, which expresses the passions, the emotions, and all the purely mental processes, must have had this beginning, and still retains much evidence of its origin. By degrees, terms thus acquire a common signification, as applied directly to the operations of the mind; and the emanations of poetry, philosophy, and eloquence, are then circulated in streams; whose pellucid flow no longer reminds us that their channels were worn out of turbid matter.[22]

And finally, Josiah Gibbs, while asserting that "there is hardly a

---

[20] W. S. Cardell, *Essay on Language* (New York: Charles Wiley, 1825), 3-4.
[21] Cardell, *Essay*, 120-121.
[22] Rowland G. Hazard, *Essay on Language and Other Papers*, ed. E. P. Peabody (Boston: Phillips, Sampson and Company, 1857), 133-134. The *Essay* was first published in 1836, under the title *Language: Its Connexion with the Present Condition and Future Prospects of Man*. Like Alexander B. Johnson, Hazard was a businessman and wrote philosophical works in his spare time.

sensual want, which language is not naturally adequate to express",
had gone on to indicate that

> when man enters the world of intellect, there is no longer a physical
> relation between sounds and the ideas he may wish to communicate. Here
> imagination comes to his aid. Words which originally belonged to the
> world of sense, and denoted sensible objects, operations, and relations,
> are transferred by a metaphor depending on a perceived analogy, to the
> world of intellect to express mental objects, operations, and relations.[23]

But to Bushnell's mind, while such observations pointed to a
critical truth, they did not recognize its implications. They spoke
of an analogy by which sensible terms could be lifted to a secondary
mental use but could only say very vaguely that the analogy was
somehow "fancied" or "perceived". But the origin of language
could be fully explained only when the mystery was recognized and
dealt with of why any two people should perceive the *same* analogous relationships. Until this mystery was analyzed and solved, no
possibility of communication had been established. For unlike a
physical object, an idea could not be pointed to, so that consent
could be gained on the word which would thereafter be associated
with it. The distinctive appropriateness of a sensibly derived word
to a non-sensible meaning had to be felt by all men in common, and
this implied some objective ground, some regular law, of analogy
inherent in nature by design. The very existence of language was
thus proof *par excellence* of the "Power, Wisdom, and Goodness of
God, as Manifested in the Creation".[24] And it was at precisely this

---

[23] J. Gibbs, *Philological Studies* (New Haven: Durrie and Peck, 1857). This
book contains pieces written by Gibbs at various times during his life.
[24] The Reverend Francis Henry, Earl of Bridgewater, directed in his Last Will
and Testament that a work or series of works be published on this theme with
the principal and interest of the sum of eight-thousand pounds sterling. Eight
works were published and came to be known as the Bridgewater Treatises. They
were the outstanding apologetic works of their day. See W. Kirby, *On the
Power* I, vii. In a manuscript written in 1832 Bushnell attempted to prove the
existence of a Moral Governor of the universe, not from the usual evidences of
design in the world, but from an ingenious use of his theory of the origin of
language. See Cheney, *Life and Letters*, 64-65. In *God in Christ* Bushnell noted
concerning the proof of God to be found in language: "No series of Bridgewater
treatises, piled even to the moon, could give us a proof of God so immediate,
complete, and conclusive." (p. 30.)

point that all merely mechanical theories of the invention of language failed.[25]

2. LANGUAGE AS A DIVINE GIFT

According to an article printed in the *Princeton Review*, "modern" defense of this theory began with a book by J. S. Süssmilch in 1766.[26] Frederic W. Farrar, in his book on the origin of language, also mentioned "an excellent review of the main opinions" in support of the theory by R. W. Zobel in 1733.[27] A much more recent defense of the theory, however, and one which could and did take into account the developments in comparative language study during the early nineteenth century, was a little book by an Englishman, George Smith. Entitled *The Origin and Progress of Language*, the book came out in an American edition in 1849, under the auspices of the Methodist Sunday-School Union. Smith stated as his main object "to prove that language was not invented by men, but bestowed at first upon them by the author of their being". Treating

---

[25] Some influential advocates of the theory of mechanical invention who have not already been noted can be listed. On the continent there was Johann G. Herder (*Abhandlung über den Ursprung der Sprache* [1772]; Herder departed from this view, however, in his later writings) and Johann Adelung (*Mithridates*, 1806-1817). In Britain there was Adam Smith (*Dissertation on the Origin of Language*, 1761), James Burnett, Lord Monboddo (*The Origin and Progress of Language*, 1773-1792), and Horne Tooke (*Diversions of Purley;* part I appeared in 1786, and another edition with a second part, in 1798). William D. Whitney expounded the theory very ably in America in his *Language and the Study of Language*. Bushnell praised this book in his essay "Our Gospel a Gift to the Imagination" (*Building Eras*, 268-269). And well he might have, for, first published in 1867, it had gone into a fourth edition by 1869. It was translated into several European languages and along with another book by Whitney published in 1874, still serves "as an excellent introduction to language study," according to Bloomfield (*Language*, 16).

[26] G. S. Süssmilch, *Versuch eines Beweiss, dass die erste Sprache ihren Ursprung nicht von Menschen, sondern allein vom Schöpfer erhalten*. See "The Origin of Language," *Princeton Review*, n.s. XXIV (1852), 410-411. The writer of this article favored the divine gift theory.

[27] R. W. Zobel, *Gedanken über die verschiedenen Meinungen der Gelehrten von Ursprunge der Sprachen*. See Farrer, *The Origin of Language* (London: John Murray, 1860), 32-33 note. Some other advocates of the theory Farrer mentioned were: MM. de Bonald, de Maistre, and de Lammenais. Ibid, p. 20.

the whole matter of the origin of language on "Christian principles", he would exhibit the complete harmony of the evidence accumulated by philological science with the statements of the Bible, thus presenting but another proof of the "authentic and inspired character" of that sacred book.[28] Thus what we essentially have in the theory of divine origin is but an instance of the familiar paradigm of a quest for an effective statement of the traditional faith against the threat of new scientific discoveries. For what seemed to be at stake here, just as when the unsettling discoveries of Darwin later came onto the scene, was the authority of the Bible, the original perfection and fall of man, and all the doctrines that hung upon those two beliefs.[29]

Some of the arguments by which the theory was defended can be mentioned. They can be divided roughly into reasoned arguments and arguments from the Scriptures. We shall take the former first. For one thing, Smith thought it "preposterous" that, if language had been invented, there should have been no recollection by subsequent ages of so momentous an event. But search as historians might, there was not even a vestige of a record pointing to the supposed benefactor or benefactors of the race who had first brought language into being.[30] Then too it was highly improbable

---

[28] Smith, *Origin and Progress*, 3-4.
[29] Smith, *Origin and Progress*, 44-45; 49; 88; *passim*.
[30] This argument could apply equally well against the invention of the wheel. It gained its cogency from the truncated sense of history then dominating the mind. Science had not yet established the great antiquity of the earth, and the theory of evolution had not yet gained credence. Coupled with these facts was the wide influence of chronologies worked out from Genesis, such as that of Archbishop Usher, which was inserted in all King James Bibles and seemed to most to be a part of the biblical record. Usher fixed the creation at precisely 4004 B.C. Smith could therefore score a point against the evolutionary ideas of Lord Monboddo by indicating that Egypt, in the mummies of its animals, had preserved "a museum of natural history which presents to us at the distance of three thousand years [!] every species then as now", *Origin and Progress*, 120-121. (Monboddo had sought to prove that society can precede language by citing the "social life" of the orangutans, who, though they were certainly "of our species," had not yet invented a language. See note 25 of this chapter.) This same truncated sense of history made it much easier to consider the Bible an historical authority on the origin of language, as witness Smith's contention that Moses' writings, by virtue of their sheer antiquity, were "the only competent

that men in a savage state (as they must have been without language) could invent a thing so highly refined and complex as language. No species of beings had ever been found which, not being endowed with speech, had made up that defect for itself; indeed every known race of men had a language complete with the intricacies of grammar. Further, the oldest languages seemed invariably to be the "richest in materials, the most perfect in analogy, the most uniform in etymological structure".[31] This argued for a gradual decline in the quality of language instead of for a development from rude beginnings. Again, Rousseau had been right when he spoke of the impossibility of conceiving of a society without presupposing an already existent language. Another argument was that since language and reason were so interdependent in man, the conclusion was inevitable that "it would be as wise to inquire when man began to see or hear, as to ask when he began to speak; and that God, who conferred on him the gift of reason, at the same time bestowed on him the power of speech, as the channel through which his reasoning powers should flow and act".[32] A final argument was that brute creatures had their natural language from the time of their creation and could use it instinctively; could it have been otherwise with man, the lord of the creation?[33]

To these reasoned arguments were added the testimony of the Bible. The naming of the animals and of his wife by Adam showed conclusively that language was coeval with the origin of man and was applied by him to the objects in his surroundings from the earliest days of his existence. The prohibition regarding the Tree of the Knowledge of Good and Evil was communicated to him in speech by God, and the first pair conversed regularly with God and heard the temptation of the serpent through language. And lest it

---

authority by which to decide the primitive history of the race", *Origin and Progress*, 95-96.

[31] Smith, *Origin and Progress*, 75. The remark was quoted from Donaldson's *New Cratylus*.

[32] Smith, *Origin and Progress*, 72-73.

[33] The arguments I have listed can be found in *Ibid*, 71-93. For similar ones see a Review of Matthew Harrison's *The Rise, Progress and Structure of the English Language* in the *Princeton Review*, n.s. XXII (1850), 322-323.

were supposed that the fall of man threw him into a savage state without language, it was to be noted that the Creator still spoke with his rebellious children, pronouncing theirs and the serpent's punishment and "couching in figurative but beautiful phraseology the promise of the Saviour's advent and victory in the fulness of time ...".[34]

Smith did not want to go so far as to say that God had put into Adam's mouth the very words he should use on all occasions, but he did want to insist that He instructed him to "use aright his powers of mind and tongue", in such a way that "the framework of language would be at once perfectly constructed, and rendered capable of whatever service should be demanded from it for the immediate uses of mankind".[35] And this language was no mere collection of words but was grammatical in form, having the five parts of speech: nouns, verbs, modifiers, prepositions, and interjections.[36]

Smith did not hold to the theory that some existing language, such as Hebrew[37] or Sanscrit, was the primitive stock from which other languages had sprung, but in other respects he viewed the evidence of the comparative study of languages quite differently than did Bushnell. Speaking of the variety of languages which grew up after Babel, he commented:

We are not told, nor is it probable, that the original Adamite language was abolished, and that all these varieties were so many new creations; on the contrary, we should expect that, however different these tongues might become by the confusion introduced at Babel, and by the incongruous habits of different tribes, there would still be traces of a common origin. It is the acknowledged tendency of philology to establish this.[38]

[34] Smith, *Origin and Progress*, 106. See 99-106 for the other arguments.
[35] Smith, *Origin and Progress*, 123-124.
[36] Smith, *Origin and Progress*, 125-126. Contrary to the assumption of Smith and most early students of language, the parts-of-speech system to be found in the Indo-European languages is by no means a universal feature of speech. See Bloomfield, *Language*, p. 17. This fact nullifies Smith's argument that a common grammatical structure in all languages establishes their derivation from a single parent tongue.
[37] For a writer who held to this view, see "Illustrations of the Elementary Principles of the Structure of Language", *Princeton Review*, 1st s. III (1827), 519.
[38] Smith, *Origin and Progress*, 44-45.

Linguistic studies had pointed, for instance, to remarkable co-incidences of words pertaining to the most necessary aspects of life, such as *ma* and *pa* and their compounds, expressing the relation of parents. And there had been a gradual discovery of a prevailing uniformity in the principles of grammar, and this applied even to languages where verbal resemblances were lacking, such as the American Indian tongues.[39] The existing diversities and conformities in languages subjected to close scrutiny by scholars could nowhere in any existing records be accounted for more adequately than in Genesis. "Identity without structural diversity would prove only a common derivation; diversity without identity would disprove a sameness of origin; but so much resemblance, and so much disparity, exactly coincide with the statement of an anterior unity, and of a subsequent confusion and dispersion."[40]

Bushnell did not bother to deal with such arguments in detail. We have seen that his reasoning from the relevant passages in Genesis differed from Smith's. We have also seen that he considered the evidence of comparative linguistics as proof of the pluralistic, rather than unitary, origin of languages.[41] But the thing he most objected to in the theory of language as a divine gift, we can infer, was that it implied that terms of sense and those of intellect had originated simultaneously, thus obliterating from view or at least obscuring the limitation upon the latter entailed by their development from the former. The theory also tended to emphasize the interdependence of speech and thought, as though the first could be coextensive with the second, and it perhaps implied that, because language was directly revealed to man by God, it was a more nearly perfect instrument than Bushnell was willing to admit. At one point, however, we can say that there was definite affinity be-

---

[39] Smith, *Origin and Progress*, 148-158.
[40] Smith, *Origin and Progress*, 181.
[41] While Bushnell felt that Wilhelm von Humboldt's researches tended to substantiate his thesis of a pluralistic origin, Christian C. J. Bunsen, in his influential and massive *Christianity and Mankind, their Beginnings and Prospects*, 7 vols. (London: Longman, Brown, Green, and Longmans, 1854), while noting that Humboldt had purposely refrained from entering upon the question of the original unity or diversity of races and languages, definitely felt that his findings pointed to a unitary origin. See III, 59-60.

tween his view and the theory of divine origin. He was unwilling to say that the development of language had been a matter of merely arbitrary contrivance; this thesis could not explain the origin of its mental and moral department. The transition from sensible words to the words of thought and feeling and from the relationships of nature to those of grammar had been in accord with the divine plan, had been, indeed, under the continual guidance of the Divine Logos, "who is in the world". To this important extent language had originated in God.

3. LANGUAGE AS AN ORGANIC DEVELOPMENT

Under the influence principally of the German scholars Karl Ferdinand Becker and Wilhelm von Humboldt this third theory of the origin of language sprang up and gained widespread recognition. Becker, in thoughts developed primarily in two works,[42] had declared that actions and relations which are caused by the life of anything are *organic* actions and relations. As such, they are subject to organic laws and cannot be arbitrary or accidental in their development and functioning. Human language has its cause in the organic life of man; it is inseparable from that life and also from the process of thinking, which is itself organically related to that life. It is by an organic process that what is external to the organism becomes internal, that is, passes into the world of perceptions and ideas. And it is by a process no less organic, in fact, by a continuation of the same organic process, that what is internal again becomes external, as perceptions and ideas become embodied in language. Thus, language proceeds necessarily from the very nature of man as a living and thinking being.[43]

This conception meant that language came spontaneously into being as soon as men began to think. As Humboldt expressed it,

---

[42] *Organism der deutschen Sprache* (1827) and *Das Wort in seiner organischen Verwandlung* (1833).

[43] "The Origin of Language": article from the *Princeton Review* XXIV (1852), 425-427. I have drawn primarily upon this article for my exposition of the thought of Becker and Humboldt.

language was not made or mechanically contrived by man but burst from his breast as naturally and easily as her warbling notes trill from the throat of the nightingale. For man to speak was not a merely outward necessity, a means of establishing contact with his fellows, but an inner necessity by which he could gain knowledge of his relation to the world. It was an aspect of that mystery by which mind and matter merge into his single being. Subjective activity has to form an object in its act of thinking; and since language is the means by which thoughts are objectified into concepts, language is absolutely essential to man's solitary musings.[44]

According to this theory, then, thought was not anterior to language. There was no period of mutism preceding the development of language, no need for a hypothetical social contract by which the meanings of terms were settled upon. And since man speaks spontaneously and in accord with organic laws of his being, it could truly be said that God gave man language even as He had created him. The theory of organic development thus neatly avoided many of the criticisms to which the theory of mechanical invention had been subjected, and it seemed at the same time more philosophical and scientific than the theory of divine origin, which savored of the *deus ex machina* solution to a difficult problem.[45]

Humboldt carried the organic development theory further than Becker had in two principal respects. The first was his significant distinction between speaking and speech, and the second, his stress upon the peculiar impress given to language by the nations and individuals who use it. Speaking is the endeavor to objectify thought, to express it in articulate sound. Speech or language is the totality of what is produced by speaking. As such, language is never static, a work which is completed, but always dynamic, always developing with the creative activity of speaking. Language

---

[44] "The Origin of Language", 424, 426 note, 432-433. The way of expressing the organic development theory contained in this paragraph was Humboldt's. His thoughts on the subject were contained in the Introduction to his *Über die Kawi-Sprache auf der Insel Java, nebst einer Einleitung über die Verschiedenheit des menschlichen Sprachbaues und ihren Einfluss auf die geistige Entwicklung des menschengeschlechts* (1836).

[45] See Plato's *Cratylus*, 425.

has, as it were, its own "spirit" or "power", its germ of never ending destiny. It prescribes path and form to the work of the mind, but does not thereby constrict it. It channels its energies, but at the same time it lures the mind to inexhaustible depths, in much the same way that nature does. This fact becomes especially clear whenever a genius wields language as his weapon, for in his hands it is no dead mass but an instrument of wondrous plasticity. Language is a mine in which things unknown can be discovered and the feelings impressed in a way not felt before. There is an endless dialectic between the mind and language, the product of its striving; the subjective becomes objective and the objective enters again into the depths of subjectivity, there to be transformed.[46]

It followed from Humboldt's analysis that a nation's language, the sum-total of its thinking and speaking, should express its own peculiar spirit. This is how he accounted for the diversity of languages. And further, it had to be the case that only in the individual does language become ultimately definite. No one understands a word in exactly the same sense as another person; all congruence in thought and feeling is therefore at the same time a disagreement, a not-understanding. And this difference, however slight and subtle, continues to undulate through all discussion.

But on the other hand, all thinking and speaking function in accord with universal organic laws. This means that beneath all the diversities there will be clearly discernible traces of unity. This accounts, then, for the remarkable similarities of languages without our having to necessarily suppose that they all arose from a single primitive stock. There is thus in Humboldt's view a dialectic between language functioning in accord with organic laws, language "as having its source in itself, divinely free and acting independently", and the freedom of men and nations. And "it may be said with equal correctness, that the whole human race have but one language, and that each man has one for himself".[47]

---

[46] "The Origin of Language", *Princeton Review*, N.S. XXIV (1852), 431-432.
[47] "The Origin of Language", 421 note, 433. The words in inverted commas are Humboldt's. As the article points out, the ideas in this and the preceding paragraph above were earlier given expression by Herder, in the work already cited (note 25 of this chapter), and by Johann G. Fichte, in the fourth of his

These ideas found a ready audience in America. One writer, opposing on the one hand the theory that language was a divine gift, and resisting even more strongly, on the other, the notion that it developed as a pure convention, took the position that it is "a living product of thought". Given the organic connection between thought and language, it was only to be expected that the word order in the Latin and Greek languages would afford insight into fundamental laws of thought, and to the explication of this idea he devoted the bulk of his article.[48]

Another writer, W. G. T. Shedd, a professor of English literature at the University of Vermont, developed at some length what he took to be the implications of the organic development theory. After dismissing as "shallow" the idea that language was invented and settled into use by a compact, he declared that he definitely favored "that nobler, more exciting, and more rational theory, which regards language to be 'a necessary and organic product of human nature, appearing contemporaneously and parallel with the activity of thought'".[49] Although he believed that the first human language was a gift of God to Adam, who in this, as in all other respects, was created full grown and in complete possession of all mature human faculties, he stressed the continual growth and development which language would have to have undergone thereafter.[50] And he insisted that this development was natural and spontaneous, "a growth, and not a manufacture".[51] For thought was as much the living and organizing principle of language as the

---

Reden an die deutsche Nation (1808). The article also links the same ideas with "a noted New England divine", who was, of course, none other than Bushnell. Ibid, 421-423.

[48] Frederic A. Adams, "The Collocation of Words in the Greek and Latin Languages, Examined in Relation to the Laws of Thought", *Bibliotheca Sacra* I (1844), 708-725.

[49] W. G. T. Shedd, "The Relation of Language to Thought", *Bibliotheca Sacra* V (1848), 663.

[50] Similarly Blair, while thinking it only right to suppose that language had had a "divine original", yet assumed that it must have been only such as suited the immediate needs of Adam and Eve. He therefore felt free to discuss its further development in terms of the mechanical invention theory. See Blair, *Lectures*, 60.

[51] Shedd, "The Relation of Language to Thought", 652.

soul is the life of the body, and since a living power merely added to a dead body was not life, it was inconceivable that language could have been produced by the "superinduction of thought upon, or by the assignation of meaning to, a mass of unmeaning sounds already in existence". Words uttered at the origin of language could not have been merely arbitrary or haphazard but must have been "*prompted* and *formed* by the creative thought struggling out of the world of mind, and making use of the vocal organs in order to enter the world of sense".[52]

This meant for Shedd that there was a fitness of the sounds of these original words to express the thoughts which gave them rise, a fitness stemming from the instinctive physiological responses elicited by the thoughts in the human organism.

The motions of the mouth, the position of the organs, and the tension of the muscles of speech in the utterance of such words as shock, smite, writhe, slake, quench, are produced by the force and energy and character of the conceptions which these words communicate, just as the prolonged relaxation of the organs and muscles in the pronunciation of soothe, breathe, dream, calm, and the like, results naturally from the nature of the thought of which they are the vocal embodiment.[53]

Thus a word, like a blush or a tear, had to be considered as having a vital and natural connection with the feeling or thought that it exhibited, and it could be said that at "the root and heart, language is self-embodied thought".[54]

It is significant, however, that Shedd did not hold that thought could embody itself in the beginning only in a single set of forms, as though those alone were uniquely and exclusively adapted to express it. All that be argued for was that every set of vocal forms which arose (since obviously many sets did arise, creating the the different languages) possessed a definite adaptedness to the thoughts to be conveyed.

All ... different languages are equally embodiments of thought and of the same thought substantially. For the human mind is everywhere, and at all times, subject to the invariable laws of its own constitution, and that

[52]   Shedd, "The Relation of Language to Thought", 653-654.
[53]   Shedd, "The Relation of Language to Thought", 654.
[54]   Shedd, "The Relation of Language to Thought", 654.

logical, immutable truth which stands over against it as its correlative object, is developed in much the same way among all nations in whom the intellect obtains a development. The vital principle — logical, immutable truth in the form of human thought — is here seen embodying itself in manifold forms with freedom and originality, and with an expressive suitableness in every instance.[55]

For Shedd, the process by which language arose was much more analogous to art than to mechanical invention. Of the Greek and English languages and, by inference, of all the rest, he said:

A creative power, deeper and more truly artistic than the inventive understanding, produced these languages. It was that plastic power by which man creates form for the formless, and which, whether it show itself universally in the production of a living language, or particularly in the works of the poet and painter, is the crowning power of humanity.[56]

Shedd's use of the term "plastic power" in connection with his theory of the origin of language is significant. For in the system of the Cambridge Platonist, Ralph Cudworth, whose metaphysics of nature had had a profound effect on the English romantic poets, the term "Plastick Nature" had stood for a kind of Platonic World Soul.[57] Since Shedd was a professor of English literature, he could hardly have used the similar term "plastic power"[58] without being conscious of its having this connotation. In saying that the rise of language was analogous to the production of a work of art he was suggesting more, therefore, than that it had been created by the

---

[55]   Shedd, "The Relation", 656.

[56]   Shedd, "The Relation", 661. Friedrich Schlegel held "that language must not be thought of as being in the first instance produced piecemeal by the con-creation of several atomistic and unconnected parts, but as moulded in one cast, and in its totality, similarly to a poetical or other creation of art". He taught too that language emerged from "the full inner and living consciousness of man". *Philosophy of Language*, 407; 402. If we ask how Shedd could have reconciled his idea that language was organic in its development with this view that it arose like a work of art, we can perhaps say that the two ideas seemed compatible in that both entailed form flowing spontaneously from thought and feeling.

[57]   See Joseph Warren Beach, *The Concept of Nature in Nineteenth Century English Poetry* (New York: Macmillan Company, 1936), Chapter III.

[58]   As Beach notes, Coleridge used the term "plastic power" in the sense of Cudworth's "Plastick Nature" in his "Religious Musings": "... ye of plastic power that interfused/ Roll thru the grosser and material mass/ In organizing surge! Holies of God!/ And what if monads of the infinite mind?"

unaided human imagination; he was suggesting that it had grown under the guidance and inspiration of God. This is confirmed by the fact that only a little further on we find him affirming that "the human mind is connected with the Divine Mind, and thereby with the whole abyss of truth".[59]

We should not ... have a complete view of the relation of language to thought, if we failed to notice that in its best estate it is an imperfect expression. Philosophy ever labors under the difficulty of finding terms by which to communicate its subtile and profound discoveries, and there are feelings that are absolutely unutterable. Especially is this true of religious thought and feeling. There is a limit within this profound domain beyond which human speech cannot go, and the hushed and breathless spirit must remain absorbed in the awful intuition. Here, as throughout the whole world of life, the principle obtains but an imperfect embodiment. There is ever something more perfect and glorious beyond what appears. The intelligible world cannot be entirely exhausted, and therefore it is the never-failing source of substantial principle and creative life.[60]

The theory of organic development also stands out quite clearly in the thought of Frederick Rauch, whose reflections on language, as we have already seen, were cited by Bushnell in connection with his own language theory.[61] Rauch noted that one of the main arguments used by proponents of the theory of language as a divine gift was that the development of reason presupposes language, and therefore men could not have had sufficient intelligence without it to enable them to invent it. But he insisted that it was equally true that reason could not have developed by means of a divinely revealed language, since that language would have had to presuppose reason for its comprehension. The truth was therefore to be found in the theory of organic development, where it was perceived that

---

[59]   Shedd, "The Relation", 662.
[60]   Shedd, "The Relation", 662.
[61]   Bushnell cited other writers in such an off-handed way that the only conclusion we can legitimately draw from such citations is that he had at least some acquaintance with them, and even that, perhaps, not always at first hand. He was not one to acknowledge his indebtedness to the thought of others, and he seems to have read not so much to comprehend their thought in its entirety as to derive hints or suggestive insights which he could incorporate into his own way of thinking. In this he was very much like Emerson. He obviously read much more widely on the subject of language than is indicated by the few works which he bothered to cite.

language and reason are identical. The Greek term *logos*, meaning both "word" and "reason", contained this very truth in germ. No person could think without speaking, if not out loud, at least to himself, though he might not be conscious of it. Feelings and sensations, it was true, could be had without language, but conceptions always required it. Thus, like Humboldt, Rauch held that not only the desire to communicate his thoughts first motivated man to the production of language, but even more fundamentally, his efforts to form his thoughts.[62] The position could be summed up in the dictum that "language is the external reason, as reason is the internal language".[63] And since that was true, it had to be maintained that "without will or design, spontaneously language proceeds from the development of reason".[64]

Rauch spoke in a vein very close to Shedd when he asserted that language does originate, in the ultimate sense, in the Deity, because reason itself is grounded in God.

As the plastic power produces at the same time *sap* and *bark*, *form* and *contents*, so reason produces *thought* and *language*. But reason has not its origin in itself; its author is God, whose will lives in it as its law. The author of language is, therefore, not *man*, but *God*.[65]

The "plastic power" of nature was, in fact, simply a more primary aspect or manifestation of God than human reason. All the impressions of the senses, out of which the conceptions of reason were formed, derived from nature. And it was only on account of an "identity of reason and nature"[66] that man was enabled to know nature at all. Thus for Rauch, an unbroken and continuous line bound together God, nature, reason and language.[67]

---

[62]　Rauch did not mention Humboldt's name in this particular connection, but he did mention him at one place. See Rauch, *Psychology*, 257.

[63]　Rauch, *Psychology*, 261.

[64]　Rauch, *Psychology*, 256.

[65]　Rauch, *Psychology*, 256.

[66]　Rauch, *Psychology*, 256.

[67]　Humboldt declared that language and mind grow out of an incomprehensible essence of the human mind. H. Steinthal, in his *Der Ursprung der Sprache, im Zusammenhange mit den letzten Fragen alles Wissens* (1851), reasoned that this incomprehensible essence could only be the identity of the human and the divine spirit. See "The Origin of Language", article previously cited from the *Princeton Review*, 440-441. Herder held a similar conviction,

But if language grows organically from reason and if reason, being grounded in nature and God, is everywhere the same, why were there so many different languages? Rauch sought to explain this fact by observing, first, that underlying all the variations in languages there were the same universal laws of grammar which reflected the universal reason. And second, each language was "the objective existence of a national spirit".[68] This was to say that each people had its peculiar cast of mind, moulded by such factors as geography and climate, of which language was the representation. This principle of diversification applied not only among nations, but also within them, as the different dialects in a country testified. And it was evidenced ultimately in the fact that the general nature of language was always being "tinged with that of the individual",[69] as each person imparted to his national language the peculiarities of his own style and point of view.

Henry M. Goodwin, a member of Bushnell's North Church in Hartford studying for the ministry at Andover Seminary, came out in the spring of 1849 with an article written in defense of his pastor's views on language. The basic ideas of this article are clearly Bushnell's. At least they were contained in his "Preliminary Dissertation" published in February of that year as part of *God in Christ*. But the development of these ideas is tighter and more cogent in the article than it had been in Bushnell's writing. The influence of the article is clearly discernible in the chapter on "Language and Dogma" in *Christ in Theology*, published two years later. It is an interesting, if unanswerable, question as to what influence Goodwin may have had upon Bushnell in discussions that the two may have had prior to the latter's writing of his "Dissertation", since Goodwin in his article is so clearly the master of his subject and seems to move so confidently and easily within the orbit of the older man's thought. We know that the two were close

---

holding that language and religion are primitive organic manifestations of the divine life in man. See Bunsen, *Christianity* III, 17. This view of Herder was contained in his *Ideen zur Geschichte der Menschheit* (1787-1791).

[68]   Rauch, *Psychology*, 259.
[69]   Rauch, *Psychology*, 258.

after 1849, as a number of letters testify, and there is a published letter in which Bushnell expressed his gratitude to Goodwin for coming to his defense amid the furor of orthodox reaction to *God in Christ*, stating: "If it were not for you, I should feel myself to be much alone." In this same letter Bushnell also predicted a bright future for the young man and suggested that he might essay to write a book on theological method from the point of view they held in common.[70] But of their relationship previous to 1849 nothing is known. The article itself is invaluable for a study of Bushnell's language theory, since it precisely states a number of assumptions lying behind that theory which Bushnell alluded to somewhat vaguely. Among these was the organic development conception.

Bushnell had noted with approval a statement he attributed to Humboldt, namely, that "Speech ... must really be considered as inherent in man: language could not have been invented without its type pre-existing in man."[71] But he did not otherwise acknowledge his indebtedness to the theory of organic development. Goodwin, however, was quite clear in siding with that theory. The theory of divine origin was, he held, "improbable, except perhaps in the sense of a Divine mental illumination".[72] The mechanical invention theory, on the other hand, made language out to be "something wholly external and artificial, which can be analyzed and put together like any other mechanical product. Words are indeed the signs of thought, but their signification is wholly arbitrary, like that of an algebraic formula. They stand for thought as its representative or substitute, not as its manifestation".[73] But there was a third, much more "philosophical" theory

according to which words are not so much the materials or instruments, as the natural *body* of thought, and language is not a dead mechanism, but a living organic *growth*, springing directly out of the life of thought, partaking of its vitality and pervaded and organized by its spirit. Accord-

---

[70]   Cheney, *Life and Letters*, 221. Munger tells us that Goodwin soon after took a professorship at Olivet College and became well known by his writings, thus fulfilling Bushnell's prediction. Munger also speaks of him as "the ablest defender of Bushnell's theology". Munger, *Horace Bushnell*, 167, note 1.
[71]   Bushnell, *God in Christ*, 19.
[72]   Goodwin, "Thoughts, Words and Things", 277.
[73]   Goodwin, "Thoughts, Words and Things", 271.

ing to this theory, words are not mere arbitrary signs, representing something beyond them, but the manifestation of a spirit that lives in them. Their power is not conventional and fixed, like the signs of algebra, something which can be measured and weighed by definitions, but is rather a spiritual and inward power, like that which resides in a human countenance. Language, in short, like man himself, is a living thing, subject to the laws and conditions of life.[74]

This organic development theory meant for Goodwin that it could only be by a natural necessity that certain words should come to express certain thoughts. Every thought has "its own body, which, if it be true to itself, it must assume".[75] This was in accord with the inward life and laws of each individual thought. To speak of the thought and the word as being joined organically, the latter germinating from the former as the plant from the vital energy of the seed, was no "mere fanciful analogy" but simply a recognition of certain fundamental principles underlying and pervading both nature and mind. And once again we find the notion of the "Plastick Nature" brought into the discussion, as Goodwin asserts: "Thought unfolded into language spontaneously, as the plastic principle in the germ unfolds itself into the tree; and this process, call it creation, development, or growth, is substantially repeated whenever a new thought is born into the world."[76]

Goodwin qualified these assertions in two respects, however. In the first place he stated that he did not deny that there was something arbitrary in the first construction of language. And by this he probably meant in the construction of words denoting physical objects. Like Bushnell and unlike most other proponents of the organic theory, Goodwin did not advocate any notion of the natural significance of sounds to express the qualities of physical objects. But an organic law did govern the selection of forms in which thought would clothe itself in what Bushnell called the "second department" of language. But even here, and this was the second qualification, there was the fact of human freedom: "We ... have it in our power to violate the law of development and disturb this organic relation, by arbitrarily imposing upon the thought a

---

74 Goodwin, "Thoughts, Words and Things", 271.
75 Goodwin, "Thoughts, Words and Things", 274.
76 Goodwin, "Thoughts, Words and Things", 277-278.

body which does not belong to it. To this, as we conceive, is to be traced all that is false and perverse in this world of letters."[77] Obviously, what Goodwin had principally in mind in making this statement was artificiality in speaking and writing. The clarity of his exposition, we might say, is somewhat marred by his habit of oscillating between the development of language and its present uses, without the maintenance of a definite distinction between the two topics. But he seems also to have meant that distortions crept into the organic relation between thoughts and their verbal forms as language was undergoing its first development. This was due to a misuse of freedom, just as one might interfere with the organic laws of his physical development.

Goodwin placed great emphasis on the distinctive stamp given to language by its individual users, holding that the degree of this distinctiveness is one of the marks of genius, and that in the way a great mind uses language the limitations of language become most apparent. We shall have more to say about this later, but it is mentioned here to show how Goodwin followed what we have been pointing up as the major characteristics of the organic development theory.

We also find in the article an important note that seems to have been lacking in most other exponents of the organic theory, namely, a discussion of how thought comes to embody itself in specific forms of nature. If it were by a fixed law in the mind that thought comes to select certain images or forms from the material world as peculiarly suited to its expression — this Goodwin took to be the essence of the organic development theory — then there seemed to be required also a similar and corresponding law in nature. Some kind of "affinity" had to exist between the mind within and the material world without.

There is, indeed, a most wonderful analogy and correspondence between the human mind and nature, as if each were created and conformed into the other; a correspondence extending to the minutest features and operations; so that not a thought can arise or be born in the world of mind, but its corresponding image or symbol forthwith presents itself in the world of nature.[78]

[77]   Goodwin, "Thoughts, Words and Things", 274.
[78]   Goodwin, "Thoughts, Words and Things", 285.

But the true relation which language held to nature could only be understood when nature itself was conceived as being "itself a language, the language of a universal mind; as the creation and embodiment of the Divine thoughts".[79] Every thing in nature embodies and represents some thought; the proponents of sensationalist theories of knowledge needed to recognize this fact as the metaphysical foundation of all knowledge. Thought could not be derived from sensation if thought were not already contained in the objects of nature, by virtue of their conception and creation by the Mind of God. Of the sensible and intelligible it had to be seen that the former was only the *phainomenon*, the outward index or symbol, and the latter, the true substance. Newtonian physics brought this fact out quite clearly, by resolving "all natural phenomena into certain elemental and vital *forces*, acting not blindly, but intelligently, or at least intelligibly, and hence called *laws* of nature".[80] That physical laws originated in the mind was evident from the fact that they are "ideal and the sole matter of science". They were nothing else but "*efficient thoughts*, thoughts made actual, or *externalizing* themselves in things". Thus modern discoveries confirmed the wisdom of Plato, whose "divine ideas", conceived as the "constitutive soul of all things", were "not a mere fiction of poetry, but the result of the calmest and deepest philosophy, and even coincident with the highest teachings of Christian faith". Nature, then, was "at once the language and living organ" of a "divine, omnipresent Spirit".[81] Such overt Platonism had only been hinted at by Bushnell, and that mainly in a writing influenced by this article by Goodwin. In writers on language such as Shedd and Rauch, as we have seen, it was clearly implied by their use of the conception of the "Plastick Nature", but the conception was not developed to any appreciable extent.

Clearly implied in this conception of the origin of language, to Goodwin's mind, was a recognition of its limitations. No finite natural form could adequately express the infinite Mind of God. This was why, though human thought naturally and spontaneously

[79] Goodwin, "Thoughts, Words and Things", 285.
[80] Goodwin, "Thoughts, Words and Things", 285.
[81] Goodwin, "Thoughts, Words and Things", 286.

seized upon fitting images for its expression, these images were not to be thought of as having only one single and well-defined meaning. There was a manifoldness of meaning in all such images, and every word, like a stone dropped into a pond, had its over-widening circles of association, implication, and suggestiveness. The scientist, who saw only definite, unvarying laws exhibited by the objects of nature, could not penetrate as deeply into the language of nature as the poet, who perceived every natural object in its manifoldness of meaning and whose own language of metaphorical suggestiveness and feeling pointed beyond nature in its outward aspects and phenomena to nature in its vital, indwelling spirit. "For this reason poets surpass other men in the use and mastery of language. A true poet reproduces nature in his own verse."[82]

But if poetry was the norm of language, this was an indication not only of its expressive power but of its limitations. For even in the many-sided language of the poet the attempt had to be made to compress the "infinite life and activity which belongs to mind within certain *terms* or limits".[83]

Behind and below all that is written, is an infinite deep of thought which cannot be embodied in words, which outreaches all possible combinations of language. ... All words are powerful according as they are symbolical or suggestive. Their value lies not so much in what they express as in what they indicate. Or, more strictly, the individual thought embodied and expressed in words, is a symbol more or less suggestive, of what lies below and is unexpressed.[84]

Since this was the case, the attempt to interpret a writer's language "by the appliances of logical or grammatical rules, or any merely external system of hermeneutics", appeared to Goodwin like trying to interpret a smile by the laws of physiology. "No one truly comprehends his author, no one is fit to be an interpreter, who cannot look as far behind and below the letter as the heart is below the countenance; who is not so penetrated with the *spirit* of the writer as to supersede in a measure the help of words."[85] Nothing was so

[82] Goodwin, "Thoughts, Words and Things", 290.
[83] Goodwin, "Thoughts, Words and Things", 282.
[84] Goodwin, "Thoughts, Words and Things", 282.
[85] Goodwin, "Thoughts, Words and Things", 281.

much required for the proper use and interpretation of words, therefore, as a keen and active imagination.

Before we try to assess the importance of the theory of the organic development of language for Bushnell's own language theory, we can take note of the fact that Josiah Gibbs, while he nowhere in any of the writings that have been cited singled out the organic development view for discussion, was undoubtedly in possession of a detailed knowledge of it, not only because of his wide-ranging philological knowledge, but also because in the Preface to his *Philological Studies* he acknowledged himself to be principally indebted to the studies of Karl Ferdinand Becker. In that work he also used such expressions as "the organic process of language" and "regular organic laws".[86] Traces of the organic view are perhaps also evident in his unwillingness to allow a merely arbitrary imposition of words as the signs of thought, by insisting upon a "perceived analogy" by which sensible terms acquire their metaphorical significations, and arguing for a "natural significancy" in words taken as sounds. His book is of a highly compact and summarized nature and concentrates mostly upon grammatical points, leaving us only to speculate on to what degree he did accept the organic theory of the origin of language. It may well be, though, that Bushnell first became aware of this theory through Gibbs, as he sat under him while a student at Yale.

Against the background of this theory, as it grew up in Germany and was interpreted by the American thinkers we have discussed, we can introduce the following reflections regarding Bushnell.

(1) While Bushnell was content to discuss the origin of the sensibly oriented noun-language in terms of the mechanical invention theory, he felt that theory inadequate to explain how the noun-language could have been structured according to the laws of grammar and its terms made to designate internal states and operations of the mind. At this point in the theory of the development of language one had to admit, with Humboldt, that language had "its type pre-existing in man", and to say that its development proceeded in accord with a universal law implanted in the mind.

[86] J. Gibbs, *Philological Studies*, 191; 18.

This law for Bushnell, of course, was the law of analogy. It was required for him, as has been said, as the bridge between individual minds, making possible initial communication for the setting up of the second department of speech.

(2) For Bushnell, as for some others who advocated the organic development theory in at least some of its phases, it was not enough to simply locate the law governing the development of language in the mind, as Becker and Humboldt had done. It had also to be located in nature, since the objects existing in nature plainly stood ready to be taken up as types for the mind.[87] Nature, in fact, was the original language, the language of God, embodying and expressing his thoughts. Recognition of this fact brought readily to mind the Platonic tradition of thought, given fresh impetus by the metaphysics of the "Plastick Nature" and "Spirit of Nature" in the thought of Cudworth and More, and by the discovery of invariant mathematical laws of nature on the part of the Newtonian physics. Humboldt had spoken of language as having its own "spirit", and Bushnell and others were convinced that that spirit was rooted not simply in the reason of man but in the Mind of God, as disclosed in the material world. To designate this key metaphysical assumption, Bushnell chose the term "logos", presumably because of its long association with the idea of an organizing, vitalizing World Principle or Spirit (the Stoics, Philo, the Gospel of John, the Hermetic literature, etc.) and also because of its double meaning of "reason" and "word".[88]

[87]   The sense of this need on the part of Bushnell and the others is in keeping with a statement contained in an unpublished paper on "The Doctrine of Analogy and Recent Analytic Philosophy", loaned me by its author, James A. Martin. The statement, made in reference to Aquinas, is "that one cannot talk responsibly about analogy in discourse without carefully considering the implications for the analogy of *being*, more recent philosophers and theologians to the contrary notwithstanding".

[88]   In his discourse on the Trinity in *God in Christ*, Bushnell characterized the Logos as "the power of self-representation in God", that "peculiar power by which God is able to represent himself outwardly, in the forms of things", "a capacity of self-expression, a generative power of form, a creative imagination", not unlike the human imagination, except that "our imagination is stored with forms, colors, and types of words from without", while "all such forms, God has in himself; and this is the Logos". This power of self-representation reached its consummate expression in Jesus Christ. See 177, 187, 145-147.

(3) At the very heart of Bushnell's positive program for the use of language was his insistence upon the need for an organic approach to language. "Organic" had for him the meaning of wholeness or comprehension, but it stood also for the need to penetrate to the organizing spirit behind any spoken or written composition. For since any good thinker's language would spring organically, as it were, from the originality of his ideas and the intensity of his feelings, it would bear the marks of his individuality and would require for its comprehension an imaginative sensitivity probing beneath its forms to that which gave it birth. It is most probable that Humboldt's distinction between speaking and speech and his emphasis upon the marked impression made upon language by the peculiar spirit of nations and individuals was a formative factor for this feature of Bushnell's thought.

(4) Shedd, arguing for the fitness of words as sounds to express given ideas, made the point that an idea was not restricted to a single sound-form, but could find embodiment in any number of them, just so long as there was *some* kind of suitability of the sound to the idea. Goodwin indicated that objects in the external world have manifold meanings, thereby implying that they could be taken up as forms by a variety of ideas, and still retain the kind of analogical fitness for which Bushnell argued. As for Bushnell himself, it is obvious that he could not mean to hold that the law of analogy demanded that there be only one sensible image suited to express every sensible idea. His language theory would be absurd in that event, since in every language on earth there would have to be precisely the same sensible images standing for the same thoughts. And his whole case for the powers and limitations of language would fail, since that rests primarily upon the metaphorical suggestiveness and ambiguities of words.

Speaking of his first discovery of the two-departmental character of language, Bushnell stated that "the second, third, and thirtieth senses of words" were all given "to be inspired by". This multipication of meanings for the uses of the mind was not unlimited or without control, however, for he added that of course words "must be genuinely used — *in* their nature and not contrary to it", and he insisted that the suggestiveness of a word must be restricted to "whatever it can properly signify".[89] In one place he noted how every dictionary illustrates an "unsheathing process always going on", whereby a complex of meanings issues from the original root image in a word.[90] And elsewhere, as we have seen, he argued that the "latent presence" of that root image stands by the word, limiting the expansions of its meanings to the analogical implications genuinely inherent in the root (by Divine intent).[91] Analogical fitness, then, was clearly compatible with multiplicity of meanings in his mind, though there was need for him to have brought the point out more clearly and discussed it more thoroughly in his writings on language.

If we protest that it is primarily usage, and not etymology, that governs the changes in meaning words undergo, Bushnell's conception of the logos still presses on us the question of why usage follows the paths it does and why some signs seem appropriate for the designation of certain of our ideas and others do not. We may not be inclined to accept his answer to these questions, but we cannot escape the fascination and mystery of the problem he has posed.[92]

[89]   Bushnell, Letter to Dr. John Sewell (n.d.) in Cheney, *Life and Letters*, 209.
[90]   Bushnell, "Our Gospel a Gift to the Imagination", *Building Eras*, 256.
[91]   See above, p. 25. C. A. Goodrich criticized this idea of the "latent presence" by bidding his readers check Facialati or Leverett's lexicon, where Bushnell's example word *gradior* or *gressus* applies to "the tripping steps of a child, to the clumsy motions of a mule, and in general, to ... mere 'movement' ... without the slightest reference to any 'measured tread'". "What Does Dr. Bushnell Mean?" second in a series of three articles under the pseudonym of "Omicron" in the *New York Evangelist*. This one appeared on April 5, 1849.
[92]   An anthropological approach to answering this question is suggested by the following remark of Pierre Maranda: "... myths (and other folkloric genres as well) map out the grooves along which thought can move in a linguistic and cultural community. They also, by virtue of this, teach which associations are permitted and which ones are not, within specific parameters." Maranda, "Structuralism in Cultural Anthropology", in B. J. Siegel, *et al.*, eds., *Annual Review of Anthropology* I (1972) (Palo Alto, California: Annual Reviews, Inc.), 340.

III

LANGUAGE AND THOUGHT

> ... a religion which is contained in precise finite
> terms is inadequate to the boundless cravings of
> the soul.... The more ethereal ... will be the first
> to feel that its abstractions are too cold to express
> their heartfelt emotions, too limited to meet their
> expanding views of moral excellence. They will be
> the first to discover that there is a spiritual refine-
> ment which it has not power to portray; a holy
> charm, a sublime mystery, which it does not ap-
> proach.
>
> Rowland G. Hazard, *Essay*
> *on Language* (1836)

In view of Bushnell's dictum about words, that it is "the mode of
their origin that reveals their power", it was perhaps inevitable that
we should already have touched upon the topic of the relation of
language to thought in our discussion of the various theories of the
origin of language. But now we have to inquire into it more thoroughly and bring its implications for Bushnell's language theory
into as clear a focus as possible.

There were two major schools of opinion, we can say, on the
question of how language is related to thought. The one school,
under the influence chiefly of Locke and the Scottish Common
Sense philosophers, assumed that language can be the precise
instrument of thought when words are carefully defined abstractions
employed according to the laws of a rigorous logical method
patterned after mathematics. Language is at its best, claimed this
school, when it is literal and not figurative, rational and not poetic
or rhetorical. The other school tended to subordinate the language
of the intellect to the language of feeling.

1. THE FIRST SCHOOL: LOGICAL METHOD THE NORM OF
LANGUAGE

Taking the former school first, we can begin by noting a few of the
statements of Locke concerning the relation between language and
thought. The subject was, of course, one of the greatest importance
to him, and he devoted the entire Third Book of his *Essay Concerning Human Understanding* to it. To his influence can be attributed much of the discussion concerning language that went on
after his time. Locke held that it was wrong to believe that there is
any natural connection between words and thoughts. Words were
connected with thoughts only "by a perfectly arbitrary imposition",
and it was only long and familiar use that made men imagine
otherwise. The fact was clearly evidenced in that the words we
assume to be perfectly clear and unambiguous often kindle in
others different thoughts than we had in mind, giving rise to
numerous controversies of a fundamentally semantic nature.[1]

What was needed to clear up confusions arising in this way was
the observance of certain rules: (1) taking care that no word is used
without a signification of some definite idea; (2) making sure
that all the words we use can be reduced to clear and simple ideas,
or if to complex ideas, being certain that these are determined;[2] (3)
applying words, whenever possible, only to those ideas they are
most commonly associated with — words are not to be altered
according to mere personal whim, even though their connection
with thoughts is merely arbitrary; (4) declaring one's meaning for
the use of very complex or ambiguous terms; and (5) using the same
word constantly in the same sense, or at least, noting clearly the
variations in sense whenever these occur.[3] This program applied
with special force to discussion of such a highly abstract subject as

---

[1] J. Locke, *Essay*, II, 12.

[2] "... by *determined*, when applied to a complex idea, I mean such an one as
consists of a determinate number of certain simple or less complex ideas, joined
in such a proportion and situation as the mind has before its view, and sees in
itself, when that idea is present in it, or should be present in it, when a man gives
a name to it". *Essay* I, 22. Simple and clear ideas for Locke were those of sensation and reflection.

[3] Locke, *Essay* II, 148-164.

morality. Here Locke urged that what was needed to avoid frequent misunderstandings was clear definitions of terms, constant uses of them as defined, and employment of the same methods of exactness and persistence in searching after moral as after mathematical truths.[4] Figurative speech, in all discourse that would aim to inform or instruct, was to be avoided altogether, for it only clouded the mind by insinuating wrong ideas and misled the judgment by moving the passions.[5]

In Dugald Stewart's widely-read *Elements of the Philosophy of the Human Mind* the ideas and spirit of Locke can be readily discerned. A thoroughgoing nominalist, Stewart virtually identified the use of language with thought itself. General ideas could not be present to the mind in his view except through the mediation of general names. Thus, although a minimal kind of reasoning could take place by means of the impressions of individual things, taken as representatives of classes, it could "be laid down as a proposition which holds without any exception, that, in every case, in which we extend our speculations beyond individuals, language is not only a useful auxiliary, but is the sole instrument by which they are carried on".[6] This fact had the fortunate result of imposing on mankind "the necessity of employing, in their solitary speculations, the same instrument of thought, which forms the established medium of communications with each other".[7] It meant, in other words, that all reasoning automatically had a public and objective character. But this same fact was also a liability, in that it forced the thinker to operate with an instrument molded by the unphilosophic temperament of the general populace.[8]

---

4 Locke, *Essay*, II, 211.
5 Locke, *Essay* II, 146.
6 D. Stewart, *Elements*, 187.
7 Stewart, *Elements*, 171.
8 Stewart stated the need for a universal philosophic language but was doubtful of the possibility of its adoption: "I am more and more convinced of the advantage to be derived from a reformation of the common language, in most of the branches of science. How much such a reformation has affected in Chemistry is well known; and it is evidently much more necessary in the Philosophy of Mind, where the prevailing language adds to the common inaccuracies of popular expressions, the peculiar disadvantage of being all suggested by the analogy of matter.... But it belongs to such authors alone, as have extended the

Reason could rid itself of this liability only by accurate definitions and consistent usage of terms. Thinking, after all, was like an algebraic operation, in that it was carried on almost entirely by the use of signs, without attention being given to the things signified by them. But the signs could not, of course, be allowed to remain ambiguous in their meaning. Figurative expressions were therefore prohibited for serious reasoning, because of their tendency to divert the attention by exciting the imagination or to bias the judgment by introducing casual associations. Nothing should be allowed to distract the mind of the careful thinker from the mechanics of his reasoning. But it was precisely this logical rigor and level of abstraction required for exact and creative thought that opened rational language to the censure of those who would read merely for amusement and who demanded a vivacity and ornament in all discourse.[9]

Although the powers of abstraction which language bestows upon men were its greatest boon, so that the benefits given to mankind by the use of machines could be said to be but a "faint image of that increase of our intellectual capacity we owe to language",[10] it was nevertheless true that, the more general the principle, the greater the extent of damage it could cause if it were false. Therefore the philosopher had to be certain that every general term employed in his discourse could be resolved into particular facts and particular objects of experience. Stewart hastened to add, however, that he did not mean to say that language depended for its meaning on the experience of individual persons. It was precisely the fact that it did *not* which made it the means of mankind's intellectual progress. For the experience of the past could be profited from by its becoming embodied in general terms and general propositions, so that what in one age was confined to the studious and learned few could become in the next, part of the elementary principles of general education. All such terms and propositions had only to be kept in close connection with the precise facts and items of experience which

---

boundaries of science by their own discoveries to introduce innovations in language with any hope of success." *Elements*, 343.
[9]   Stewart, *Elements*, 162; 425.
[10]   Stewart, *Elements*, 190.

they represented, since their value as abstractions rested upon that of which they were the generalized expression.[11]

In sharp contrast to his elevation of abstract, logical language as the proper instrument of thought and means of intellectual progress, stands Stewart's treatment of the language of the imagination. He observed that this form of language depended for its effectiveness upon the principle of association, and that its power to elicit readily a complex of associations in the mind stemmed from its connection with sensible objects, concerning which latter he had this to say:

The effect of perceptible objects, in awakening associated thoughts and associated feelings, seems to arise, in a great measure, from the permanence of the impressions which such objects produce. Before one idea can suggest another idea, it must itself disappear; and a train, perhaps, succeeds, to which the first bears a very slight relation. But, in the case of perception, the object remains before us; and introduces to the mind, one after another, all the various ideas and emotions with which it has any connexion.[12]

Men especially adept at using language in this concrete, associative way Stewart termed "men of fancy", and he claimed that while they used language primarily "to please" men, it was the office of the philosophers "to inform and enlighten mankind".[13] This subordination of poetic and metaphorical language to the language of the intellect was carried further by his distinction between two types of association, a distinction which, to his knowledge, no other philosopher had perceived. One type comprised relations of resemblance and analogy, which require little exertion for their perception and spring almost spontaneously to mind. This was the type of association upon which the poet depended. But the other type was discovered only in consequence of sustained efforts of attention. This was the association discerned by the philosopher between premises and conclusions, the association which regulated the train of thought in his mind as he was engaged in his investigations. The latter, clearly, was the more important of the two types.[14] And, in

[11] Stewart, *Elements*, 191; 195-197.
[12] Stewart, *Elements*, 245.
[13] Stewart, *Elements*, 419-420.
[14] Stewart, *Elements*, 254.

order to further subordinate the imaginative form of language, Stewart pointed out that progress in the philosophy of the human mind depended much more upon the severe and discriminating judgment which attempts to *separate* ideas which nature or habit had caused to be associated in the mind. The important philosophic distinction between sensations and perceptions was a case in point,[15] as was the necessity of separating permanent principles of morality and religion from those transient notions or practices which had become associated with them because of the influence of convention, fashion, or authority.[16]

Carrying further his analysis of the relation between imagination and morality, Stewart was willing to grant that "the faculty of imagination is the great spring of human activity, and the principal source of human improvement".[17] He attributed this to the capacity of imaginative language to present to the mind scenes and characters more noble and elevated than those found in everyday life, thus serving as a stimulus toward greater moral attainment. But a serious moral danger also lurked in imaginative forms of expression. For one thing they could so captivate the mind with ideal situations that contact with real life was lost, morality thereby degenerating into pipe dreams and ceasing to be a matter of active duties. For another thing, while the enthusiasm engendered by passionate speech could lead to heroic actions and an exalted character, it had also to be recognized as a "temper which is one of the most fruitful sources of error and disappointment".[18] Moreover, imagination could be a positive detriment to morality by exciting enthusiasm for wrong acts. The rash of "fictitious histories" and their effect in misleading the passions of youth "with respect to the most interesting and important of all relations" was "one of the many instances of the inconveniences resulting from an ill-regulated imagination".[19]

---

[15]   According to Stewart *sensations* are excited in the mind by external objects, and *perceptions* are of the material qualities designated by these sensations.
[16]   Stewart, *Elements*, 299-311.
[17]   Stewart, *Elements*, 448.
[18]   Stewart, *Elements*, 448.
[19]   Stewart, *Elements*, 441-442.

To sum up then, Stewart had many misgivings and reservations about the language of the imagination. The philosopher, with his careful definitions and abstract terminology, stood on much firmer ground than the poet, and it was to the philosopher's kind of language that mankind had primarily to look for its moral and religious, as well as scientific, instruction and advancement.

By clear implication, we find a similar subordination of imaginative language to abstract, rational language in the thought of Hugh Blair. But in his case the subordination was not so complete or ruthless as it was in the case of Stewart. Blair, in discussing figurative speech, noted that it was not a refinement of language, invented after it had advanced to its later stages and mankind had acquired culture and polish, as might have been supposed, but that it was in fact in its greatest profusion right at the beginning, when men had hardly any words for expressing their thoughts. For in order

to signify any desire or passion, or any act or feeling of the mind, they had no precise expression which was appropriated to that purpose, but were under a necessity of painting the emotion or passion which they felt, by allusion to those sensible objects which had the most relation to it, and which could render it, in some sort, visible to others.[20]

But despite this observation, which for Bushnell would have been a conformation of the metaphorical character of *all* speech relating to the mind or feelings, he went on to affirm that, as mankind had advanced, the understanding had gradually gained ground on the imagination, and language had lost most of its figurative character. Clarity, instead of figurative suggestiveness, came to prevail as the number of words increased, and in place of the poets, philosophers became the instructors of men. As prose finally came to predominate over poetry, the ancient metaphorical dress of speech was laid aside, to be employed only on those special occasions when ornament was desired.[21]

---

[20] H. Blair, *Lectures*, 66.
[21] Blair, *Lectures*, 67-68. Barbara Cross has not presented Blair's view fairly in saying that he "hoped that eventually metaphors and imagination would disappear, as intellectual progress made language more precise". See her *Horace Bushnell: Minister to a Changing America* (Chicago: University of Chicago Press, 1958), 98. For actually Blair gave a large place to the role of metaphors

It was true that ordinary language still preserved clear traces of its ancient figurative character, and Blair mentioned that it was impossible to compose any discourse without having rather frequent recourse to figures of speech. Still, the bulk of words had lost their figurative character entirely and had come to be regarded by long use as "simple and literal expressions".[22] Tropes and other figurative expressions thus had for Blair an important, but plainly subordinate, function. They were a specialization or refinement of speech rather than its norm. They could be described in general "as that language which is prompted either by the imagination or by the passions".[23] They contributed to the beauty of grace and style, and they could "render an abstract conception, in some degree, an object of sense", surrounding "it with such circumstances, as enable the mind to lay hold of it steadily, and to contemplate it fully".[24] Still, they were simply aids to thought and not, as in bygone days, its sole or primary vehicle.

This subordination of figurative language to a logically precise form of discourse, along with the Lockean and Scottish philosophers' conception of just what constituted such discourse and what were the rules governing its proper use, entered as unquestioned assumptions into the thinking of nearly every New England theologian in the first half of the last century. The fact helps to account, as Bushnell so shrewdly perceived, for much that was characteristic in their theology. For if they transposed the warm and vital language of the Scriptures into the coldest and most colorless kind of abstractions and subjected these, in turn, to a mechanical

---

and imagination in language, as might be judged from the title of his book: *Lectures on Rhetoric and Belles Lettres.* And he expressed no hope that stylistic writing and speaking would eventually disappear. Writers who employed figurative style wisely were those who did "not despise the beauty of language". (Ibid, 202). He recognized the dangers of artificiality and distortion in such discourse, to be sure, and devoted his lifework to warning of them and inculcating into his students proper habits in the use of imaginative speech. He did this, it is obvious, because he was convinced of the vital and continuing contribution of this specialized way of using language.

[22] Blair, *Lectures*, 152.
[23] Blair, *Lectures*, 147-148.
[24] Blair, *Lectures*, 154.

method of reasoning reminiscent of a geometrician's handling of his theorems, it was not simply because they had lost sight of the religion of the heart, but because they were honestly convinced that this was how language should be used. In this way, it was thought, the Scriptures could be rid of the ambiguities and troublesome contradictions inherent in their figurative and loose-knit style, and correct doctrines could be set before the faithful in consistent, easily understandable prose. Such formulations might seem dry to the heart, but it was more important that they be clear to the head. But unfortunately, the method did not fulfil its promise. It did not clear up misunderstandings and allay controversy as Locke had said it would. Instead it provoked a period of bitter dissension unparalleled in American religious history. As one historian has put it, "This conception of theology trained a race of giant wrestlers; but it tended to magnify intellectual differences in the apprehension of relatively minor aspects of Christian truth into barriers scarcely to be passed."[25]

One of the theologians of the period in whose writings this conception of language stands out quite plainly was Edwards Park. Just one year after beginning what was to be a distinguished career as a teacher of theology at Andover Seminary, he published an article in which he contended, in the spirit of Blair, that the writers of the Bible had been forced to express themselves figuratively because of the sparse supply of words in their ancient languages. But now that language had greatly advanced and a more copious vocabulary lay ready at hand, it was the task of the theologian to "analyze and spread out the hints coiled up in these figures".[26] And that meant reducing the biblical language to a "more compact, scientific, and even scholastic" style, extracting literal truths from their poetic embodiments.[27]

Of more interest to us, however, is an article written by Park a year after the publication of *God in Christ*. For in this article, though

[25] Williston Walker, *Great Men of the Christian Church* (Chicago: University of Chicago Press, 1908), 359.
[26] Edwards Park, "The Proper Mode of Exhibiting Theological Truth", *Biblical Repository* X (1837), 462.
[27] Edwards Park, "The Proper Mode", 468.

it nowhere made mention of Bushnell's name, Park was making a serious effort to grasp and appropriate the insights of Bushnell's critique of the prevailing conception of language, and even to achieve some kind of synthesis between the apparently quite opposite views. In this attempt he stood almost alone among the older theologians of Bushnell's day. For they were for the most part content merely to pour scorn on his language theory, perhaps because they sensed that if it, and the general approach and attitude toward theology it implied, were to be acquiesced in even to a slight degree, it could mean the death-knell for the kind of theology known and practiced in New England for the past one-hundred years.[28]

In this article, entitled "The Theology of the Intellect and That of the Feelings", Park set out to distinguish between two basic types of theological exposition and to discover some of the influences they exert upon one another. Subserving the reason, the theology of the intellect comprehended religious truth "just as it is, unmodified by excitements of feeling", and "as accurate not in its spirit only, but in its letter also". It rested its statements carefully upon evidence which was "either internal or extraneous", by which Park presumably meant evidence either of the senses or of the ideas of reflection, in keeping with the Lockean method of verification of statements. But since he was speaking of theological statements he must also have had in mind the evidence of revelation. At any rate, in order that these statements might be fitted to act as "premises for subsequent trains of proof", the theology of the intellect naturally preferred "general to individual statements, the abstract to the concrete, the literal to the figurative". Its terminology was intended to be so exactly defined that no "ambiguous, mystical, or incoherent sentence" could be found in it. And it would be "in entire harmony

---

[28]   It is a question of organization as to whether Park's article should have been discussed here or after we have gone into our discussion of the second school of thinking on language, since his views do presuppose the ideas of that second school. But since we have already discussed Bushnell's language theory in detail, and it catches up the themes of the second school, and since Park's final position is with this first school, it seemed best to discuss him here. I might also point out that N. W. Taylor's views on language — never put in the form of a definite theory of language — are discussed in Chapter VI below.

with itself, abhorring a contradiction as nature abhors a vacuum".

But of course, because it purposefully avoided the dash of an imaginative style, it was quite to be expected that the mass of men would find it dull and dry.[29]

The theology of the feelings, on the other hand, was "adapted to the well-trained heart". Literally interpreted, it might or might not be false. It was satisfied with embracing what it conceived to be the "substance" of truth, studying not the exact propositions of doctrine, but only those features of it which appeal to the feelings. It sacrificed abstract statements "to visible and tangible images" and was "satisfied with vague, indefinite representation". Its very power was the looseness of its style, whereby, pressing a passage through or over mere logical rules, it aimed directly at the feelings. Because it feared monotony far more than want of consistency or of comprehensive breadth, it made free use of discordant forms, suiting these to the changing moods of the heart. And in the process it not infrequently strained "a word to its utmost significancy".[30]

In saying these things Park meant no disparagement to the so-called theology of the feelings. He felt that it had its definite place and was, indeed, the natural expression of profound religious emotions. Concerning it he wrote:

It is no play, but solemn earnestness. It is no mere fiction, but an outpouring of sentiments too deep, or too mellow, or too impetuous to be suited with the stiff language of the intellect. Neither can its words be called *merely* figurative, in the sense of arbitrary or unsubstantial. They are the earliest, and if one may use a comparison, the most natural utterances of a soul instinct with religious life.... This form of theology, then, is far from being fitly represented by the term imaginative, still farther by the term fanciful, and farther still by the word capricious. It goes deeper; it is the theology both of and for our sensitive nature; of and for the normal emotion, affection, passion. It may be called poetry, however, if this word be used, as it should be, to include the constitutional developments of a heart moved to its depths by the truth.[31]

The Bible itself made it obvious that "all warm affection ... over-

[29] E. Park, "The Theology of the Intellect and That of the Feelings", *Bibliotheca Sacra* VII (1850), 534-535.
[30] E. Park, "The Theology", 536-537.
[31] E. Park, "The Theology", 538.

leaps at times the proprieties of a didactic style". In a word, the theology of the feelings was inevitable, simply because the "nice language of prose" was "too frail" to express the bursting sympathies of the soul.[32]

According to Park, these two legitimate forms of theology could be expected to interact in several ways. First, the theology of the intellect could gain entrance into the sensibilities and thus make its appeal to the whole man only when it was combined with the theology of the feelings, that is, only when its literal truths were clothed, for the sake of illustration and force, in appropriate images.

Second, the theology of the intellect enlarged and improved that of the feelings, while the theology of the feelings corrected and adjusted that of the intellect. A system of doctrine logically drawn out could not only make its own appeal to the heart, by its sheer symmetry and precision, but it could also provide the imagination with materials to clothe in making its appeal to the emotions. Moreover, it needed to be recognized by those who exalted an emotional theology at the expense of and to the detriment of speculative theology that

Our faith becomes a wild or weak sentimentalism if we despise logic.... If the intellect of the church be repressed, that of the world will not be, and the schools will urge forward an unsanctified philosophy which good men will be too feeble to resist, and under the influence of which the emotions will be suited with forms of belief more and more unworthy, narrow, debasing.[33]

On the other side of the coin, however, it remained true that when the feelings were grossly offended by some item of theological teaching — for instance, a doctrine portraying the divine government as "harsh, pitiless, insincere, oppressive" — it was obvious that somewhere the doctrine had gone wrong.[34]

Third, the theology of the intellect served to qualify and bring into harmony the extreme and frequently contradictory statements of the theology of feeling. For instance, when the emotive theology,

[32] E. Park, "The Theology", 538-539.
[33] E. Park, "The Theology", 543.
[34] E. Park, "The Theology", 545.

expressing the repentance of a sinner looking back at some past misdeed, laid great emphasis on the fact of human responsibility, it was not only true "in substance" but also in point of literal fact. But when that same theology, expressing the frustrations of a sinner looking forward and knowing he will sin again, emphasized the utter inability of man to choose in favor of the right, then it was only partially true and had to be qualified and corrected by the intellectual theology. The latter had the function, therefore, of making "the eloquent style of the feelings at one with the more definite style of the reason".[35]

It had this function especially with reference to the Bible, where incommensurate figures of expression were common. For example the Bible portrayed the sinful human heart as a stone needing to be exchanged for flesh; as flesh needing to be turned into spirit; as a darkened spirit needing to be lightened by knowledge; as dead and needing to be made alive; as needing to die, to be crucified, and buried; as needing to be circumcised or inscribed with a new law. Then again, these forms were inverted, and man was called upon to make himself a new heart; to arise from death; to open his blinded eyes to see; to open his deaf ears and give heed. The theology of the intellect could educe "light from the collision of these repugnant phrases", modifying and reconciling them "into the doctrine, that *the character of our race needs an essential transformation by an interposed influence from God*". This definition, however, emphatically did not make the figures superfluous, for "how soon would this doctrine lose its vivacity, if it were not revealed in these dissimilar forms, all jutting up like the hills of a landscape from a common substratum".[36]

In the fourth and final place, Park claimed that the theology of the intellect and of the feelings tended "to keep each other within the sphere for which they were respectivaly designed, and in which they are fitted to improve the character".[37] Such a biblical expression as "Behold! I was shapen in iniquity, and in sin did my mother conceive me", had great meaning for the feelings, but it

---

[35] E. Park, "The Theology", 548-549.
[36] E. Park, "The Theology", 546-547.
[37] E. Park, "The Theology", 550-551.

could not meet the test of cold rationality, for it then implied the absurd doctrine that man was "deserving of punishment for the involuntary nature which he has never consented to gratify; really sinful before he actually sins".[38] But when it came to creeds, though there were those who would claim that these should be taken in a similar symbolical or emotional way,[39] and not literally, Park insisted that each one,

if true to its original end, should be in sober prose, should be understood as it means, and should mean what it says, should be drawn out with a discriminating, balancing judgment, so as to need no allowance for its freedom, no abatement of its force, and should not be expressed in antiquated terms lest men regard its spirit as likewise obsolete. It belongs to the province of the analyzing, comparing, reasoning intellect; and if it leave this province for the sake of intermingling the phrases of an impassioned heart, it confuses the soul, it awakens the fancy and the feelings to disturb the judgment, it sets a believer at variance with himself by perplexing his reason with metaphors and his imagination with logic; it raises feuds in the church by crossing the temperaments of men, and taxing one party to demonstrate similes, another to feel inspired by abstractions. Hence the logomachy which has always characterized the defense of such creeds. The intellect, no less than the heart, being out of its element, wanders through dry places, seeking rest and finding none.[40]

So keen was Park's sympathetic insight into Bushnell's point of view that he could speak at times almost like him. This statement is a good example:

The literal doctrines of theology are too vast for complete expression by man, and our intensest words are but a distant approximation to that language, which forms the new song that the redeemed in heaven sing; language which is unutterable in this infantile state of our being, and in comparison with which our so-called extravagances are but feeble and tame diminutives.[41]

But in the final analysis he sided unmistakably with the conception of language we have been discussing in this section, as the following quotation makes plain:

[38] E. Park, "The Theology", 552.
[39] I hardly need point out that Park had Bushnell in mind here and was criticizing him at this point, just as when he said that an emotional theology without the check of an intellectual one degenerates into sentimentality. (see p. 90 above).
[40] E. Park, "The Theology", 554.
[41] E. Park, "The Theology", 549.

But while the theology of reason derives aid from the impulses of emotion, it maintains its ascendency over them. In all investigations for truth, the intellect must be the authoritative power, employing the sensibilities as indices of right doctrine, but surveying and superintending them from its commanding elevation.[42]

This clearly meant that logic, not poetry, was the norm for the language of theology. Moreover, it must be admitted that Park's attempted synthesis, for all of its ingenuity and suggestiveness, did not really probe to the heart of Bushnell's view, because it did not take his language theory fully into account. For while Park gave a prominent place to emotional or symbolical language, he nowhere came to grips with the question of whether there actually is a "literal" way of speaking about mental and moral matters, in which the ambiguities in words and their metaphorical imprecision can be quite overcome. He simply assumed, in line with the conventional theory, that words could be so defined as to have this "literal" character.

Bushnell himself, writing nineteen years later in his "Our Gospel a Gift to the Imagination", took note of this crucial omission in Park's article by citing the formula by which Park had tried to reduce to logical consistency the contradictory utterances of the Bible on the sinful heart. To say that "the character of our race needs an essential transformation by an interposed influence from God", said Bushnell, was no great clarification, for the statement itself was shot through with vague and inexact terminology. For instance, "could we but settle this one word *influence* alone, about all the great church controversies of eighteen centuries would be settled".[43] The gospel revelation was one such influence, the power of the Spirit another, the power of the sacraments another, and the human example of Jesus still another. The relationship among these various forms of influence was by no means a settled question among Christians; hence, it was futile to claim that the word or the proposition of which it was a part could be "literal" or unambiguous in its meaning. The only literal meaning the word had, in fact, was its physical sense of "motion" of "flow". All else required meta-

42 E. Park, "The Theology", 545.
43 Bushnell, *Building Eras in Religion*, 271.

phorical application and entailed organic interpretation. The word "character" was another case in point. Literally it meant "mark" or "distinction", but as to its mental applications it could be said without exaggeration that "There is almost nothing we conceive so variously, and unsteadily, and advance upon by so many rectifications, even to the end of life, as this matter of character".[44] The argument applied with similar force to every other word in the formula, including even its prepositions.

One may get the impression of quibbling from these remarks of Bushnell. And yet, when taken against the background of the conception of language we have been trying to bring into view, it would seem to have been a necessary kind of criticism. If nothing else, it served to display the difference between language and mathematics. For no matter how precisely words are defined, they always remain words, and they will probably continue to color the thought of the reader and even of the writer with ambiguous connotations working below the level of clear consciousness, simply because of long familiarity with the words in other senses than the nicely defined ones. These connotations can mislead thought in many subtle ways. Moreover, definitions themselves are made up of words, and there is a kind of infinite regress required in giving definitions for the terms of the definitions, then defining the terms of the definition of the definition, and so on. Also, abstract propositional statements can arrest depth analysis of a problem, because their succinctness and simplicity so easily creates an illusion of saying something absolutely precise or immensely profound, an illusion that can be dispelled only when the statements are themselves subjected to analysis or when one enters into debate with someone else on what it is exactly that they do mean. Then too, there is obvious point to Bushnell's observation (which, of course, he was not alone in making) that the whole mental set and temperament, past experience, and system of thought adhered to enters decisively into the meanings and relative values a person tends to attach to terms and propositions. Furthermore, the conventional view of language certainly did not make sufficient allowance for

44 Bushnell, *Building Eras*, 270.

the meanings which are inevitably lost when poetic statements are paraphrased into prose. If the "literal" meaning of such poetic utterances be conceived of as their *essential* meaning, as was no doubt the case for the adherents of the conventional view, then that essential meaning is almost always lost in such a paraphrase, as Bushnell so clearly saw.

And finally, Bushnell was certainly right in saying that religious language, resting upon and reflecting a dynamic experience as it must, is emotional in character, at least to a significant degree, and is subject to important individual variations, which means that it can never be as objective and coldly logical as it was generally supposed in his day. Even if the point be granted, purely for the sake of argument, that theology is a deductive system working from objective Scriptural propositions, still it will never be the case that theological statements will remain objective as they are responded to and used in the discourse of a believer. For him they are statements of profound and urgent moment, and they will become tinctured with his feelings and transformed into something quite unobjective when he employs them. The point has been well brought out by Wilfred Cantwell Smith, in a recent statement which is close in a number of ways to Bushnell's view of theological language. Smith called an image "a representation pointing beyond itself and capable of meaning different things to different people, depending upon their capacity and insight, and the quality of their personal life". He then went on to say:

We know that an image means more to a believer than to an outsider, much more to a profound and devout believer than the same image does or can to a lukewarm or superficial one, and indeed that the meaning lies not in the image itself, but in what the man of faith brings to it. We are not quite so trained to recognize that this sort of thing is true also of a theological system, for instance, though it too, I personally take as a symbol, an intellectual one this time, something whose meaning lies beyond the immediate sense of its statements. The phrases in themselves mean something, but symbolize something more, as in poetry.[45]

---

[45] W. C. Smith, "The Faith of Other Men", a lecture series broadcast over WRVR (Riverside Church Radio in New York City), March 4 - April 15, 1962. The statement is taken from Lecture V: "Confucian and Taoist Traditions".

Surely apropos also is the point, made by John Wilson among others, that knowing *that* a theological statement is true presupposes our knowing *how* it is true in our own experience,[46] for this signalizes quite a breadth of possible interpretations, as well as indicating that the verifiability of religious statements cannot be nearly so direct or, at least on the level of language itself, even so convincing as that of scientific or mathematical statements. In recovering such insights, as he definitely did, Bushnell through his language theory spoke a much needed word to his own time and also made what can be regarded today as a significant contribution to the ever crucial discussion of how language is related to thought, particularly to religious thought.

2. THE SECOND SCHOOL: FIGURATIVE SPEECH NORMATIVE

Despite the overwhelming prevalence of the conception of language just discussed, there was another trend or school of thought which regarded the figurative way of speaking, rather than the logical or "literal" way, as normative for language in its relation to thought, or at least gave much greater place to this than had Locke or the Common Sense philosophers and their followers.

The Kantian criticism of "pure" or speculative reason gave impetus to this alternate way of conceiving the connection between language and thought, as did the appearance of Romanticism. Americans found a vigorous exponent of both, particularly the former, in Samuel Taylor Coleridge. His influence on the Transcendentalist Movement in America is well known, and Transcendentalism can be regarded, in one aspect, as a resurgence of symbolical consciousness, as over against the anti-symbolism of the bulk of American Unitarians, who applied the Lockean, Common Sense conception of language to theology with a vengeance. Similarly Bushnell, himself profoundly impressed with Coleridge's thought, sought to inaugurate a symbolical reformation among

---

[46] John Wilson, *Language and Christian Belief* (London: Macmillan and Company Ltd., 1958), esp. Chapter IV.

New England Congregationalists. It was also his fond hope in delivering the lectures that were later included in *God in Christ*[47] to recall the Unitarians to the symbolical character of Christian theology and thus to bring the sundered rationalists back into the Congregational fold. But more on this later.

Coleridge was introduced to America in 1829 by James Marsh, then President of the University of Vermont and later Professor of Moral and Intellectual Philosophy at that institution. In that year Marsh brought out a heavily annotated edition of Coleridge's *Aids to Reflection*, together with his own lengthy introduction and excerpts from other writings of the English poet-philosopher. As Theodore Munger has said: "It may almost be said that is it to this book that we are indebted for Bushnell."[48] He read the book while still in Yale College but did not comprehend it. Some time later he came to it again, and this time it helped to produce a profound reorientation of his thought. Here he conceived of that distinction between the literal and figurative usages of words that was to form the basis of his theory of language. But we can let him speak for himself:

By-and-by it fell to me to begin the reading of Coleridge. For a whole half year I was buried under his "Aids to Reflection", and trying vainly to look up through. I was quite sure that I saw a star glimmer, but I could not quite see the stars. My habit was only landscape before; but now I saw enough to convince me of a whole other world somewhere overhead, a range of possibilities in higher tier, that I must climb after, and, if possible, apprehend. Shortly after, a very strong lift in my religious experience came as a waft upon my inspirations, to appraise me more distinctly of their existence, and of the two-fold range that belonged to me. My powers seemed to be more than doubled; and where was the language to serve me in such higher thoughts as I might have? In this mood or exigency, I discovered how language built on physical images is itself two stories high, and is, in fact, an outfit for a double range of uses. In one it is literal, naming so many roots, or facts of form; in the other it is figure, figure on figure, clean beyond the dictionaries, for whatever it can properly signify.[49]

---

[47] These lectures were delivered in 1848: "Discourse on the Atonement" before the Divinity School at Cambridge on the 9th of July; "Discourse on the Divinity of Christ" as *Concio ad Clerum* at Yale College on the 15th of August; "Dogma and Spirit" at Andover Seminary in September.
[48] T. Munger, *Horace Bushnell*, 46.
[49] Bushnell, Letter to John T. Sewall, in Cheney, *Life and Letters*, 209.

Bushnell was often to say thereafter that he was more indebted to Coleridge than to any other writer outside of the Scriptures.[50]

In the *Aids to Reflection* edition published by Marsh we do find many strains of thought and attitude which figure prominently in Bushnell and make up the background of his theory of language. But first, we should note the similarities between the two men, Coleridge and Bushnell. They were much alike in temperament. Both were poetic and mystical, rather than rational and analytical. Both had a romantic fascination with and attachment to nature. Both laid stress on the religious experience itself as the ground of theology and deplored efforts on the part of speculative theologians to reduce the living truths of the Christian faith to a tightly-laced system of cold definitions and constructive formulas. Either one of them could have written:

Too soon did the Doctors of the Church forget that the *Heart*, the *Moral* Nature, was the beginning and the End; and that Truth, Knowledge and Insight were comprehended in its expansion. This was the true and first apostasy — when in Council and Synod the divine humanities of the Gospel gave way to speculative Systems, and Religion became a science of Shadow under the name of Theology, or at best a bare skeleton of Truth, without life or interest, alike inaccessible and unintelligible to the majority of Christians.[51]

Finally, both faced up to a similar religious situation in their respective countries. In New England, Edwardian theology, after a near-hundred year reign, was losing its hold. Ever since Edwards men like Bellamy, Hopkins, Emmons, the younger Edwards, Dwight, and Taylor had tinkered with and modified the Edwardian system in the hope of accomodating it to the rapidly changing attitudes of a robust, expanding America. But the times had moved too rapidly, and the frustrations of theology toward the mid-nineteenth century were betrayed by an atmosphere of defensiveness and negative antagonisms. The prevailing conception of language entered importantly into this atmosphere, as we have seen. In England, the situation was even more stagnant: "Piety was gone,

---

[50]   Cheney, *Life and Letters*, 499.
[51]   S. T. Coleridge, *Aids to Reflection* (ed. James Marsh, Burlington, Vermont: Chauncy Goodrich, printer, 1829), 123.

and that intellectual life which always accompanies piety was also gone. The church confessions were dead, the liturgy monotonous, the hierarchy deadening."[52] But Coleridge and Bushnell were pious souls, and the intensity of their religious feelings was wont to burst the bounds of traditional orthodoxy and speculative rationalism surrounding them. It was only fitting, then, that both should give impetus to new movements in the life of the Church: Coleridge to the Broad Church Movement in England, and Bushnell, to the "new" or liberal trinitarian theology in America.

Right at the outset of the *Aids* was an emphasis upon the importance of a right understanding of the nature and uses of language. As the first and most important of the book's "aids" its author listed:

To direct the Reader's attention to the value of the science of Words, their use and abuse, and the incalculable advantages attached to the habit of using them appropriately, and with a distinct knowledge of their primary, derivative, and metaphorical senses. And in furtherance of this Object I have neglected no occasion of enforcing the maxim, that to expose a sophism and to detect the equivocal or double meaning of a word is, in the great majority of cases, one and the same thing. Horne Tooke entitled his celebrated work *epea pteroenta*,[53] Winged Words: or Language, not only the *Vehicle* of Thought but the *Wheels*. With my convictions and views, for *epea* I should substitute *logoi*, i.e. Words *select* and *determinate*, and for *pteroenta*, *zōontes*, i.e. living words. The *Wheels* of the intellect I admit them to be; but such as Ezekiel beheld in "the visions of God" as he sat among the Captives by the River of Chebar. "Whithersoever the Spirit was to go, the Wheels went, and thither was their Spirit to go: For the Spirit of the living creature was in the wheels also."[54]

The correspondence between this passage and one, already partly quoted, in which Bushnell described the effect of his reading of Coleridge upon his thoughts is striking: "Finding the air full of wings beyond me, bouyant all and free, I have let them come under

---

[52] Winfield Burggraaff, *The Rise and Development of Liberal Theology in America* (New York: Board of Publication and Bible Work of the Reformed Church in America, n.d.), 89.
[53] This was the alternate title of Tooke's *Diversions of Purley;* see Chapter II, note 25 above. It means "winged wheels", an allusion to Ezekiel 1: 15-21.
[54] Coleridge, *Aids*, lviii-lix.

and lift. The second, third, and thirtieth sense of words — all but the physical first sense — belong to the empyrean, and are given, as we see in the prophets, to be inspired by."[55]

Bushnell's interest in etymology, which had a fundamental relation to his discovery of the physical image inherent in words, was no doubt spurred by an admonition such as this one: "... accustom yourself to reflect on the words you use, hear, and read, their birth, derivation, and history. For if words are not THINGS, they are LIVING POWERS, by which the things of most importance to mankind are actuated, combined and humanized".[56] Marsh himself commented significantly in this connection about Coleridge:

To those, who are unaccustomed to the language of the author, it may be of service to remark once for all, that he often aims to attain a greater degree of precision, and to secure the advantage, enjoyed so eminently in the Greek and German languages, of presenting a thought in a form, that is picturable to the imagination, by recalling compound and derivative words to their original and etymological import.[57]

Bushnell's notion of the analogy of nature to mind likewise follows a trend of Coleridge's thought. "... there is something in the human mind", the Englishman had reflected, "which makes it know (as soon as it is sufficiently awakened to reflect on its own thoughts and notices), that in all finite Quantity there is an Infinite, in all measures of Time an Eternal; that the latter are the basis, the substance, the true and abiding reality of the former ...".[58] And commenting on what he called "the great book" of Nature, he had also stated the following:

That in its obvious sense and literal interpretation it declares the being and attributes of the Almighty Father, none but the *fool in heart* has ever dared gainsay. But it has been the music of gentle and pious minds in all ages, it is the poetry of all human nature, to read it likewise in a figurative sense, and to find therein correspondencies and symbols of the spiritual world.[59]

---

[55] Letter to Sewell, Cheney, *Life and Letters*, 209.
[56] Coleridge, *Aids*, lxi.
[57] Coleridge, *Aids*, 252 note 3.
[58] Coleridge, *Aids*, 55.
[59] Coleridge, *Aids*, 376.

Coleridge also asserted that in discussing the workings of God in human life it was permissible to do so in terms of cause and effect, but only when it was clearly understood that this way of speaking was metaphorical, not literal. For the whole question involved the interaction of transcendent divine Act and human Powers, an interaction occurring quite above and outside of the natural order of determined events.[60] The confusion of a merely *similar* situation with one in which the two kinds of action were regarded as *identical* had bred endless confusion and led to the absurd extreme of abrogating the experienced fact of human freedom, in order to remain consistent with the belief in divine sovereignty. This only gave grist to the mills of infidels and skeptics.[61] In like manner, it had to be realized that "Before and After, when applied to such Subjects, are but allegories, which the Sense or Imagination supply to the Understanding".[62] As we have seen, Bushnell also cited the fallacy of speaking of the workings of the will in mechanical terms conceived of as literally applicable, and he branded as erroneous the attribution of temporal sequences in any other than a figurative way to facts of consciousness.[63] The point was an especially potent one in New England, where theology since Edwards had struggled primarily with the problem of the freedom of the will. There were seed-thoughts, then, in Coleridge's statements which entered into the development of Bushnell's conception of the analogy of nature to mind and his conviction that the analogy is validly employed only when it is not stretched beyond a strictly metaphorical sense.

Coleridge likewise viewed the Bible in a vein close to Bushnell's thought. He referred to what he called the "just and pregnant Thought" of Archbishop Leighton that "The Word of God speaks the language of the Children of Men". Expanding the remark, he said:

---

[60] Cf. Kant's principle that freedom of the will is a noumenal fact transcending the Understanding, based as that latter is upon sensible experience mediated through the category of causation.
[61] Coledridge, *Aids*, 135.
[62] Coleridge, *Aids*, 45.
[63] See above, pp. 26–28.

On moral subjects, the Scriptures speak in the language of the Affections, which they excite in us; on sensible objects, neither metaphysically, as they are known by superior intelligences: nor theoretically, as they would be seen by us were we placed in the Sun; but as they are represented by our human senses in our present relative position.[64]

This clearly implied that the purpose and intent of the Scriptures was not to declare upon metaphysical mysteries or scientific facts but to speak forth what was most natural and helpful for man in his religious life. The point of view was reflected in Bushnell's approach to the three major theological doctrines of Atonement, Trinity, and Nature of Christ, where he focused entirely upon the expressive, rather than metaphysical character of those doctrines. Coleridge also regarded the Bible as primarily "a gift to the imagination", to use the phrase of Bushnell, as was shown in his allegation that the histories and political economy of the Scriptures were

the living *educts* of the *Imagination;* of that reconciling and mediatory power, which incorporating the Reason in Images of the Sense, and organizing (as it were) the flux of the Senses by the permanence and self-circling energies of the Reason, gives birth to a system of symbols, harmonious in themselves, and consubstantial with the truths, of which they are the conductors.... Hence, by a derivative, indeed, but not a divided influence, and though in a secondary yet in more than a metaphorical sense, the Sacred Book is worthily intitled *the* Word of God. Hence, too, its contents present to us the stream of time continuous as Life and a symbol of Eternity, inasmuch as the Past and the Future are virtually contained in the Present.... In the Scriptures therefore both Facts and Persons must of necessity have a two-fold significance, a past and a future, a temporary and a perpetual, a particular and a universal application. They must be at once Portraits and Ideals.[65]

From these comments to Bushnell's conception of revelation, as constructed from his language theory, is not a very large step.

But Coleridge did more than influence Bushnell at these isolated, though highly significant, points. He transmitted a theological and philosophical orientation, rooted in German thought, that was compatible with Bushnell's own developing thought and experience. And it is this which explains why he turned to a theory of language

---

[64] Coleridge, *Aids*, 56.
[65] Coleridge, *Aids*, 295-296.

in the first place. He took it as a method of giving structure and cogency to those convictions which were closest to his heart. Coleridge, like one of his own mentors, Schleiermacher (who also, as we have seen, influenced Bushnell), regarded Christian truth not so much as a set of propositions to be logically demonstrated as something to be perceived primarily by spiritual feeling. The evidence for the faith was in the inner consciousness of the individual Christian.

While a tutor in Yale College, preparatory to entering the legal profession, Bushnell underwent a religious crisis which caused him to enter upon theological studies. And the struggle was between the head and the heart, the inner conviction of the truth of Christianity in conflict with a host of intellectual doubts. But the heart won out, for as he said at that time to his students:

O men! What shall I do with these arrant doubts I have been nursing for years? When the preacher[66] touches the Trinity and when logic shatters it all to pieces, I am all at the four winds. But I am glad to have a heart as well as a head. My heart wants the Father; my heart wants the Son; my heart wants the Holy Ghost — and one just as much as the other. My heart says the Bible has a Trinity for me, and I mean to hold by my heart.[67]

But it had to be shown for him that there was a valid way of perceiving and expressing religious truth beyond the cut-and-dried logical techniques of the theologians. His mind revolted from the contradictions of such doctrines as the Trinity, and he instinctively knew that those contradictions could never be resolved and be made acceptable to the mind by sheer intellectual argument. When Coleridge showed how the center of religious truth is in the religious consciousness and that no amount of logic could discount its testimony — when he exposed the near-irrelevance of the speculative reason for matters of conscience and morality, the pieces of the whole puzzle at once fell into order for Bushnell, and he was possessed of an approach to theology that was to be characteristic of him for the rest of his life.

[66] A revival was then in progress at the college; Bushnell stubbornly resisted its influence as long as he could, but then finally gave in.
[67] Recollection of Dr. McEwen, Cheney, *Life and Letters*, 56.

What Coleridge did was to posit, as Kant had, a distinction between the "Reason" and the "Understanding". The distinction Coleridge held to be the keystone to his entire system of thought. The Understanding he took to be faculty by which the mind, through categories or forms inherent in itself, reflects upon and inductively generalizes from sense experience, arriving at maxims or rules more and more general and highly probable, but never absolutely certain. This was the faculty in terms of which the sensationalist system of Locke and the Scottish philosophers had been worked out. But there was another faculty of the mind which had been left out of account by them as a distinct faculty. This faculty was the Reason, and unlike the Understanding, whose judgments were binding only in relation to the objects of the senses, it was the source and substance of truths above sense, having its evidence entirely in itself. Its presence was marked in the mind by *a priori* force, by the necessity of the positions it affirmed. The ascendency of the Reason over the Understanding could be aptly illustrated, thought Coleridge, by the contrast between the Ptolemaic system, the "highest boast" of the faculty of the Understanding, with its dependence upon sensations, and the Newtonian system, which was clearly "the Offspring of a yet higher Power, arranging, correcting, and annulling the representations of the Senses according to its own inherent Laws and constitutive Ideas".[68]

But following Kant again, Coleridge went on to argue for a distinction between abstract Reason (speculative or notional Reason, he also called it) and practical Reason. With regard to its own data taken in themselves, Reason's necessity was absolute. Here it was

[68] Coleridge, *Aids*, 145. Cf. Kant's statement of the distinction between the Reason (*Vernunft*) and the Understanding (*Verstand*): "Understanding may be regarded as a faculty which secures the unity of appearances by means of rules, and reason as being the faculty which secures the unity of the rules of understanding under principles. Accordingly, reason never applies itself directly to experience or to any object, but to understanding, in order to give to the manifold knowledge of the latter an *a priori* unity by means of concepts, a unity which may be called the unity of reason, and which is quite different in kind from any unity that can be accomplished by the understanding." *Critique of Pure Reason* (trans. Norman Kemp Smith, London: Macmillan and Company Ltd., 1958), 303.

the ground of formal principles, the abstract Reason. But that necessity could be only conditional when applied to facts of experience or to the rules and maxims of the Understanding; here it was the practical Reason. The double conviction that, on the one hand, the sensibly oriented Understanding could not apply its judgments to aspects of experience not sensible in character, and, on the other, that judgments of the Reason could only be conditional with respect to all experience, meant that the claims of religion could neither be supported nor denied by the abstract Reason or the Understanding. Whenever dictates of the abstract Reason or the Understanding conflicted with such experienced facts as the "Will, the Conscience, the Moral being with its inseparable Interests and Affections",[69] the experience was the deciding factor. Religion depended for its proof, therefore, upon experience and faith, not upon logic.[70] The practical Reason founded its inferences upon that experience and that faith, thus giving the required reasonable character to belief. It was thus for man "the organ of *Wisdom*, and ... the source of living and actual Truths".[71] Still, the abstract Reason did have its role for theology, according to Coleridge. It determined on the negative truth of whatever was required to be believed; that is, it insured that it did not contradict any universal principle, since that would be a doctrine that contradicted itself.[72]

But as against applying the judgments of the abstract Reason in any other way to religious data Coleridge had the following to say. He observed that the human mind formed "certain Essences, to which for its own purposes it gives a sort of notional *Subsistence*. Hence they are called *Entia rationalia:* the conversion of which into *Entia realia,* or real Objects, by aid of the imagination, has in all

---

[69] Coleridge, *Aids*, 115.
[70] Cf. Kant: "I have ... found it necessary to deny *knowledge*, in order to make room for *faith*. The dogmatism of metaphysics, that is, the preconception that it is possible to make headway in metaphysics without a previous criticism of pure reason, is the source, of all that unbelief, always very dogmatic, which wars against morality." *Critique*, 29.
[71] Coleridge, *Aids*, 115.
[72] Coleridge, *Aids*, 120. Coleridge's discussion of the points contained in this and the preceding paragraph can be found primarily on pp. 135-145.

times been the fruitful stock of empty Theories, and mischievous Superstititions, of surreptitious Premises and extravagant Conclusions". It was too easily forgotten or overlooked "that the stablest and most indispensable of these notional Beings were but the necessary *forms* of Thinking taken abstractedly ...", and subsisting "wholly and solely in and for the Mind, that contemplates them. Where the evidence of the Senses fails us, and beyond the precincts of sensible experience, there is no *Reality* attributable to any notion, but what is given to it by Revelation, or the Law of Conscience, or the necessary interests of Morality". Somewhat further on he urged:

Let the Believer never be alarmed by Objections wholly speculative, however plausible on speculative grounds such objections may appear, if he can but satisfy himself, that the *Result* is repugnant to the dictates of Conscience, and irreconcilable with the interest of Morality. For to baffle the Objector we have only to demand of him, by what right and under what authority he converts a Thought into a Substance, or asserts the existence of a real somewhat corresponding to a notion not derived from the experience of his senses.[73]

But although Bushnell was deeply indebted to Coleridge, it would be a mistake to suppose that he followed him slavishly and had little originality of his own. Coleridge had thrown out hints and suggestions which were taken up by Bushnell's fertile mind, transformed, supplemented by his own insights, which were many, and applied in an independent way. His theory of language is outstanding proof of that fact. For although Coleridge had provided seed-thoughts pointing to the sensible roots in words, the limitations of language, the analogous relation of the physical and mental worlds, the danger of presuming that that relation can be literal instead of merely metaphorical, and the limitations of speculative logic, he had actually concerned himself very little with the problem of language as such. He had concentrated rather on the epistemological problem, primarily in its relation to morals and religion, and on making, in his aphoristic and disconnected way, what amounted to a general attack upon the sensationalist philosophy of Locke and the

---

[73]   Coleridge, *Aids*, 109-111.

Scottish philosophers. It was left to Bushnell to develop a theory of language and ingeniously to make use of it as a fresh and engaging way of putting the Kantian conclusions about the speculative reason and laying the proper stress on immediate intuition and the inner consciousness. Bushnell could not even with full propriety be regarded as a disciple of Coleridge, for he was first and foremost a disciple of his own experience, and put stock only in what accorded with that. He found a brother in the Englishman, not a master.

An American who came to conclusions similar to those suggested by Coleridge and stated by Bushnell on the relative place of poetic or figurative diction in comparison to the logical was Rowland Hazard, whose *Essay on Language*, written in 1836, has already been mentioned. His thought has been gone into in some detail in the following pages, not because there is any evidence for his having had any direct influence upon Bushnell, but rather because of the importance of his views as exemplifying and giving lucid expression to this second school of thought of which we have been speaking.[74]

Hazard used the term "ideals" to designate "impressions of things, and all the images, sensations, and emotions of the mind, which are really independent of words".[75] It was these ideals which had induced men to develop language, since by means of language they could be communicated and also be compared more easily with one another in the individual's own mind. And according as the ideals themselves or the signs designating them were made objects of greater or less attention, three types of language arose.

If the verbal signs and the ideals were kept equally in mind and kept clearly separated from one another, this was what Hazard called the language of *narration*. This was the instrument of the memory, since its use required neither reason nor imagination but simply an exercise of the memory in recalling particular observed events and associating them with the appropriate conventional signs by which they could be narrated. But if the greatest attention came to be concentrated upon the signs, instead of the ideals, then there was what could be called the language of *abstraction*. This was the instrument of the reason, since it was the reason which discerned

---

[74] See point (3) on p. 47 above.
[75] R. Hazard, *Essay on Language*, 10.

traits of similarity among the observed facts stored up in the memory and grouped them into categories, designating those categories with generic or abstract terms. These abstract terms then served the reason as a kind of short-hand, enabling it to found its inferences much more upon the relations implicit in or suggested by the signs themselves, than upon ideals immediately present to the mind. Mathematics was the purest example of this language of abstraction.

But if the converse were the case, and the terms of language were so managed that attention was directed principally to the ideals they called up in the mind, then it was the language of *ideality*, the instrument of the imagination. Here it was not generic similarity or symbolic inference but the principle of "association" which was called into play, which was to say, the relation of observed facts, not to one another, but to those feelings, ideas, or impressions (ideals) they tended to arouse in the mind, and the intuited relation among ideals, quite apart from signs. The intent of the language of ideality was to call ideals into consciousness afresh and with their original vividness. Therefore it would not do to utilize those terms of abstraction which men had come to conventionally associate with the ideals; in fact, in many cases there might not even be such terms available, so novel might be the ideals in question. Bold and forceful images would have to be resorted to; new and vivid resemblances or analogies would have to be traced, in order that the imagination of the hearer could be deeply stirred, and the same ideals brought to life in him as were in the mind of the speaker, or in order that ideals could be given some kind of suggestive embodiment for the use of the thinker who wished to call them into consciousness again. Hazard sought to express the distinction concisely by saying that while the modes of narration or abstraction could make *known* the facts that were to be stated or proved, the mode of ideality could cause one to *perceive* and *feel* those facts as if they were occurences passing before him. The distinction could be illustrated quite well in the poet's not being content to state as a simple fact, "all was still", but wanting to add, "still as the breathless interval betwixt the flash and the thunder".[76]

[76]   R. Hazard, *Essay on Language*, 11; 13; 22-24.

Having laid down these distinctions, Hazard went on to make some rather provocative comments[77] about the relationship between the language of abstraction and the language of ideality, both for the progress of thought in general and for various kinds of thought. On the former he held that the language of ideality was the cutting edge by which all thought advanced,[78] because it could extend itself beyond precise terms, which themselves represent only the present

[77] This provocative quality was not recognized or appreciated by the writer of a review of Hazard's *Essay on Language and other Papers* in the *Christian Examiner*. For while praising Hazard for his interest in scholarly matters, despite the fact that he was only a businessman, the reviewer was in general unimpressed with his writings, stating: "The Essays give us the impression of a mind that excels in sincerity of moral purpose, rather than in freshness and force." LXIII (1857), 139. The review carried a tone of condescension toward Hazard because he was not a professional scholar, but it is notable that the three most original writings on the philosophy of language to come out of the first half of the nineteenth century in America were the work of men who were not professional scholars: Hazard's *Essay*, A. B. Johnson's *A Treatise on Language*, and Bushnell's language theory. This perhaps suggests that the professional scholars were so enmeshed in the traditional conception of language and scholarly method that they lacked the critical distance for perceiving weakness and limitation in it.

The *Dictionary of American Biography* surmises that Hazard's *Essay* possibly had its inception in his discussions with his friend and the friend of Poe, Mrs. Sarah Helen Whitman, on the nature of poetry. When the *Essay* was first published in 1836, it attracted the attention of William E. Channing, and he and Hazard subsequently became intimate friends.

[78] Hazard did not have sufficient appreciation for the role of mathematics as an instrument of discovery. He apparently conceived of its importance only as a means whereby men of science could communicate their views accurately and precisely, and thus focus their thoughts in common on a given problem. See his *Essay*, 34. But as Whitehead has reminded us, mathematics often points us to relationships which could not have been imagined; thus, in this case, reason would be in the vanguard of imagination: "Nothing is more impressive than the fact that as mathematics withdrew increasingly into the upper regions of ever greater extremes of abstract thought, it returned back to earth with a corresponding growth of importance for the analysis of concrete fact.... The paradox is now fully established that the utmost abstractions are the true weapons with which to control our thoughts of concrete fact." *Science and the Modern World* (New York: New American Library), 36-37. All Hazard could say by way of qualifying his contention that the language of ideality always precedes the language of abstraction in the progress of knowledge was: "if poetry has not always presented the first indications of remote truth, it is because of the superior discipline and perseverance of men of abstraction..." *Essay*, 52.

stage of knowledge. This was to say that "the imagination, being the most excursive faculty, and describing that which it rapidly glances over, by analogies to what was before known, and by refinements of the language which already exists, has a greater celerity than reason, which follows with assured and cautious steps, and has to adapt a language of terms to every new discovery".[79] The genius, the man in advance of his age, was marked by nothing so much as his keen powers of intuition. And intuition was an aspect of the process of ideality, the discerning of ideals and associations below the level and beyond the reach of the language of abstraction. Thus he characteristically defied or ignored the accepted rules of logical thought, occupying "a sphere too far advanced for their application, and in which the processes of ideality are alone availing".[80] He was like the poet, whose "discoveries are primitive perceptions, and a skilful use of the language of ideality" was all that could "enable him fully to impart them to others".[81]

Abstract language followed upon and condensed into precise terms the vague and conjectural language of ideality. Demonstration followed "on the rear of fancy";[82] "every effort and advancement of reason" was preceded by "great strides of the imagination".[83] And just when the scientist or philosopher had developed a language of abstraction to consolidate the truths laid open to view by the imaginative thrust of the language of ideality, that abstract language or settled system of thought served as a springboard for still loftier flights of ideality and genius into the unknown: "as philosophy is extended, poetry, always occupying the circle beyond it, recedes, ... and to make what is already within the sphere of concrete science the subject of poetry, would be to retrograde".[84]

An implication of what Hazard had to say about the language of abstraction following upon and consolidating the gains made by the

[79] Hazard, *Essay*, 52.
[80] Hazard, *Essay*, 74.
[81] Hazard, *Essay*, 54.
[82] Hazard, *Essay*, 80.
[83] Hazard, *Essay*, 122.
[84] Hazard, *Essay*, 82, 80.

language of ideality was that neither the poetic or prosaic modes of impression and investigation was sufficient unto itself. All thought required a combination of them both. In taking this position Hazard stood close to Park, who had said virtually the same thing with regard to theological thought in particular. It was one of the greatest defects of those who relied exclusively upon the intuitive principle to the exclusion of reasoning, according to Hazard, that they could not distinguish true intuition "from other impressions unconsciously received". Hence, they were "as tenacious of traditional error as of revealed truth". What was needed in their case was a frequent application of the test of reasoning, an expression of the ideals or primitive perceptions of the mind in terms, together with an examination of their relations.[85] "The votaries of abstraction", on the other hand, were

more liable to be led astray by the bewitchments of prohibition, and the plausibility which their reasoning gives to new opinions insufficiently investigated. They, moreover, of necessity, acquire a habit of regarding only the signs, and, however clearly and certainly they may arrive at conclusions, are apt to forget that these conclusions are founded on hypotheses involved in the definitions of their terms. They do not see *things* vividly, but perceive only the *signs* which they have substituted for them; and hence their power of examining actual existences is lessened. By degrees, abstractions obtain in their minds the place of realities, to such a vicious degree, that in some instances they become the ultimate objects of thought, and the signs are invested with all the attributes which belong to that which they signify.[86]

These opposite evils could only be avoided when ideality and abstraction were allowed to work in concert, each correcting the deficiencies and excesses of the other. Of course, in given individuals one or the other mode would naturally predominate, but it was the predominance of one over the other, and not the presence of one to the exclusion of the other, which distinguished the able philosopher from the gifted poet.

Hazard departed from Park and the prevailing language view, however, in holding that "ideality is ... in the ascendant",[87] and

[85] Hazard, *Essay*, 88.
[86] Hazard, *Essay*, 89.
[87] Hazard, *Essay*, 91

that its power "is the highest endowment of humanity".[88] In the following statement of the impact of the scientific revolution upon thought and language he showed keen insight, and his protest was of a piece with the romantic protest, then manifesting itself in so many ways, against an extreme rationalism:

In this process [of scientific development] ideality has performed its part; but the results have been reduced to the more definite form of abstraction. The great magnitude of those results, and the universal interest felt in them, has produced a corresponding effect on the age. Abstraction has acquired a supremacy, and is made the test of rationality on every subject. Ideality is not permitted to range far beyond its precincts. The noble sallies of the soul are repressed. Mind, limited to a particular mode of action, exerts itself on subjects to which that mode is best adopted. Physical science is the order of the day.[89]

But now that successful inquiry had been made into the laws of nature, the world was ready for another enterprise: an investigation of the laws of the mind, which would yield a better understanding of the workings of the language of ideality and of its supremacy over abstract discourse. To be sure, those who reduced the discoveries of poetic vision to terms and a system of terms did much good. They brought knowledge to a form in which it could be easily imparted and made useful; they had improved the means of social intercourse, and given to words a power and subtlety little short of the original thoughts they represented. Such men of abstraction were inspired by a fearless love of truth and never flinched at exposing error, whether it presented itself under the "imposing forms of mystery and superstition" or fought them with "the arms of prejudice and the armor of ignorance".[90] But despite their important contribution to thought and the high elevation to which they attained, they took second place to the poets or men of ideality. These occupied a yet higher sphere, "far beyond this little circle where every idea is clothed and made palpable in words, as a soul animating its embodying clay".[91]

[88]   Hazard, *Essay*, 112.
[89]   Hazard, *Essay*, 122.
[90]   Hazard, *Essay*, 114.
[91]   Hazard, *Essay*, 115.

Hazard was convinced of this ascendancy of poetic diction on several grounds, some of which have already been spoken of. One was that it was closest to concrete thought and feeling. Ideals, not words, were the primary instruments of thought,[92] and while any language could be "but an approximation"[93] to thought and feeling, the language of ideality was a much nearer approximation than the language of abstraction, which turned away from them to move on the level of formal realtionships among terms, taken in themselves. Another reason was that the language of ideality was best fitted to express moral and religious truths, since it had "its source in the deepest recesses of mind", and sprang "from those feelings which quicken and stir the soul, and the aspirations which lead it forward into the infinite".[94] The language of abstraction was well adapted to material things. In the physical sciences it could communicate with great accuracy and precision. But it was "wholly inadequate to a subject which, of all others, must most interest a world of spirits …".[95] This rootage of figurative speech in the deep recesses of spirit was an all the more awesome proof of its superiority when one believed, as Hazard did, that "our finite minds are blended with the infinite" and that "we hold communion with omniscience".[96] Still another reason for the subordination of the abstract to the ideal language was that the former was restrictive, while the latter was expansive and bound to grow with the soul in every new state of its development. This was why it could be the cutting edge of thought, moving swiftly to give articulation to new discoveries and insights, transcending the limits of the more cumbersome abstract or logical mode.

We can conclude this discussion of Hazard's philosophy of language by noting what he had to say about the limitations of

[92]   On this point Hazard took a position in sharp opposition to that of Stewart. (See above, p. 83). This marks the watershed between the two conceptions of the relation between language and thought. Similarly the stress of Bushnell and Coleridge upon the inner consciousness and experience was a departure from the prevailing view, at least so far as religious language was concerned.

[93]   Hazard, *Essay*, 11.

[94]   Hazard, *Essay*, 32.

[95]   Hazard, *Essay*, 35.

[96]   Hazard, *Essay*, 109. This same kind of immanentalism was, as we have seen, proof for Shedd of the limitations of language. See above, pp. 67.

language, particularly the language of abstraction, as far as religious thought was concerned. Religion was adapted to the wants of the "ethereal nature", he held, and this meant that it possessed, like that nature, "a susceptibility to never-ending expansion". It always exhibited, in other words, a higher and better state of thought and existence than that to which its adherents had come. To make of it "a rigid finite system" by reducing it to abstractions could only hamper its progress and distort its true nature:[97]

... a religion which is contained in precise finite terms is inadequate to the boundless cravings of the soul. The ardor of discovery, the fervor of improvement; the confidence of demonstration; the pleasure derived from clearer, self-reconciling, systematic views, may, for a time, be sufficient to sustain its votaries; but these very causes will at length bring them to a point at which terms will fail to bear them forward, or even to express what their enlarged views have enabled them to discover of the numerous and delicate relations which exist between the finite spirit and the infinite. Their advancement in thought has then outstripped their improvement of its signs.[98]

"The more ethereal" would be the first to feel that the abstractions of such a religion were "too cold to express their heartfelt emotions too limited to meet their expanding views of moral excellence". They would be the first, therefore, to discover that there was a "spiritual refinement" which it had "not power to portray; a holy charm, a sublime mystery" which it could "not approach".[99] These would turn forthwith to the language of ideality, as the mode best suited to their need and to the integrity of their faith, only stopping now and again to apply the test of abstract reasoning to that mode, lest it fall into gross excesses, absurdities, or contradictions.[100] As for morality taken in itself, Hazard noted that "in the formation of character, ideality exerts an influence of the highest importance. It is the channel by which the conceivable objects of desire or aversion are brought nearest to the springs of voluntary action".[101] The sense of the demands of morality always outstripped

[97] Hazard, *Essay*, 67.
[98] Hazard, *Essay*, 90.
[99] Hazard, *Essay*, 91.
[100] Hazard, *Essay*, 88; 92.
[101] Hazard, *Essay*, 98.

any attempted reduction of it to a narrow, abstract legalism.[102] It is interesting to note too that, in keeping with his general insistence upon the supreme importance of ideality and the language of ideality, Hazard thought it cheering news that romantic novels, such as those of Scott and Bulwer, had met with such wide reception. This indicated that the principle of ideality had not been eradicated by the encroachments of physical science. Nor was it confined to a few who successfully cultivated it, but happily, it was still diffused through all classes of society.[103] The contrast between these statements and the misgivings of Stewart about ideality and the moral life, particularly the ideality of novels, is striking.[104]

Two other men, now familiar to us, who stood in this general school of thought where figurative language was held to be normative, or where it was at least recognized as having a much larger role for thought than was accorded it by Locke and the Scottish philosophers,[105] can be mentioned. Goodwin's ideas on the relation of language to thought were discussed in the last chapter, and we saw how he elevated poetry over logic.[106] To that discussion we can add that he declared of the imagination that "there is no element so absolutely essential to language, so constantly active in the use and interpretation of it, and at the same time so little understood ...".[107] He then went on to speak of it much as Hazard did, holding that it

is not, as sometimes represented, a false and lawless faculty, but the truest of all, since it pierces into the inmost laws and spirit of nature, and does not stop with the bare truth of science. It is no less sure in its operations

---

[102]   Hazard, *Essay*, 67.
[103]   Hazard, *Essay*, 82.
[104]   Barbara Cross has given an excellent account of the influence of the gift books in cultivating a romantic spirit and a romantic approach to language in mid-nineteenth century America. *Horace Bushnell*, passim.
[105]   I have also characterized the school in this more qualified way in order to include those who, like Coleridge, were less than specific on the question of whether poetic or logical modes of expression are ascendant. Obviously, in this qualified sense, Park also belongs in the second school. But I have put him in the first because he expressly elevated the language of the intellect over that of the feelings. The categorizations are not so important as our understanding that there were these two trends of thought concerning language which made up a background against which Bushnell's own theory was developed.
[106]   See above, p. 74.
[107]   H. Goodwin, "Thoughts, Words and Things", 292.

than reason, but it works more directly and intuitively. It reaches its conclusions, not by slow deduction or calculation, but by direct insight. It is the pioneer and torch of reason, which she sends on before to explore the way and guide her footsteps...[108]

Gibbs also belongs in this school, because he insisted, as Bushnell did, that language is quite metaphorical. He only wanted to distinguish "rhetorical metaphors, which are used for embellishment" from those ordinary words which are "faded metaphors", the literal or physical sense being lost in the mind of him who uses the term.[109] The fact of pervasive metaphor in language meant that "the person addressed is not a passive recipient of thoughts and ideas from the speaker, but by an independent activity of his own he reproduces the thoughts and ideas out of what is presented to him".[110] What Hazard called ideality was thus inevitably called into play, and as Bushnell said in a passage closely similar to this one, words "do not literally convey, or pass over a thought out of one mind into another, as we commonly speak of doing. They are only hints, or images, held up before the mind of another, to put *him* on generating or reproducing the same thought ...".[111] A one-to-one correlation between symbol and thought, in other words, was not possible, given the fact that so many words are metaphors. Gibbs also maintained that the want of a "nice sense of the metaphor" was the source of error and confusion in discussion of religious matters.

Some of the most difficult problems of Christianity depend entirely upon understanding the nature of this figure; as the return of the Jews; the millennial reign of Christ; in short, all the prophecies and declarations of God in respect to the future, all the imagery in respect to the invisible

[108] H. Goodwin, "Thoughts, Words and Things", 293.
[109] J. Gibbs, *Philological Studies*, 16. Bloomfield's comment in this connection is interesting: "Poetic metaphor is largely an outgrowth of the transferred uses of ordinary speech. To quote a very well chosen example, when Wordsworth wrote: 'The gods approve / the depth and not the tumult of the soul', he was only continuing the metaphoric use current in such expressions as *deep*, *ruffled*, or *stormy* feelings. By making a new transference on the model of these old ones, he revived the 'picture'. The picturesque saying that 'language is a book of faded metaphors' is the reverse of the truth, for poetry is rather a blazoned book of language." *Language*, 443.
[110] J. Gibbs, *Philological Studies*, 191.
[111] Bushnell, *God in Christ*, 46.

world, and all the language in respect to the attributes and actions of the Most High.[112]

The attack upon alleged anthropomorphisms in the Bible was an instance of this lack of understanding, as was the argument of Universalists that because the primary meaning of the biblical word *gehenna* was the Valley of Hinnom near Jerusalem, it could not denote hell or the world of punishment. Those who resorted to such arguments seemed not to be aware "that all language relating to the intellectual world is derived from the sensible world", and to be consistent they would have to "hold that *paradise* never means *heaven*, that the Greek *hamartia* (sin) is always *a missing the mark* ...". In short, by their destruction of metaphor, they "should blot the whole spiritual world out of existence".[113]

Since we have already taken note of some of the specific elements of validity in the protest of this second school, as typified in the thought of Bushnell, against the prevailing language theory, we can bring this chapter to a close by looking at some of the liabilities of Bushnell's way of elevating the language of the feelings over that of the intellect.

While the conventional theory erred on the side of placing too heavy a reliance upon the accuracy and non-ambivalence of definitions and tended to overlook the limitations of language and the many levels of consciousness reflected in it, Bushnell's theory erred perhaps as badly in failing to assign anything but a minimal role to definitions and to attempts at clarity of argument and exposition. Bushnell bandied the term "imagination" about endlessly, for example, but just what did he mean by it? We are bound to ask how imagination is to be distinguished from reason, what is the distinction, if any, between poetic, scientific, and religious imagination, and even how imagination as an intuitive grasp of the real is to be differentiated from the merely "imaginary".

Hazard provided material for a distinction between imagination and reason when he suggested that reason is thought by means of mathematics or by means of language as a system of abstract signs.

---

[112]   J. Gibbs, *Philological Studies*, 198.
[113]   J. Gibbs, *Philological Studies*, 16.

If we follow this lead and say that imagination is thought by means of verbal images, then we run into the problem that Bushnell declared that all words are images when applied to mind and spirit. This means that reason as well as imagination has to depend on images, if it uses language to any appreciable extent. Bushnell claimed that there are only two kinds of imageless language, the language of mathematics and language applying rigidly to physical occurrences. But with regard to the latter, he overlooked the point that physical occurrences cannot be fully analyzed or explained without using such terms as "power" and "causality", terms which seem to invert his theory of language in that their primary sense would seem to be mental or volitional, while their application to physical occurrences is secondary, derivative, or "metaphorical".[114] If the complete absence of images be the criterion for distinguishing reason from imagination, therefore, only the most elemental kind of physical descriptions, together with pure mathematics or formal logic, could lay claim to being rational in Bushnell's theory. But this narrows the term in the extreme, and, conversely, it assigns to the term "imagination" such an all-inclusive application that it becomes bereft of any definite sense. It is obvious that Hazard's distinction between reason and imagination in terms of the type of language used by each will not do for Bushnell; it puts him in an untenable and extreme position.

The question still remains, then: how did he intend his key term "imagination" to be understood? On occasion he used the term "imaginative reason",[115] by which he probably meant to suggest Coleridge's practical Reason, as over against the abstract Reason (also called the notional Reason by Coleridge) and the Understanding. But in place of those latter two terms Bushnell seems to have set the single term "notional understanding",[116] showing that he was not following the Kantian or Coleridgean epistemology with any great precision. His epistemological assumptions were left very

---

[114] Frazer, in his edition of Locke's *Essay*, has noted that Maine de Biran made this observation in support of the contention that there are apparent exceptions to the origin of all words in sensation. See II, p. 5, note 1.
[115] See Chapter I, note 92, above.
[116] See Chapter I, note 83, above.

vague in fact, despite their critical importance for his whole theory of language.[117] In this same general connection we are led to ask what role language has, in his view, for restraining, as well as giving vent to, the imagination. The dialectic between logical and imaginative diction in the theories of Park and Hazard provided language with such a role, as we have seen. But where was the check against what Park called "a wild or weak sentimentalism"[118] in the theory of Bushnell?

Now if it be argued that we are demanding that in defense of his language theory Bushnell should have adopted the techniques of that conventional conception of language he was opposing, replete with abstract definitions, then our only rejoinder must be that clear thought at some point seems to demand such definitions. We need to recognize their inadequacies and tendencies to mislead, to be sure. But we still require them. Even Bushnell admitted as much. He only wanted it understood that even in the most carefully drawn definitions the inevitable limitations of language cannot be completely surmounted; some metaphorical ambivalence will remain.[119] Apart from an understanding of just what is meant by such a term as "imagination", all claims for its role in language suffer from a deficiency of clarity and convincingness. A similar critique could be made of Bushnell's use of terms like "symbol" and "metaphor", terms which, although absolutely crucial to his language theory, he failed anywhere to define.

Language can deceive when precise definitions are lacking just as much and perhaps far more than when they are depended upon too uncritically. For we often discover that, having been left to surmise the meaning of the key terms used by a thinker, we have been relying upon vague and conflicting guesses, many times assuming that he means to say one thing when in fact he intends quite another. And frequently serious flaws will lurk undetected in those systems of thought where the problem of providing precise definitions of key terms has not been confronted. Considerations like these were the

---

[117] The same kind of mystical vagueness characterized Emerson's term "Reason", which was in many ways the correlate of Bushnell's "imagination".
[118] See above, p. 90.
[119] See above, p. 27.

burden of Locke's plea for reform in the use of language among philosophers.

Definitions of the sort we are now arguing for would not have been a violation of Bushnell's spirit or of his convictions regarding language, nor was it inevitable that, thinking in the vein he did, he should have failed to provide them. Lacking them, his theory is suggestive but not adequate. As a counterweight to the exaggerations of the prevailing language theory, it played a vital and necessary role, but as a theory of language in its own right, it suffers from its own overstatements and is at times nebulous and overwrought. Like so many reforms, it steers so resolutely from one extreme position that it unwittingly runs aground on another.

IV

LOGICAL SKEPTICISM, BIBLICAL POETRY, AND ELOQUENCE

> ... the notions, so frigidly and distortedly aggregated in our doctrinal compends, are one thing; the notions so beautifully and gracefully diffused over the sacred page another thing. They are spirit, they are life.
>
> Edwards Park, "The Proper Mode of Exhibiting Theological Truth" (1837)

The purpose of this chapter is to introduce three factors, in addition to those already spoken of, which help to account for Bushnell's theory of language. The first factor is the implication of skepticism regarding the conclusions of logical method contained in the reductionist verification principle of the Lockean, Common Sense conception of language. The second and third factors no doubt had their influence, not only upon Bushnell, but upon other proponents of what we termed the second school of thought regarding language in the preceding chapter. These factors were the emphasis that came to be laid upon the Bible as a work of poetry; and the trend toward thinking of eloquence as the natural manner in which all deep thought and honest conviction would express itself.

1. SKEPTICISM TOWARD LOGICAL METHOD IMPLICIT IN THE LOCKEAN, COMMON SENSE CONCEPTION OF LANGUAGE

The reaction against the prevailing conception of language which we took note of in the previous chapter had implied in it a skepticism about the adequacy of logical discourse to at least some forms of thought, but this skepticism arose from a ground outside of the prevailing conception of language itself. We have now to speak of a protest against Locke and the Scottish philosophers which arose, not in the form of a pitting of different principles than theirs against them, but precisely in the form of applying their own principles with complete consistency and rigor, especially the rule of empirical verification of the meaning of terms. The man who entered this protest was an American, Alexander Bryan Johnson, in the work which we have already mentioned and which Bushnell read, A *Treatise on Language: or The Relation which Words Bear to Things* (1836).

Locke had insisted that those who would use language with clarity and precision must be certain that their words were built upon and reducible to simple ideas of sensation or reflection. In other words, language, like knowledge, was dependable only when it was rooted very definitely and distinctly in experience. This same empiricism was the core of Johnson's theory of language. He held that words are significant only to the extent that they can be shown to refer either to "sensible information" or to other words. Under "sensible information" he included not only the five physical senses, but also the inner feelings, or what we are conscious of experiencing within ourselves. Failure to recognize and discriminate these three types of reference and hence, significance, in words was the cause of no end of confusion for thought.[1]

Taking first those words which refer to information provided by the five senses, Johnson contended that it was of the utmost importance to recognize that these words have no inherent signification. They can supply the place of no sense. They simply refer us to what our senses disclose. The most forcible language cannot infuse into the blind a knowledge of colors, and this is because colors are sights and nothing can reveal to us sights but the actual process of seeing.

---

[1] A. B. Johnson, *Treatise*, 159; 165. Barbara Cross has stated that Johnson believed that "language that could not point to sense data was gibberish", and has held that he was the proponent of "a rigorous sensationalism". *Horace Bushnell*, 100-101. These statements are not quite correct, in view of the fact that Johnson included the testimony of the inner consciousness in his empiricism and also asserted that words can refer significantly to other words.

The same conclusion had to be applied to every other item of our knowledge of the external world. Still philosophers were continually falling into the trap of interpreting nature by their language, instead of interpreting their language by nature.

"The most important characteristic of language" was "that every word possesses as many meanings, as it possesses application to different phenomena".[2] Ambiguity was inevitable in language, in view of the fact that there are only a finite number of words available to express the infinite number of particular facts of human experience.[3] That was why the meaning of a word had always to be ascertained in terms of those elements of experience, if any, to which it referred at a given time, and why the nature of reality could never be adequately apprehended by means of verbal formulations.

Johnson believed that Locke's distinction between primary and secondary qualities was an instance of what can happen when philosophers overlook or seek to eliminate this ambiguity in words. For Locke had, in effect, restricted the meaning of "external object" to the sensible signification of feeling and had assumed, though he was unconscious of doing so, that the significations of the other four senses were invalid for that term. Thus, taking the word "porphyry" as exclusively the designation of something to be felt, it was inevitable that he should have insisted that the presence or absence of light could produce no alteration in porphyry as thus defined, and that color could not be in it or a part of it.[4] After determining that the phenomena of feeling alone constitute every external object, Locke and other philosophers were naturally led to ask, where is color located? And a philosopher like Stewart could speak for them all by saying: "a few moments' reflection must satisfy any one that the sensation of color can reside in the mind only; yet our constant bias is to connect color with external objects".[5] Here Stewart was assuming, suggested Johnson, that

---

[2]   Johnson, *Treatise*, 35.
[3]   Bushnell made this point, as we have seen, as proof of the limitations of language. See above, pp. 23-24.
[4]   Johnson, *Treatise*, 66-67. See also Locke, *Essay*, I, p. 176.
[5]   Johnson, *Treatise*, 271. The quotation from Stewart can be found in his *Elements*, Chapter I, section 2, paragraph 4.

"connect" can have only the meaning of a tangible connection; he was forgetting that it can also have the perfectly valid signification of a visual connection. Who had ever wanted to contend, after all, that colors could be connected with anything in other than a visual way? Were not colors visual phenomena? The testimony of the senses thus exploded a problem which was only a creature of the "latent sophistry in language",[6] and which resulted from being "misled by not knowing the chameleon character of words".[7]

Failure to perceive the need for reducing words to their concrete empirical references had created any number of additional problems or delusions, such as the comments of Hume on causation. He had declared that there was no visible union between any cause and its effect. But the union which he had in mind was the sight and feel exhibited by the links of a chain. And this kind of union could never be seriously intended by a person holding that a cause and its effect are united, simply because cause and effect can exist only successively, never simultaneously. To talk, therefore, of seeing a cause and effect united, as when we see the union of two links, was to talk of seeing at the same time a present phenomenon and a past one, or a present one and a future one. It was to speak absurdly. Language could not explain or disprove the experienced fact of cause and effect; it could only point to that experienced fact.[8] This crucial last point had also been overlooked by Thomas Brown. For his definition of causation as "an immediate invariable antecedent" could only simplify causation when the meaning of the phrase was sought from another source than the revelations of the senses, which would be to seek a fallacious meaning anyhow. The experienced fact of causation was the only meaning that phrase or its more terse counterpart, the word "causation" itself, could legitimately have.[9] For Johnson held that to transmute a word into a group of words (a definition) was not to transmute the sensible fact itself into words. That could never be contained in language; language could only

---

[6]   Johnson, *Treatise*, 66.
[7]   Johnson, *Treatise*, 273.
[8]   Johnson, *Treatise*, 84-85.
[9]   Johnson, *Treatise*, 122. Bushnell made a similar criticism of Brown on this point. See above, pp. 27-28.

refer to it.[10] Attempts to define or penetrate into the mystery of matter beyond what is disclosed of its nature by the senses met with similar objections from Johnson, and he had here in mind the Cartesian allegation that extension is the essential property of matter, as well as Newton's notion that all material bodies are a congeries of uniform and like corpuscles, arranged in various shapes and masses by the forces of attraction and repulsion. Philosophers and scientists all too easily overlooked the fact that when their words went beyond what their senses could perceive, they were no longer talking about nature but were simply drawing verbal consequences from verbal premises.[11]

There was in fact in most of science what Johnson called a "bo-peep game" between nature and language, the verbal meanings of words and propositions becoming so confounded with their sensible meanings "that a reader usually acquires by his study, a knowledge of the verbal ingenuity of man, but not a knowledge of the sensible realities of the universe".[12] It was an observed fact, for example, that when the air was evacuated from a tube standing in a pool of mercury, the mercury would rise a certain distance in the tube. When as an explanation for this sensible fact it was said that it is the pressure of the atmosphere which makes the mercury rise, this was what Johnson called a "theoretical agent"[13] or "a verbal cause to account for a sensible effect".[14] It was verbal both because it did not refer directly to a sensible fact but was an inference from a sensible fact and because the pressure of the atmosphere thus inferred could not itself be felt. When from this verbal cause the scientist went on to infer a verbal effect, computing that every man of ordinary proportions sustains a pressure of fourteen tons of atmosphere, it was not generally realized how far he had moved from the original sensible fact which was the only certain meaning or reference of his theory. His conclusion excited wonder because it was overlooked that it rested upon a quite ordinary fact and

[10]   Johnson, *Treatise*, 177.
[11]   Johnson, *Treatise*, 179-182.
[12]   Johnson, *Treatise*, 174-175.
[13]   Johnson, *Treatise*, 226.
[14]   Johnson, *Treatise*, 259.

because it was not recognized that the word "pressure" in this instance had only a verbal meaning and not the same sensible meaning it had in other contexts.[15]

Theoretical agents resorted to as explanations for observed facts were always such as experience had taught could produce effects similar to those an explanation was sought for. If the phenomenon of attraction had not been experienced in magnets, it should never have been attributed to the earth.[16] It could be said of Newton's laws of philosophizing that they "are properly rules for the construction of theories: — that is, rules for the finding of verbal causes".[17] And of every theory of science, however sweeping and wondrous it was, it needed to be understood that its illustrations were in point of fact the limits of its sensible meaning and the sole measure of its dependability. When new discoveries were made, new theoretical agents were suggested and the adequacy of the older ones often called into question; and when a theory, in some of its results, conflicted with experience, the theory usually had to be abandoned.[18] All of which served as a strong reminder of the fact that "Theories are human contrivances by which we artificially associate sensible realities, and by familiar processes, account for their production."[19] Men of science, however, were always overlooking this merely verbal or hypothetical character of their theories and slipping into the habit of treating them as statements of sensible fact or even as units of the natural world.[20]

In making these points Johnson declared that he did not wish to deprecate scientific theories, which were important and useful

---

[15]   Johnson, *Treatise*, 226 note 1; 225-227; 259.
[16]   Johnson, *Treatise*, 230.
[17]   Johnson, *Treatise*, 257.
[18]   Johnson, *Treatise*, 232-235.
[19]   Johnson pointed out that "the word gravity names many interesting and important phenomena", but that it was a mistake to look for it or speak of it as an actual unit or entity of nature. It was a verbal aggregation, not a thing. The search for the identity of the mind betrayed the same delusion, for "the consciousness of a man is the many phenomena to which the word refers, — precisely as the wealth of a man is the various items of his property to which the word wealth refers". *Treatise*, 76-78.
[20]   Johnson, *Treatise*, 238.

when validly employed, but only "to mark distinctly the boundaries between what is verbal and what is sensible. Our senses alone can reveal to us sensible realities; and the moment words attempt to express more than our senses discover, the words lose all sensible signification, how much so ever they may retain a verbal signification."[21] To state the matter differently, he wanted to bring to the attention of scientists and readers of science how crucial it was for them to have a proper understanding of the nature of language, lest they "mistake words for things".[22]

Johnson argued in much the same vein when he came to deal with the language relating to the inner consciousness. Since even fewer words were available for this aspect of experience than for the sensible aspect, the possibilities for error and misunderstanding were proportionately increased.[23] Then too, the propositions of this type of language depended for their significance upon particular items of experience in the inner consciousness, and if the hearer did not have in his experience those items to which the speaker wished to make reference, there could be no communication. This explained why religious language could not be understood by irreligious men. They had not the requisite internal feelings upon which the statements of religion depended for their meaning.[24]

Because he believed religious language to be grounded in internal feelings or in the statements of revelation, themselves interpreted and corroborated by feeling,[25] Johnson considered it obvious that logic could have little effect against it. Logic referred only to the verbal meanings of words. In logic "conclusions respond verbally to premises, as a parrot responds to questions which we may ask it. Whether the answer shall be significant or not, depends on something other than the parrot."[26] Logic could "effect nothing", till it could succeed in preventing "the Scriptures from exciting religious feelings".[27]

[21] Johnson, *Treatise*, 175.
[22] Johnson, *Treatise*, 181.
[23] Johnson, *Treatise*, 163.
[24] Johnson, *Treatise*, 126; 160.
[25] Johnson, *Treatise*, 165.
[26] Johnson, *Treatise*, 217.
[27] Johnson, *Treatise*, 160.

If logic could not disprove religious statements, neither could it shore them up. Johnson held natural theology in low regard. It was a clear case of using words insignificantly, because the matters with which it tried to deal were wholly beyond the range of experience. This was indicated by the fact that logical processes, when pursued to their ultimate limits, ended up in absurdity.

"Since something must have existed from eternity", says Paley, in his Natural Theology, "why may not the universe be that something?" He answers thus: "the contrivance which we perceive in the universe proves that it was preceded by a contriver, and hence it existed not eternally." But why does a contrivance imply a contriver? Because both words refer to our operations. In them only the implication possesses a sensible signification. I would ask (but reverently) whether the appearance of Deity would not exhibit a contrivance as evidently as the universe? If it would, even Deity could not have been eternal: for a contrivance implies a previous contriver. Language is inadequate to such speculations; they are even impious. The heathen make graven images — we make verbal ones; and the heathen worship not more ardently the work of their hands, then we the work of our pens.[28]

The truths for which natural theology sought in vain were to be found only in revelation, and Johnson avowed that he was "fully impressed with the paramount authority of the Holy Scriptures" and could "admit that no repugnant doctrine can be true".[29] His philosophy of language, while it crumbled natural theology, thereby made greater room for faith. Yet he insisted, in words akin to Bushnell's on the same subject, that

a revelation must necessarily be adapted to our capacity. What we could not understand would be no revelation. It was given for the regulation of our conduct, and not for the gratification of our curiosity.... All that belongs to life is revealed in intelligible language, and what belongs to another life could not be intelligible in any language.[30]

With regard to logic in general Johnson insisted upon a clear distinction between the propositions experience forced men to make and those the mere forms of language compelled them to give assent

28   Johnson, *Treatise*, 205.
29   Johnson, *Treatise*, 208.
30   Johnson, *Treatise*, 210.

to. The latter were purely verbal.[31] But philosophers seemed to put great stock in these latter, and their speculations often turned out to be "nothing but verbal deductions from names and definitions".[32] And this had the result of causing whole philosophical positions to hang upon the thread of a single term or definition. If we employ language simply to refer to phenomena, no serious evil can arise from the terms we adopt; but if we select words to draw from them logical deductions, the slightest change of phraseology may produce in philosophy revolutions which no man can foresee till he has found all the consequences that may be logically deduced from the new names which he introduces. The metaphysician who concludes his book by asserting that nothing exists exterior of his mind, might have concluded it by asserting that everything is exterior, if he had only named the objects of his knowledge impressions instead of ideas.[33]

Philosophers, like scientists, needed to be warned away from the seductions of their logic to the testimonny of their senses and internal consciousness. Descartes had acted, for example, as if verbal formulas, and not experience, were the ultimately dependable things. He had not seen that "the silent realities of our experience alone teach us the realities of our nature".[34]

Johnson's comments on analogy are interesting for us. He was convinced that analogies and allegories from the physical world, when applied to the facts of consciousness, were invariably crude and misleading. Locke's analogy of the *tabula rasa* was a clear case in point. It was in the nature of a theory for Johnson, as we have seen, that it be "the predication verbally of some means which we have experienced to be capable of producing a result like that which we are striving to explain".[35] But since nearly all theories were derived from physical experience, they could not be applicable to mental operations. The two departments of creation were not "sufficiently analogous".[36] Language, therefore, was not adequate to explain the workings of the mind and spirit; it could

---

31 Johnson, *Treatise*, 198.
32 Johnson, *Treatise*, 222.
33 Johnson, *Treatise*, 224.
34 Johnson, *Treatise*, 263. See also 293-294.
35 Johnson, *Treatise*, 263.
36 Johnson, *Treatise*, 261.

only call attention to them as facts incapable of being verbally analyzed.

David Rynin has pointed out that Johnson's theory of language suffered from a basic flaw. He failed to distinguish the sense or *connotation* of a word or a proposition from its referent or *denotation* and to see that the first can yield meaning apart from the second. By limiting the significance of a statement to the evidence that can be adduced for it — what is known today as one of the versions of the "verifiability principle" — he made some remarkable discoveries, and foreshadowed, probably more than any other nineteenth century thinker, the linguistic analysis movement of the current century.[37] But another consequence of this was less dazzling. For by failing to perceive that words can convey knowledge reaching beyond the direct awareness of the individual, that they can state the conditions or properties which a fact must fulfil in order to qualify as the fact named or stated, his system made no provision for false (but nevertheless significant) statements or for meaningful ones about the future.[38] To this we can add that it also prohibited the transmission and accumulation of knowledge from one generation to another, the possibility of language's being what Locke called "the great conduit, whereby men convey their discoveries, reasonings, and knowledge, from one to another".[39] Stewart sought to get around this last difficulty, as has been noted, by saying that the verifiability principle demands only that words refer to the collective experience of mankind,[40] but it cannot really work in this way unless words have more than a

---

[37]   This movement, in its early stage of "logical atomism", suffered like Johnson's theory from a too intense preoccupation with reductive empiricism as the test of statements. As J. O. Urmson has noted, its "view of philosophy as having its task in the reductive analysis of the puzzling statements of our ordinary everyday language to the simple atomic report of immediate experience had to be abandoned". And with this "the ancient doctrine of British empiricism that all non-simple concepts are complexes of simple concepts must finally go". *Philosophical Analysis* (Oxford: Clarendon Press, 1958), 160-161. See in its entirety Chapter 10 on "The Impossibility of Reductive Analysis".

[38]   Johnson, *Treatise*, 17-24.

[39]   Locke, *Essay* II, 149.

[40]   See above, p. 82.

referential significance for each of the individuals hearing and making use of them.

Some of the elements which Johnson's theory of language had in common with Bushnell's can now be listed.

(1) Both warned of the tendency of logic to beguile and mislead the mind through substituting the forms of language for the realities of experience. They both saw pitfalls and dangers in abstract definitions and the deductive method of reasoning.

(2) Both were empirical in religious tendency. Like Bushnell, Johnson laid great stress upon religious experience and firmly denied the right of logic to encroach upon its testimony. Johnson even conceived of the Scriptures as addressed principally to the feelings, and he stated that they were meant to influence conduct, not to satisfy metaphysical curiosity. This fits in with Bushnell's conception of the expressive character of the Scriptures and of theological doctrines, and especially with his moral-renovation interpretation of the Atonement.

(3) Both were extremely wary of natural theology, because it tended to make religion a matter of the head rather than the heart, replacing faith with reason, and because logical language was just not competent to deal with the ultimate mysteries which revelation alone could decide upon. The only kind of natural theology Bushnell was willing heartily to endorse was that which grew out of contemplation of the existence and powers of language.

(4) Both insisted that religious statements could not communicate unless speaker and hearer shared in the same kind of experience. The purpose of religious language was to call up in the mind of the hearer those truths which he himself had already felt; it was not to "literally convey" truths from one mind into another. This meant for Bushnell that a figurative and organic language was required for religious discourse, but on this particular point Johnson made no comment. Both did point out the possibilities for misunderstanding involved in religious language, in view of the fact that its general terms might not always evince in the mind of the hearer those particular felt truths which the speaker meant to have reference to. Or to put the point somewhat differently, both wanted it recognized that it was by no means an easy matter to

translate feelings into words.

(5) Both laid emphasis on the ambiguity of words and stressed the importance of determining their meanings from the context in which they were used. This ambiguity also implied the all-important realization of the limitations of language and of its unsuitability as the material of a hard-and-fast logic. Both warned that attempts to rid words of their ambiguity, if pressed too far, would make thought one-sided and even cause communication to break down completely. As Johnson stated the matter: "To compel all men to employ the same collocation of words is impracticable. The attempt has filled the world with controversy, and not brought us to the desired uniformity."[41]

(6) Finally, both could find truth in nearly all statements, however contradictory to one another. The point has not been mentioned specifically for Johnson, but it followed from his general position that "nearly every proposition is true when interpreted as the speaker interprets it",[42] for what was at stake really was not general propositions, but the particulars to which they referred or were meant to refer. Bushnell made a similar claim for the partial truthfulness of all creeds.

It is in a way quite remarkable that these two men should have come out so close to one another at so many points. For their backgrounds and the framework of thought from which each operated were dissimilar. Johnson was a philosophically-minded businessman, and Bushnell, a theologically-minded preacher. Johnson stood for scientific rigor in the application of Locke's principle of verification to language, while Bushnell stood for poetic and romantic freedom in the use of language, and his guiding spirit was Coleridge. The important elements of agreement suggest, however, that Bushnell's indebtedness to his countryman must not be minimized. And this despite the very meager reference he made to Johnson in his *God in Christ*.[43]

---

[41]　Johnson, *Treatise*, 133.
[42]　Johnson, *Treatise*, 133.
[43]　The elements of agreement and similarities at many points, especially as regards the relation of language and religion, makes it incorrect to say, as Sherman Paul has, that Johnson's *Treatise* "could have been used by Bushnell's numerous opponents to silence him, but Johnson's limitations on language-use

He commended Johnson for the "acuteness and industry" with which he had argued the limitations of language "in reference to matters purely physical". But he complained of him that "to language in its more comprehensive sense, as a vehicle of spirit, thought, sentiment, he appears to have scarcely directed his inquiries".[44] The charge as it stands is hardly justified, and yet Bushnell's meaning is clear. He meant that Johnson had taken no account of that power by which words, all originally physical in their reference, become fit instruments for the expression of mental and spritual facts. The momentous metaphysical principle of the logos, of the law of analogy, had been left out of his analysis, and the role of figurative language, as over aginst logical, had not been brought into focus. Johnson's comments on analogy show him to have been sympathetic to the negative lessons Bushnell drew from his doctrine of the two-departmental character of language, for he deplored the literal application of sensible analogies to mental operations, and if he failed even to allow for the necessity of a figurative application, it was no doubt because he, like Bushnell, feared so much the way language has of distracting the mind from the concreteness of experience to inferences based on its own abstract forms. Still, in not recognizing the positive role of analogy as linking together what he himself referred to as "the two departments of creation",[45] Johnson did fail to strike out in a direction of thought which Bushnell considered absolutely essential to a theory of language. He consequently left unanswered and unposed those problems which Bushnell's conception of the logos of nature and mind was meant to deal with.

---

were less desirable because they were less 'liberal'; the *Treatise* would have gagged the great majority who believed in the spiritual as the highest hope of man". Johnson actually sought to free the spiritual from the confines of false conceptions of language. It is also inaccurate to state that Bushnell "would look back [today] and find that Johnson's *Treatise* and his own dissertation marked the extremes of meaning in his day and ours". The prevailing conception of language, not Johnson's, was regarded by him as the opposite extreme from his own point of view. Paul, "Horace Bushnell Reconsidered", *ETC*, VI (1948-49), 259.

[44] Bushnell, *God in Christ*, 43-44.
[45] Johnson, *Treatise*, 261.

2. THE BIBLE AS A WORK OF POETRY

The influence of Lowth and Herder,[46] revealing the Bible as a
poetic book rather than merely a prose composition concerned
with propositions of dogma, did much to instill in nineteenth
century American thinkers a new sense of the poetic and imaginative quality of religion and religious language which logical forms
of dogma tended to exclude from view. The American editor of
Lowth's *Lectures on the Sacred Poetry of the Hebrews*, Calvin E.
Stowe of Andover Seminary, stated the matter quite clearly in
these words:

On the importance of the subject of the following pages I trust I need
say but little. The principles here discussed are radically connected with
the interpretation of the Word of God. The greater part of the Old
Testament is poetry, and poetry too of a very peculiar and most impassioned kind; and by rules applicable only to poetical language, ought
this poetry to be interpreted. Yet many pay very little regard to this
important peculiarity; they make scarcely any distinction between the
poetic and prosaic portions of the Bible, and employ quotations from
both as if they had been written with the closest attention to metaphysical
precision, and in view of all the subtilties of modern philosophy.[47]

To the defense of essentially the same point the writer of an article
in the *Biblical Repository* devoted himself. Acknowledging his
deep indebtedness to Lowth, Michaelis, Herder, and De Wette,
men whose "poetic perceptions" and right understanding of "what
is Hebrew" had enabled them to "elegantly reproduce the ideas of
the Bible", he painted the effects of a lack of their perspective
upon the Scriptures in the following passage:

It is much to be regretted that, to the mass of readers, the Bible is all
prose. Nearly one third of it, indeed, is poetry. Yet there it lies, cut up
into false divisions, as falsely called "verses," and marred by figures as a
work correlative to the Concordance — a book of texts; a quiver of

---

[46]   Robert Lowth, *De Sacra Poesi Hebraeorum Prelectiones Academicae* (1st
ed. 1753; 2nd ed. 1763). An American edition of this work, with the translation
of G. Gregory and Introduction and notes by Calvin E. Stowe, appeared in
1829 (Andover: Flagg and Gould). J. G. Herder, *Vom Geist der ebräischen
Poesie* (1783). James Marsh brought out a translation of this work in America
in 1833 (2 vols., Burlington, Vt.: Edward Smith).
[47]   Lowth, American edition cited, xv.

equal arrows for the preacher's bow; and by some regarded as a Homoeopathic medicine box, with doses duly numbered, and each for best effect, to be taken carefully by itself. How unlike the manner in which the Word of God was received by the Hebrews! It came to the mass of that people most often, through the poetic sensibilities of men, kindled by the Holy Spirit. It touched men's hearts as poetry, and it was used as such to inspire the nation with heroic sentiment, and lift it up in devotional ardor.[48]

This new view of the Bible was made all the more appealing in view of the threats posed for faith by the advance of science and the development of biblical criticism. In an article on Herder, the transcendentalist George Ripley noted how quickly the thorny problems of the opening chapters of Genesis would vanish if men were willing to say, with the German philosopher, that these were poetry and to stop taking them wholly in a doctrinal sense.[49]

When the Bible came to be thus regarded, it was inevitable that a contrast should be sensed between "the notions, so frigidly and distortedly aggregated in our doctrinal compends" and those "so beautifully and gracefully diffused over the sacred page". Only of the latter could it be said: "They are spirit, they are life".[50] For a man like Bushnell this discrepancy was intolerable, and he felt the pressing need to revise conceptions of theological method in order to bring theology into closer accord with the language and spirit of the Scriptures, themselves now so obviously "a gift to the imagination". He accomplished this revision, at least to his own satisfaction, by his theory of language.

3. THE TREND TOWARD THINKING OF ELOQUENCE AS THE NATURAL MANNER IN WHICH ALL DEEP THOUGHT AND HONEST CONVICTION WOULD EXPRESS ITSELF

We have seen how Blair regarded figurative discourse as but a

[48]   George H. Hastings, "Lyrical Poetry of the Bible", *Biblical Repository*, 3rd s. III (1847), 323-324.
[49]   "Herder's Theological Opinions and Services", *The Christian Examiner*, XIX (1835). Quoted in Perry Miller, *The Transcendentalists: An Anthology* (Cambridge: Harvard University Press, 1950), 95-96.
[50]   Edwards Park, "The Proper Mode of Exhibiting Theological Truth", *Biblical Repository*, 1st s. X (1837), 445.

specialized form of speech meant to ornament and assist language in its its fundamental form of literal statements and reasoned arguments, and how Locke and Stewart distrusted the bewitchments of a florid style. A force which worked to undermine this type of attitude and hence to prepare the way for a theory of language such as Bushnell's was the coming into prominence in nineteenth-century America of the orator. He was the man of the hour. Lyceums and lecture halls were filled to overflowing with audiences eager to thrill to his passionate declamations on a great variety of subjects, ranging from abolition to self-culture. It was an era of reforming zeal, romantic sentiment, and strong individualistic reaction to authority and tradition, and this combination of factors tended to cause protracted arguments in the deductive manner and all merely "literal" or rational ways of speaking to pass into disfavor and be identified with a bygone day, while fervent appeals to the heart and will came to be regarded more and more as the "normal" way of speaking. Eloquent discourse even became the accepted form for the printed page, as can be seen most readily in the prose of Emerson, Parker, and Thoreau, as well as Bushnell.[51]

Articles analyzing the secrets of effective eloquence proliferated during the period, and in them there was a definite reaction against the academic conception of eloquence as comprised in a set of external and formal techniques and a strong trend toward conceiving of it simply as the kind of language in which all deep thought and honest conviction would naturally express itself. Stress was placed upon the personal involvement of the speaker in that of which he spoke, and out of this, it was thought, would proceed a spontaneous embodiment of ideas and feelings in appropriate words and images. An additional result would be that the language of the speaker would be an original expression of his own distinctive personality. All of this tended to relegate logical exposition such as was upheld in the conventional language theory far into the background.

The stress upon personal involvement can be seen in an article

---

[51]   B. Cross, *Horace Bushnell: Minister to a Changing America*, 85.

written by H. N. Day, a professor at Western Reserve College. He declared that eloquence was to be distinguished from poetry, on the one hand, and philosophy on the other, because it sought neither the beautiful nor the true for their own sake but used both as the means "to win the right, the good, the lovely in character".[52] He came down especially hard on the confusion of eloquence with poetry, because this meant giving almost exclusive attention to beauty of form, with the result that the mind of the would-be orator was "turned chiefly on the outward for its own sake; on the style and manner, and hence, unavoidably, the almost irresistible tendency to mannerism".[53] The antidote to this artificial concentration on form was recognition of the fact that eloquence had an ethical, rather than aesthetical, end. It was not meant merely to dazzle and adorn, but to persuade to the good. This end could not be effectively accomplished, however, until the speaker himself became deeply involved in that of which he spoke.

It is in vain to think of eloquence without having the soul of eloquence. The statesman must have a true love of country; the legal counsellor and advocate must be animated with a true love of right and equal justice; the preacher must burn with a true love of holiness and all its correlate ideas, or he cannot be eloquent.[54]

A like note was sounded by Leonard Bacon, writing on "Some of the Causes of the Corruption of Pulpit Eloquence". One of the principal causes he cited was the confusion of genuine eloquence with "rhetorical exhibition", and he spoke with withering satire of those neophyte preachers who thought that fine style could grow out of anything but solid content. These were "well read in Bulwer and Cooper, profoundly familiar with Childe Harold and Lalla Rookh, and always among the first to try the merits of the last new novel". But so intent were they upon emulating the style of their favorite romantic authors that they quite ignored Baxter and Edwards, Dwight and Hall, and the whole deposit of Christian doctrine.[55] Their trouble was that they did not perceive that elo-

[52] H. N. Day, "Eloquence a Virtue", *Biblical Repository*, 2nd s. X (1849), 208.
[53] H. N. Day, "Eloquence a Virtue", 218.
[54] H. N. Day, "Eloquence a Virtue", 219.
[55] Leonard Bacon, "Some Causes of the Corruption of Pulpit Eloquence", *Biblical Repository*, 2nd. s. I (1839), 36-37.

quence must issue from a personal involvement of the preacher in the truths he was bound to proclaim. Only the preaching of the doctrines of the faith "from a mind that perceives their evidence, their meaning, their grandeur, and from a heart that feels their power" could issue in true eloquence, could "be full of life and unfailing interest".[56]

Edwards Park also spoke out on behalf of this personal involvement when he averred that the minister's success in preaching depended "not on his graces of delivery, or his beauties of style, so much as on his enlarged and familiar acquaintance with the principles of religion".[57] He had no doubt, however, that beauty of style would flow quite naturally from such a direct acquaintance, for he stated elsewhere that a preacher's discourse would be "abstract and inefficient" unless he had secured the moral influence of doctrines upon his own heart. He also declared that though there were various means by which truth could be effectively presented, they were all but "modifications of the general one, a vigorous prosecution of study under the influence of pious emotions".[58]

Out of this involvement of the speaker in his subject matter would stem, it was believed, a natural and spontaneous embodiment of ideas and feelings in peculiarly appropriate words. Bacon attested that nothing was more necessary to eloquence than words — the command of language. But how were words to be had? "Not surely by committing a dictionary to memory. Not by being conversant with wordy people, whose flow of language without thought is a disease, instead of an accomplishment. But by having thoughts. The living thought will seize for itself the winged word. 'Thoughts that breathe' will find, or will create "words that burn".[59] Similarly, Park asserted that the "man who lets a doctrine live on his heart until the influence of the doctrine is transformed through his heart, will shape all his words in the likeness of that doctrine", with the result that "his transitions, his metaphors, his arguments,

---

[56]   Bacon, "Some Causes", 28.
[57]   E. Park, "Connection Between Theological Study and Pulpit Eloquence", *Biblical Repository*, 1st s. X (1837), 170.
[58]   E. Park, "The Proper Mode of Exhibiting Theological Truth", 450-451; 446.
[59]   Bacon, "Some Causes", 35.

will all be tinctured with the one pervading and transforming truth which he designed to portray. The sermon is then symbolical of its theme; a picture of it; of course, its manner is just what it should be."[60] This kind of thinking ran closely parallel to some of Goodwin's statements in his article on language. He asserted that anyone who considered "the almost miraculous charm and potency of 'a word fitly spoken', and the pernicous and baneful effect, both upon speaker and hearer, of a word *un*fitly spoken or *un*true to the thought", would be "able to appreciate that power which gives the right word to the thought, which is the sealing and witnessing bond that *unites* the two, and is therefore the only true interpreter and mediator between them".[61] This for him was proof of the kind of organic connection between thoughts and words for which he had been arguing. And this power of which he spoke was the power of imagination, but its exercise presupposed personal involvement or what he called integrity. Integrity he defined as

that which connects or links together in one vital whole the inmost power and being of a man with the outermost expression of it. A man possessing it, is not one thing in himself, another in his thoughts, and another in his words, but the stream of life and personality, so to speak, flows out through all in the one unbroken current, just as we see it in childhood, which is the truest type and symbol of genius. Hence the spontaneousness which always characterizes this power.[62]

The language of the genius was constituted of "living words", because "the same spirit which animates and informs the body, which looks out through the countenance, informs and dwells also in his words".[63] Goodwin even affirmed that it could be taken "as a criterion of the true expression of a thought, that it cannot be otherwise expressed; that whenever a thought can be expressed equally well in two forms of language, so as to admit of choice or arbitration in the writer, it indicates a want of individuality, and

---

[60]   E. Park, "The Proper Mode of Exhibiting Theological Truth", 451.
[61]   Goodwin, "Thoughts, Words and Things", 297.
[62]   Goodwin, "Thoughts, Words and Things", 281.
[63]   Goodwin, "Thoughts, Words and Things", 281.

hence, of vitality in the thought itself".[64] This fact was well borne
out in the work of a genius, such as Milton. Behind Goodwin's
ideal of the genius lurks the ideal of the orator which emerged
from many of the articles on eloquence during the period. He
went beyond the writers of these articles in statement, but not
always in spirit, in saying that the language of the genius (or
orator) is indicative of what language itself really is.[65]

This eloquent language to which a more fundamental role was
being assigned relied heavily, of course, upon illustrations and
figures. According to Bacon the power of illustration, which was
"nothing else than the ready perception of analogies", was absolutely essential to the orator, and he contrasted the vivid, down-to-
earth language of the the effective speaker with the style of those
"scholastic" preachers "whose propositions, and arguments, and
language, all savor of the technicalities of the schools", and
"whose talk is of major and minor propositions, of subjects and
predicates, of entities and quiddities, of substratum and acci-
dents".[66] Park declared that it was "indeed to be lamented, that
the biblical manner, in distinction from the biblical matter of
instruction" was not more attentively studied, and he pointed

[64] Goodwin, "Thoughts, Words and Things", 276. This is another way of
saying that the meanings of symbolic expressions cannot be separated from the
expressions themselves, without serious loss to the meanings. The idea figured
importantly in Bushnell's conception of symbolism, as witness his comments on
the attempt to paraphrase a great literary work or religious symbol. See above,
p. 36. See also below, pp. 171; 174.
[65] Goodwin, "Thoughts, Words and Things", 277. Humboldt had made a
similar point. See above, p. 63.
[66] Bacon classified Coleridge's philosophy as another species of scholasticism,
asserting: "there is something in its air of profundity, in its appeals to the
imagination, in its very obscurity and incomprehensibleness; there is something
too in its lofty contempt of Edwards, and Locke, and the great morning star
of modern science, — which strangely and strongly fascinates the mind of young
men of a scholastic turn, and of an inactive [sic!] imaginative temperament.
But nothing is more fatal to an effective eloquence in the pulpit, than the
fascination of such a philosophy; for nothing more effectually cuts off the
communion of sympathy and mutual confidence between the preacher and the
people. The preacher exalted above common sense by transcendentalism, will
be likely to shoot above the heads, not only of ignorant men, but of all men...",
"Some Causes", 38-39. In the view of Coleridgeans like Bushnell, of course, the
Common Sense philosophy epitomized scholasticism.

out that effective speech "must illuminate, and with its light which cheers must emit the heat which melts".[67] This was to say that a richness of imagery was required. Goodwin spoke in the same spirit when he insisted that nothing could compensate for lack of a figurative imagination in the preacher, not even piety itself. For there were preachers on every hand, eminent for godliness and orthodoxy, whose words were powerless because they were not "living and embodied realities" but only "ghostly abstractions". To be seen and embraced, truth had to be "clothed in a sensible and living form" so that it could "meet and satisfy the whole being of man, and not the intellect alone". This fact explained the universal appeal of fables, ballads, romances, and allegories.[68]

Supplementing and growing out of these features of effective oratory was the premium placed upon originality and individuality in the speaker. "In all true oratory," declared Day, "there appears a personality in all the concrete fulness of personal relations, communicating itself to a personality in all the concrete fulness of personal relations; — a living moral man acting in the present with acting, moral men".[69] The stress was in a sense a reflection of the spirit of the times. "Once tradition and faith had carried the weight of the argument; now it rested heavily upon the individual."[70] Thus Bacon warned ministers that they were "to preach in an age of revolution, an age alive with the excitement and progress of changes greater and more rapid than ever before agitated the world". And in such an age it had to be realized that "dull, prosy dogmatism, supercilious authority, merely traditionary answers to traditionary questions, will not serve his turn, who has to deal with freemen, accustomed to free thought. He must commend himself to their consciences by the MANIFESTATION of the truth."[71] Oratory and Jacksonian democracy went hand in hand, as it were. The time of meek submission to authority was past, and if a man wanted to gain a hearing, even if he was a man of the

[67]   E. Park, "The Proper Mode of Exhibiting Theological Truth", 455; "Connection Between Theological Study and Pulpit Eloquence", 172.
[68]   H. Goodwin, "Thoughts, Words and Things", 299; 276.
[69]   H. N. Day, "Eloquence a Virtue", 209.
[70]   Cross, *Horace Bushnell*, 88.
[71]   Bacon, "Some Causes", 42-43.

cloth, he would have to learn to persuade, to present his case by direct confrontation, drawing upon his personal experience and all the powers of his own unique personality. Something of the same sentiment lay behind Goodwin's statement that true language would express not what a man had, nor simply what he thought, but what he *was*; it would be "a direct and spontaneous growth or development" of his individual being. Mere conformity to conventional standards of style and traditional ideas would be a compromise of that integrity which was the hallmark of the genius and of all effective users of language.[72]

There are distinct correlations between the conception of eloquence which came into prominence in Bushnell's time and his theory of language. The fact that he himself was a preacher is of definite importance for our understanding of his theory, for it helps to explain why he should consider the fiery eloquence of a Beecher, rather than the ponderous arguments of a Taylor, the standard by which the nature and valid uses of language should be gauged. As a preacher he would be much more concerned with effectiveness of expression than with accuracy bought at the price of dullness, which was, of course, a direct reversal of the position of Locke and Stewart. Bushnell's pulpit style also instanced, as did that of Beecher and Brooks, a rather general transition taking place among American preachers, from and older type of doctrine-centered, "systematic, logical, exhaustive, and frequently irrelevant" sermon, to one which centered upon life, suggested an idea, caused the hearer to feel it emotionally, and left much to his imagination.[73] Moreover, most of Bushnell's theological writings were

---

[72]   Goodwin, "Thoughts, Words and Things", 279-280. The stress upon originality and individuality in the orator also stands out in Emerson's famous words of advice to the students of the Harvard Divinity School: "Yourself a newborn bard of the Holy Ghost, cast behind you all conformity, and acquaint men at first hand with Deity. Be to them a man." It is evident also in his claim that "The true preacher can always be known by this, that he deals out to the people his life, — life passed through the fire of thought." *Works* (12 vols., Boston: Houghton, Mifflin and Company, 1887), I, 143; 136.

[73]   Donald Niswonger, *Nature and the Supernatural as Reflected in the Theological Works and Sermons of Horace Bushnell* (New York: Union Theological Seminary S. T. M. Thesis, 1961), 41-42. See also Munger, *op. cit.*,

prepared originally for the pulpit or lecture platform, and considerations of eloquence did not fail to influence the conviction he came to hold of the kind of language best suited to theology. His language theory, like his theology, has a strong homiletical strain. Some of the correlations between the view of eloquence coming to the fore in Bushnell's day and his language theory can be stated. Because eloquence was thought to grow out of personal involvement and passionate conviction, it was natural to assume that it was the type of true *religious* language, at the very least. In contradistinction to logic, with its disinterested aloofness and abstractedness, eloquence welled up out of the soul of a man and told what he really believed and was. Eloquence also seemed akin to vital religion in that it was the language of the preacher, the politician, and the reformer, as they confronted the burning issues of the day in the public arena. It had not the musty smell of the cloistered scholar with his tomes. Moreover, the orator, much more than the logican, was sensible of the limitations of language, for he had bursting thoughts which strained and stretched words to their utmost capacity,[74] and he had to rely on words to win from his hearers not a mere intellectual agreement but commitment to a cause. Oratory was not without its dangers, however, for there was danger that form should become a fixation and eloquence degenerate into mere rhetorical display. In eloquence, as in logical rea-

---

Chapter XV; and Ernest T. Thompson, *Changing Emphases in American Preaching* (Philadelphia: The Westminster Press, 1943), chapters on Bushnell and Beecher. Eleazar T. Fitch, who filled the Chair of Homiletics at Yale when Bushnell was a student there, delivered a series of doctrinal sermons on a four-year cycle which were typical of the old, "plain style" of preaching. They were didactic in content rather than emotional in appeal and were so minutely divided into numbered heads and subheads that one undergraduate complained of being subjected to mathematics not only during the week but also on the Sabbath. Fitch was also retiring and extremely nervous and self-conscious in the pulpit — hardly a standard bearer for the new age of eloquence! Fitch was probably much in Bushnell's mind, as N. W. Taylor was, as he set about to develop a new conception of the relation of language to religious thought. See Roland H. Bainton, *Yale and the Ministry* (New York: Harper and Brothers, 1957), 83-84.

[74]   Cf. the statement of Bushnell: "if one can have great thoughts, let these

soning, therefore, formalism was the great assailant of the authentic religious spirit, as it sought to find expression in language.

Writers on eloquence also maintained that the surging thoughts of the orator would find spontaneous embodiment in fit and appropriate words; greatness of matter would instinctively manifest itself in greatness of manner. It was but a step from this conviction to Bushnell's thesis of a hidden law of analogy, rooted in nature and mind, which caused ideas to clothe themselves in images and metaphors uniquely apt for their expression. Any one who had listened to an accomplished orator or had aspired himself to speak on some important occasion knew full well the difference between "a word fitly spoken" and one inappropriate to the thought.

And since the power of illustration was such an elementary requirement for eloquence, the suggestion was that deep thinking and fervent feeling, such as were especially to be found in religion, demanded figurative, rather than abstract, logical discourse, and even that all of language was a storehouse of metaphors, waiting to be unlocked by him who had a feel for analogies and a capacity for picturing forth his ideas. Was language not meant to be used in this figurative way? Did living thoughts not require "winged words" with which to soar? Compared with the orator's magnificent whirling wheels of imagery did the formulas of the logician not seem like so many of Ezekiel's dry bones?

The presence of these three correlations in Bushnell's thought can be sensed from a passage in an address he delivered before the Porter Rhetorical Society at Andover in 1866. There he contrasted a shallow concern with the externals of style with the true eloquence which grows naturally out of possession by great ideas, affirming that "No man has a right to say a beautiful and powerful thing until he gets some thoughts beautiful and powerful enough to require it. Only good and great matter makes a good and great style." But if a man had something really strong enough to say, "angels of imagery" would present themselves for his use, and there would be "no kind of symbol observed by him in heaven

---

burst the shells of words, if they must, to get expression." Cheney, *Life and Letters*, 210.

above, or in the earth beneath", that would not be at hand "to lend him wings and lift him into the necessary heights of expression".[75]

Finally, the compelling individuality with which the orator handled words served to remind of that distinctive coloring which every penetrating thinker or system of thought and even, though to a lesser degree, every person gives to words. The formulas of logic were designed to circumvent this individualizing power, to make language the same for all men. But the nature of language would not allow it, and the very attempt to achieve it betrayed a lack of comprehension of how communication in the concreteness of life really takes place. It revealed an ignorance of what every true orator is well aware of — that language in its primary and best use is a plastic material to be worked and shaped at the thinker's will, that the speech which is common to all men undergoes many subtle transformations in the dynamic process of speaking.

[75]   Bushnell, "Pulpit Talent", *Building Eras in Religion*, 190.

V

THE LANGUAGE OF NATURE

> Have mountains, and waves, and skies, no sig-
> nificance but what we consciously give them when
> we employ them as emblems of our thoughts?
> The world is emblematic. Parts of speech are
> metaphors, because the whole of nature is a
> metaphor of the human mind.
>
> Ralph W. Emerson,
> "Nature" (1836)

This chapter shall be concerned with two topics designed to eluci-
date the background of thought implicit in such statements of
Bushnell as that nature is "a vast menstruum of thought" and
"itself language, the power of all language", and that "all things
out of sense get their names in language though signs and objects
in sense that have some mysterious correspondence or analogy,
by which they are prepared beforehand to serve as signs or vehicles
of the spiritual things to be expressed".[1] The two topics are (1)
nature as a language; and (2) the Puritans and Jonathan Edwards
on natural imagery.

1. NATURE AS A LANGUAGE

Sampson Reed, a Boston disciple of Emanuel Swedenborg, did
for his master what Coleridge did for Kant; he transmitted and
interpreted his thought to Americans. The eighteen-year-old

---

[1] Bushnell, *God in Christ*, pp. 34; 30; 25-26.

Emerson heard him give an "Oration on Genius" at Harvard in 1821, and the mood and content of it stirred him to the depths. He borrowed the manuscript from Reed, copied it, and treasured it for years, circulating it about among his friends, upon many of whom it had an equal impact. Five years later Reed published a pamphlet entitled "Observations on the Growth of the Mind", which Emerson extravagantly characterized as "the best thing since Plato". The pamphlet was held in high regard by the Transcendentalist, and it went through many editions and wielded a pervasive influence in Boston and beyond.[2]

The importance of these two writings of Reed for us is that they exhibit several striking parallels to Bushnell's theory of language, particularly as that was grounded in a metaphysics of correspondence or analogy between physical things and mental and spiritual ideas.

In his "Oration" Reed announced in cryptic, oracular style that a revolution in human thinking was on the horizon. A break was about to be made with a materially oriented science and philosophy, and a religion expounded in their terms, and a new discovery made of the "unison of spirit and nature". In an age when the finger of death rested on the church because of its abortive attempt to combine its spiritual realities with an associationist psychology, it was not strange that "genius... should take its flight to the mountains", finding in nature what the poets and men of eloquence had always found — goodness, blood-warmth, and inspiration. No longer would it be thought a thing unlike religion when poetry was written from a heart immersed in the spirit of nature. The revolution could not fail to affect men's understanding of language: "The genius of the mind will descend, and unite with the genius of the rivers, the lakes, and the woods. Thoughts fall to the earth with power, and make a language out of nature...". Words would "make one with things", and language become "lost in nature".[3]

These themes were developed at greater length and with more clarity in "Observations on the Growth of the Mind", where Reed

[2] Perry Miller, *The Transcendentalists*, 50; 53.
[3] Exerpts from Reed's "Oration" are contained in Miller, *The Transcendentalists*, 50-53.

declared that a fundamental change was taking place in the character of men's mental outlook, a change requiring a new conception of reason. Few minds could now endure the tedium of syllogistic reasoning; there was a universal longing to view the parts of a subject not only separately and sequentially, but together, and to apprehend each subject in its organic relatedness to other things. Men wanted to grasp reality as they found it in nature, warm and vibrant with life. They had no enthusiasm for reducing it to the static and abstract form of "an anatomical plate of bare muscles".[4] This new conception of reason that was coming to the fore called for a different language too than that formerly associated with mental inquiry, a language "blood-warm" and akin to the language of the orator: "reason will be clothed with eloquence as nature with verdure".[5]

If the language of the new reason was akin to eloquence, it was in even closer accord with poetry, because the latter depended so completely on natural imagery for its power. In their changed frame of mind men would come to regard poetry no longer as a pleasant fiction but as a means of serious penetration into the secrets of nature. Science, with its abstract mechanical laws and laboratory techniques, was a perception of those secrets on one level, but poetry probed them even more deeply. For nature was not only a system of interacting forces but a *language*, and poetic images were but the interpretations of that language: "There is a language, not of words, but of things"; "...truth presented in natural imagery, is only dressed in the garments which God has given it"; "By poetry is meant all those illustrations by natural imagery, which spring from the fact that this world is the mirror

---

[4]   This brings to mind Wordsworth's complaint about a scientific and rationalistic age: "We murder to dissect." Like Wordsworth and other romantics Reed wanted, as Whitehead has put it, "to grasp the whole of nature as involved in the tonality of the particular instance". He had a feeling for nature "as exhibiting entwined prehensive unities, each suffused with modal presences of others", and he was convinced that science, by its absorption in abstractions, left out of account the most important facts about nature. *Science and the Modern World* (New York: New American Library, 1960), 79-80.

[5]   S. Reed, "Observations on the Growth of the Mind" (Boston: Cummings, Hilliard and Company, 1826), 36-37.

of him who made it.''[6] Once the correspondence of idea and object, of word and thing, was understood, the gaps between science, religion, and poetry would no longer exist. For it was after all the same Divine power which acted "simultaneously to develop the soul itself, and to develop nature — to form the mind and the mould which is destined to receive it".[7] So far from misleading thought, poetry was "the soul of science". For without it science was "a cheerless, heartless study, distrusting even the presence and power of Him to whom it owes it existence".[8] It belonged to the true poet to feel the creative Spirit of God in nature and to raise the soul to it as nature's origin, "to be governed by it; to be raised above the senses; to live and breathe in the inward efforts of things ...".[9] The time was coming, indeed, when "the laws by which poetry is tested, will be as fixed and immutable as the laws of science; when a change will be introduced into taste corresponding to that which Bacon introduced into philosophy, by which both will be confined within the limits of things as they actually exist".[10]

In the stress of Reed upon such themes as the need for a break with abstract modes of reasoning and a comprehension of subjects in their organic relatedness, the elevation of eloquent and poetic language, and the correspondence between ideas and objects, words and things, woven into nature and mind by the Divine Spirit, we can immediately recognize parallels to the thought of Bushnell. What is of most interest to us here is the doctrine of correspondence, since that was probably one of the ingredients in the ferment out of which Bushnell came to the metaphysics of nature lying at the base of his theory of language. It is altogether

---

[6]   Reed, "Observations", 24; 22; 21.
[7]   Reed, "Observations", 40.
[8]   Reed, "Observations", 22.
[9]   Reed, "Observations", 22. There is a good deal of resemblance between Reed and Goodwin on the relation between science and poetry. Goodwin too claimed that poetry penetrates deeper into nature than science can, because it perceives the metaphorical and spiritual import of natural objects. See above, p. 74.
[10]   Reed, "Observations", 21-22. Hazard also called for an investigation into the laws of poetic thought which would supplement the work of science in the laws of the physical universe. See above, p. 112.

possible that he had read at least this second work of Reed,[11] given its wide diffusion and given Bushnell's close friendship with Cyrus Bartol, who was a member of the so-called Transcendental Club, the group holding Reed in such high esteem. In *Christ in Theology* Bushnell made mention of Swedenborg as one of those who had discovered "this correspondence or analogy". He had reference specifically to the analogies in the Holy Scriptures, wherein there was "a gradual unrolling or spiritualizing to us of figures and forms that envelop and represent the deeper truths of the spiritual life". But these instanced the larger truth that "the world of space and time is a medium to the world of mind; that what exists, in form, is prepared, by a certain mysterious and perfectly uninvestigable relationship, to represent what is out of form. We live in the visible; we speak, reason, worship, in terms that are of the visible."[12] Certainly there is close affinity between the following statement of Swedenborg (which Emerson quoted in *Representative Men*), and the nature metaphysics of Bushnell:

... you would swear that the physical world is merely symbolic of the spiritual world, and so much so that if you express in physical terms ... any natural truth whatever, and merely convert those terms into the corresponding spiritual terms then ... will come forth a spiritual truth or a theological dogma...[13]

Swedenborg also held that speech is "pictorial," that it is formed "from the visible objects in the world." Language originates, he believed, in the pictorial ideas of the interior memory, and when man desires to speak these ideas fall naturally into the language he has acquired.[14] Bushnell thought, however, that Swedenborg had brought the truth of correspondence into discredit by his extreme mysticism and his "fancies".[15]

---

[11] Reed's "Oration" was not printed until 1849.
[12] Bushnell, *Christ in Theology*, 36-37.
[13] E. Swedenborg, *Animal Kingdom*, para. 293. Quotation given in Signe Toksvig, *Emanuel Swedenborg* (New Haven: Yale University Press, 1948), 288. See esp. Chap. XXII of this work for a discussion of Swedenborg's theory of correspondence.
[14] E. Swedenborg, *Spiritual Diary*, paras. 5585, 5589-90. Toksvig, *Emmanuel Swedenborg*, 265.
[15] Bushnell, *Christ in Theology*, 37.

A most influential American thinker who openly drew upon Swedenborg was Ralph Waldo Emerson, and in his writings, especially in the essay on "Nature" of 1836, a metaphysics of language quite similar to that of Bushnell is presented. Among the ways in which nature subserves man, he affirmed in "Nature", is that is is the vehicle of his thought, yielding him a language. It accomplishes this in a three-fold way: words are signs of natural facts; particular natural facts are symbols of particular spiritual facts; and nature is the symbol of spirit.

Discussing words as signs of natural facts Emerson declared that natural history gives us aid in illuminating "supernatural history". Every word used to express a moral or intellectual fact could be found, if traced to its root, to be borrowed from some material thing. That this was in accordance with a fundamental law of the mind was well borne out by the fact that "children and savages use only nouns or names of things, which they convert into verbs, and apply to analogous mental acts".[16]

But it was not only words that were emblematic. The possibility of their being so rested upon the emblematic character of things. Every natural fact was a symbol of some spiritual fact. A stone cast into the water produced ever-widening circles that man immediately recognized as the physical type of all influence. A river was the spontaneous reminder of the flux of all things. The blue sky with its eternal calm and everlasting spheres was the type of Reason. There was nothing capricious in the discernment of such analogies. They welled up from the universal soul within or behind man's individual life and testified to a "radical correspondence between visible things and human thoughts".[17] This correspondence was the ground and possiblity of all language.

As we go back in history, language becomes more picturesque, until its infancy, when all is poetry; or all spiritual facts are represented by natural symbols. The same symbols are found to make the original elements of all languages. It has moreover been observed, that the idioms of all languages approach each other in passages of the greatest eloquence and power. As this is the first language, so is it the last. This immediate dependence of

16   R. W. Emerson, *Works* I, 32.
17   Emerson, *Works* I, 34.

language upon nature, this conversion of an outward phenomenon into a type of somewhat in human life, never loses its power to affect us.[18]

Language in its pristine purity was picturesque and alive; language in which imagery was suppressed and words used abstractly was not only corrupt itself but revealed corruption in those who used it. It was no mere accident that strong-natured and honest men used language that was full of metaphors drawn from nature; such language was "at once the commanding certificate that he who employs it is a man in alliance with truth and God".[19] Good writing and brilliant discourse abounded with spontaneous imagery and evidence "the working of the Original Cause through the instruments he has already made".[20]

There was no question but that nature was the symbol of spirit. The relation between matter and mind was no mere poetic fancy but stood rooted in the will of God. Recognition of this fact had "exercised the wonder and the study of every fine genius since the world began; from the era of the Egyptians and Brahmins to that of Pythagoras, of Plato, of Bacon, of Leibnitz, and Swedenborg".[21]

There seems to be a necessity in spirit to manifest itself in material forms; and day and night, river and storm, beast and bird, acid and alkali, preexist in necessary Ideas in the mind of God, are what they are by virtue of preceding affections in the world of spirit. A fact is the end or last issue of spirit. The visible creation is the terminus or the circumference of the invisible world.[22]

Grammar pointed to the correspondence: "Parts of speech are metaphors, because the whole of nature is a metaphor of the human mind." As new scientific discoveries were made they added to the reservoir of metaphors expressive of important spiritual truths and had "a much more extensive and universal sense when applied to human life, than when confined to technical use".[23] But in

---

18 Emerson, *Works* I, 34-35.
19 Emerson, *Works* I, 36.
20 Emerson, *Works* I, 36.
21 Emerson, *Works* I, 39.
22 Emerson, *Works* I, 40.
23 Emerson, *Works* I, 38.
23 Emerson, *Works* I, 38.

order to read the vast picture-book of nature one had to be attuned with its spiritual Author. That meant loving natural beauty and living a life of truth and virtue. The parallels in "Nature" to Bushnell's writings on language are obvious. The two men shared in a belief that there is a law of analogy implanted in nature and mind by the Divine Spirit which lies behind them both; they noted that words and grammar are founded on this law and traced the origin of language to its operation; they were convinced that figure-filled language is the natural expression of honest piety and true conviction, and they were doubtful of the spiritual integrity of men who stuck to a language of spiritless abstractions; they linked an advance in language with the advance of the physical sciences. These parallels and many other similarities at detailed points are surely more than coincidental. Moreover, in view of the attention attracted by Emerson's essay, it is difficult to see how Bushnell could have avoided reading it at some time during the twelve-year period from the time of its publication until he came to the writing of his own dissertation on language. Yet he made no mention of Emerson there, possibly because he knew the Boston romantic was regarded as an arch-heretic by the majority of those to whom he spoke and wrote, Congregationalists and Unitarians alike, and feared that mention of him could only do unnecessary damage to his own cause.[24] Heretic or not (and Bushnell did not escape the epithet himself) the two men moved in much the same orbit and gave expression, in the same ebullient and freedom-loving spirit, by their respective writings on language, to a protest against what they regarded as an intellectual and spiritual sterility and bondage, and which they traced, in good part, to false conceptions and uses of language.[25]

[24] Another possible reason for Bushnell's omitting to mention Emerson, assuming that he had read him and was influenced by him, is that he found nothing in his views on language to take issue with. An acknowledgement of indebtedness for its own sake was not a matter of honor for him or for most other writers of his day. When other authors were mentioned, it was generally either to bolster one's own case by their authority or to bat them down as opponents.

[25] Cf. in this connection the statement of Emerson in "Intellect", reminiscent of Bushnell's attacks on logical language: we "perceive the superiority of the spontaneous or intuitive principle over the arithmetical or logical. The first

In regard to what chiefly concerns us in this chapter, the metaphysics of language, they wrote almost as one man. An exception to this, however, was that Emerson claimed that every particular natural fact is a sign of a particular spiritual fact and that the same symbols will be found to make the original elements of all language. Bushnell did not go so far.[26] Nor did Emerson stick to his position, for he declared in his essay on "The Poet" that "all symbols are fluxional" and that the poet could not stop at one meaning read out of an object but had to go on to make it an exponent also of new thoughts, for a symbol nailed to one sense soon became old and false. The essence of religious error was in point of fact the mistake of making symbols "too stark and solid".[27] He spoke also in this essay, in words close to Bushnell's own on the subject, of "the double meaning, or shall I say the quadruple or the centuple or much more manifold meaning, of every sensuous fact".[28]

But Emerson never went against the basic conviction, held in common with Bushnell, that there is power in images to signify certain meanings "because this power is in nature. It so affects, because so it is... The selection of the image is no more arbitrary than the power and significance of the image. The selection must follow fate".[29] This metaphysical belief seems to have been rooted in significant part for Emerson, and one suspects equally for Bushnell,[30] in what we have spoken of in the preceding chapter: the psychological experiences of the poet or orator, who feels himself to fall spontaneously and, as it were, quite inevitably onto just the "right" image when he is inspired.

---

contains the second, but virtual and latent. We want in every man a long logic; we cannot pardon the absence of it, but it must not be spoken. Logic is the procession or proportionate unfolding of the intuition; but its virtue is as silent method; the moment it would appear as propositions and have a separate value, it is worthless." *Works* II, 307.

[26]   Cf. the discussion of this point above, pp. 77-78.

[27]   Emerson, *Works* III, 37-38.

[28]   Emerson, *Works* III, 10.

[29]   Emerson, *Works* VIII, 25.

[30]   An additional and even more basic factor contributing to the belief for Bushnell, as we have tried to show, was the problem of how the second department of language could ever have come into being without some kind of fixed law of analogy in nature and mind.

There lie the impressions on the retentive organ, though you knew it not. So lies the whole series of natural images with which your life has made you acquainted, in your memory, though you knew it not; and a thrill of passion flashes light on their dark chamber, and the active power seizes instantly the fit image, as the word of its momentary thought.[31]

The conception of nature as a language was widespread in America in the nineteenth century and was by no means confined to Reed, Emerson, and the Transcendentalists.[32] Rowland Hazard gave it expression when he asserted that the highest productions of poetic genius were "but imperfect copies of this original language, in which nature appeals to our sensibilities; the beautiful, the poetic language in which God, through the medium of his works, holds communion with the soul, and shadows out the mysterious relations which exist between the visible and the invisible, the finite and the infinite". Jesus had applied this universal language when he uttered his nature-parables and drew from the lily, for instance, the lesson of the universal care of Providence.[33] The conception was also echoed by H.N. Day when he observed: "There is, indeed, an oratory of the most perfect kind, ever open to our study; the oratory of nature. There the All-Perfect is ever speaking. His Divine person, ever holding forth the high moral end of his teachings, appears everywhere." When nature was studied for this moral end and for the mode by which it was to be accomplished, good sermons would be found not only "in stones" but everywhere.[34]

A year before Emerson brought out his essay on "Nature",

---

[31] Emerson, *Works* II, 311.

[32] Other Transcendentalists, most notably Alcott and Thoreau, shared heart and soul in Emerson's conception of a symbolic universe. Thoreau complained, for example, that "in all the dissertations on language, men forget the language that is really universal, the inexpressible meaning that is in all things and everywhere, with which the morning and evening teem", and he declared that natural "types almost arrange themselves into words and sentences as dust arranges itself under the magnet". Alcott believed that "God publishes himself in facts, whether of the corporeal or spiritual world. These are his words." Thoreau, *Writings* (Walden ed., Boston, 1906), VII, 386-387; XII, 133. Quoted in Feidelson, *Symbolism*, 140. Alcott, *Journals* (ed. Odell Shepard, Boston, 1938), 100. Quoted Feidelson, 104.

[33] R. Hazard, "The Adaption of the Universe to the Cultivation of the Mind", a lecture delivered at a lyceum in Kingston, R.I. (n.d.), in his *Essay*, 131.

[34] H. N. Day, "Eloquence a Virtue", 222-223.

another Bostonian, F. M. Hubbard, recalled that men in every age had understood in the appearances surrounding them a meaning deeper than that which meets the eye. This was proof "that the Author of Nature designed them to be so understood".[35]

The material world in which we live is full of meaning. It is written all over, within and without, with characters of wisdom and mystery and beauty. Every fragment is of itself a true and appropriate symbol.... To the practised eye, every flower, every crested surge, every existence animate and inanimate through the whole range of nature, is a sentence traced by the finger of God; to the tuned ear, every voice of melody, and of discord too, is an utterance which the fitting sentiment within interprets.[36]

The meanings in nature could be reduced to two fundamental classes: the logical, addressing itself to the understanding and comprehended by the reason, and the tasteful or moral, addressed to the sentiments and apprehended and shaped by the imagination. The first class comprised nature as viewed by the scientist or philosopher, and the second, the way in which nature spoke to the poet. Great progress had been made in discovering the meanings of the first class, and Hubbard calculated that it would hardly be possible to go beyond the Newtonian theory of the universe. Yet the whole system of physical truth was "enclosed and sustained by a circle of superior and transcendent truth".[37] This was the second class of meanings, which, unfortunately, had been almost entirely neglected or forgotten in the preoccupation of men with what ministered most directly to their physical necessities and convenience.

Both types of meaning in nature presupposed "an outward and natural correspondence"[38] in it to the mind. Nature's laws, as

---

[35]   F. M. Hubbard, "Study of the Works of Nature", *Biblical Repository*, 1st s. VI (1835), 175.

[36]   Hubbard, "Study", 173. Hubbard noted that not every moral truth has an adequate representation in nature, "but the resemblances are numberless, our poetry and common language are full of them, and the mind that searches cannot fail to find them. Light is a symbol of knowledge, the water lily of hope and faith. The relation of a child to its parent is an earthly similitude to the high and cheering truth that God is 'the Father of our spirits'." Ibid, 183.

[37]   Hubbard, "Study", 179.

[38]   Hubbard, "Study", 181.

discerned by the scientist, had been found to be constituted on the principles of mathematics, the elements of which were not in nature (though its materials were) but in the mind.[39] Similarly, the sentiments of order, beauty, grandeur, harmony, the feelings of interest and attachment, were in the soul alone, but it was nature which elicited them in the mind and occasioned their development. This correspondence between mind and matter was a mystery inherent in man's nature as a creature who, though a spirit, was yet akin to earth, was fashioned of it, and made to reach knowledge through his organic connection with it.

Benjamin Taylor's *Attractions of Language*,[40] though ostensibly concerned with language in the usual meaning of the term, had over a fourth of its contents taken up with illustrations of how nature acts as a language. Early in the book Taylor invited his readers to "Go with me, if you will, and as we wander forth, we will listen to the language of nature; talk with the flowers, the stars, the seasons and the winds, for strange as it may seem, they all *can* talk. This is the language of Inanimate Nature..."[41] He then proceeded to provide various illustrations of the truths flowers, stars, the seasons, and other natural phenomena convey to the receptive spirit. A bit of ivy which had wrapped around an oak and then been crushed when the oak had fallen seemed to say: "cling not to earthly things, for even *oaks* will not last forever".[42] The aspen poplar, which would quiver at the tiniest breath of wind, warned of the duty to be careful and kind with one's companions, since there would always be some sensitive spirits among

---

[39] Hubbard's statements in this connection bear a close resemblance to those of Coleridge in the Fifth Essay of *The Friend*. There the Englishman announced the "remarkable fact" that "the material world is found to obey the same laws as had been deduced independently from the reason", and he inquired, with Plato, into the "ground of the coincidence between reason and experience; or between the laws of matter and the ideas of the pure intellect". He spoke also a bit further on of the "principle of connection given by the mind and sanctioned by the correspondency of nature". Cited in Beach, *The Concept of Nature*, 323. Hubbard himself hailed Coleridge in passing as a "profoundly meditative mind", "Study", 183.
[40] See above, Chap. II, note 8.
[41] B. Taylor, *Attractions*, 20.
[42] B. Taylor, *Attractions*, 21-22.

them whom the slightest unkind word or look would unsettle.[43] So distinct was the message of each type of flower that a Floral Dictionary could be offered, where the language of the Amaranth is Immortality, of the Beech, Prosperity, of the Bramble, Envy, of the Flax, Domestic Industry, and so on through the alphabet.[44] Taylor called flowers "the stars of this lower world" and then went on to contrast their collective lesson with that of the stars of heaven:

The stars of Heaven and Earth! Look on these, and see life's shifting scenes; three words express them: budded, blossomed, — blasted! and these three are all. Gaze up to those, and in their quenchless light, still shining on through clear and cloud the same, read of immortality.... Turn to these; their faded forms remind you, you must die; then look on those; they tell you, *you will live!*[45]

But the stars had their separate messages too. The polar star, for instance, said: "Life is a troubled sea, and all men, mariners; when earthly guides and hopes are almost gone together, that star whispers, 'Look aloft! look aloft!'".[46] With the seasons, as with the trees, flowers, and stars, there was a language. Winter covered the earth with a snowy shroud and made all cold and desolate. But there was life beneath that robe, and the spring would again call it forth. "Who, with winter's language sounding in his ear, thinks death a sleep that knows no waking?"[47]

Taylor was, of course, a poet. And inspiration for this kind of thinking was in part the poetic love of nature which has found in it meaningful images since the dawn of human consciousness. But as Barbara Cross has suggested, this mystic fascination with nature had an unusually poignant appeal in America during Bushnell's time because of the nostalgia which newly urbanized citizens felt for their country origins. The industrial revolution seemed to be taking its toll in enduring values of the human spirit, values associated with rural life and childhood, amid the serenity of natural beauty. We catch a glimpse of this nostalgia in both Taylor and

[43]   B. Taylor, *Attractions*, 24-25.
[44]   B. Taylor, *Attractions*, 26.
[45]   B. Taylor, *Attractions*, 39.
[46]   B. Taylor, *Attractions*, 40.
[47]   B. Taylor, *Attractions*, 55.

Hubbard, and its role in the thought of Emerson is well known. When one wandered away by himself into the woods and fields and felt a strange deep companionship with nature, Taylor reflected that "the din of the city would sound unpleasantly".[48] And Hubbard observed that in the love of nature there was also a sensitivity to the settled values of childhood and the home: "The lover of nature can hardly be an undutiful son, he can hardly fail to be a better father, a more obedient subject, and a holier Christian."[49] By contrast, the popular fiction of the day painted lurid pictures of the corruption of young men who had left their country homes for life in the city.[50] Emerson echoed the nostalgic sentiment of his times when he said of the farmer: "The uncorrupted behaviour which we admire in animals and in young children belongs to him, to the hunter, the sailor, — the man who lives in the presence of Nature. Cities force growth and make men talkative and entertaining, but they make them artificial."[51]

The notion that nature is a language grew also out of a complicated intellectual heritage. The belief that spirit informs the universe and that sensible objects are images of intelligible ideas is as old as Plato and Plotinus. As we shall see presently, some of Bushnell's Puritan forebears came to lay strong emphasis on the symbolical role of natural facts as pointing to Deity, and Cudworth and More gave large place in their influential systems to a "Plastick Nature" or Soul of the World which permeates every natural object, giving it a spritual significance. Spinoza made extension and thought attributes of the one substance God or Nature, and Fichte and Schelling, working under his and Kant's inspiration, opposed the mathematical-physical conception of nature as a self-sufficient mechanism independent of mind and substituted for it a teleological conception where nature subserves mind and exists for the sake of mind. Schelling even conceived of spirit as invisible nature and nature as visible spirit, and he spoke of nature as a great poem,

[48] B. Taylor, *Attractions*, 19.
[49] Hubbard, "Study", 187.
[50] B. Cross, *Horace Bushnell*, 58.
[51] Emerson, *Works* VII, 148.

whose secret could only be revealed by art.[52] This kind of thinking provided a way to unify man's emotional and intellectual life (nature's "spritual" meanings were no less real than its "physical" ones) and to escape the painful dualisms of God and nature and man and nature that science and the Cartesian and sensationalist philosophy had created. The idealistic metaphysics and the deeply felt need for unity which had been its driving force was reflected in the plea of Wordsworth and Coleridge for a "marriage of words and things",[53] and in the dictum of Carlyle that "Matter exists only spiritually, and to represent some Idea, and body it forth".[54] It stood out also in the many statements by which Friedrich Schlegel, in a work which Bushnell may have read, urged the general thesis that creation is the thought, the image, the expression and the impress of the hidden essence of the Deity, and that there is a designed harmony between the external sensible world of nature and the inner conceptual world of consciousness.[55] To this catalogue of names must also be added that of Emanuel Swedenborg, whose odd visions were dismissed by most, but whose doctrine of correspondence was eagerly seized upon as a perfect rubric for the times.

The idea that in the act of speech nature is internalized and humanized and then again made external figured importantly in the thought of Wilhelm von Humboldt, as we have seen,[56] and it is very much to the point here, because it gives language a central role in unifying nature and mind. The following summary of Humboldt's position by G. J. Adler, in a book on the German philologist and philosopher of language published in 1886, shows quite clearly the resemblances between him and Bushnell, so far

---

[52] See Frank Thilly and Ledger Wood, *A History of Philosophy* (New York: Henry Holt and Company, 1951), 472.
[53] The phrase occurs in Emerson's *Journals* (ed. E. W. Emerson and W. E. Forbes, Boston and New York, 1909-1914), III, 519, but it is the basic image, Feidelson remarks, of Coleridge's "Dejection" Ode and of the "Prospectus" to Wordsworth's *Excursion*, 11. 62-71. See Feidelson, *Symbolism*, 126; 295.
[54] Thomas Carlyle, *Sartor Resartus*, Book I, Chap. XI. Cited in Beach, *The Concept of Nature*, 306.
[55] F. Schlegel, *The Philosophy of Language*, 508, 516, 525, 547.
[56] See above, p. 63. Becker had a similar view. See above, p. 61.

as the latter's metaphysics of a correlation between nature and mind is concerned.

The most general and characteristic function of language is that it is a medium or link of communication. ... It bears the imprint of the double nature of man blended into a symbol. In language our spontaneity and receptivity act together, and the subjective unites itself with the objective. By the act of speech the external world becomes converted into an internal one; and it is thus that nature, its individual objects as well as the laws by which we conceive it regulated, becomes translated into something that is human. Language is thus a perpetual prosopopoeia. As the isolated sound establishes a relation between the object and ourselves, so language, as a totality, constitutes a medium between us and nature, as the latter produces its impressions on us either from without or within. It is an intellectual world linked to sounds and occupies a sort of middle ground between man and the external; and it not only represents objects to the mind's eye, but it also gives us the impression produced by them, thus blending and uniting our receptivity with the self-determining, active energy of our being.[57]

In addition to this background of thought implicit in Bushnell's conception of nature as a language we can also make mention of the approach to nature he took in his book of 1858, *Nature and the Supernatural*. For this work, though written at a later time than two of his three main writings on language, may shed light on some of the assumptions present in his mind when he produced those writings.

Though he did not want to take the position of pantheism, Bushnell was nonetheless anxious to countermand the rigid dualism, as he conceived it, of the conventional theological attitude toward the relation of nature and the supernatural, where it was believed "that they existed in antithesis one to the other, and when the supernatural 'invaded' the natural, there must necessarily be the suspension of the natural order or natural law".[58] In place of this attitude he urged the conviction that the two realms are necessary phases of the one system of God. To consider them otherwise

---

[57]   *Wilhelm von Humboldt's Linguistical Studies* (New York, 1866), 16. Quoted in Feidelson, *Symbolism*, 75.
[58]   Niswonger, *Nature and the Supernatural*, p. 25.

was to "see things only in a partial manner"[59] and to overlook the all important fact that nature, although it is a "created realm of being or substance which has an acting, a going on or process from within itself, under and by its own laws",[60] still has meaning only in reference to the purposes of God and the needs of man as comprised within those purposes. The rift between the two realms was healed, in other words, when nature was teleologically conceived, and when man was regarded as standing in dominion over it in keeping with the Genesis account of his creation.

For Bushnell included under the term "supernatural" whatever does not issue from within nature's causal order but acts upon it from without. Man was therefore a supernatural being, or to use the Coleridgean term, a "Power", and not just a "Thing".[61] Nature was so constituted that it was pliable to human freedom as well as prepared to be acted upon by the Divine Power, as, for instance, in the raising of Lazarus. Bushnell characterized "Powers" as beings

... moving out from nature and above it, consciously superior; ... subduing it, developing or detecting its secret laws, unharnessing its forces, and using it as the pliant instrument of their will; first causes all, in a sense, and springs of action, side by side with the Creator, whose miniatures they are, whose footsteps they distinguish, and whose recognition they naturally aspire to.[62]

Given the existence of these supernatural Powers or free agents in the universe, standing above physical nature and subduing it for their ends, it was obvious that nature alone could not be the complete system of God — a refutation of pantheism. And it was also obvious that the system of God centered much more in man than in nature, that nature was but the stage for the development of men's "final glory and completeness as persons".[63]

Bushnell left behind him no complete or consistent system of

[59]   Bushnell, *Nature and the Supernatural* (New York: Charles Scribner's Sons, 1903), 19.
[60]   Bushnell, *Nature and Supernatural*, 36-37.
[61]   S. T. Coleridge, *Aids to Reflection*, 40-46.
[62]   Bushnell, *Nature and the Supernatural*, 88.
[63]   Bushnell, *Nature and the Supernatural*, 58.

thought, and it was perhaps characteristic of him that he did not try to connect his notion of nature as a language with this Coleridgean, teleological conception he advanced in *Nature and the Supernatural*. But the two do fit together. Both, in effect, bring matter, mind, and God into close connection, without identifying them, and what is most important for our purposes, both entail a view of nature as adapted to the uses of the human spirit. It is no mere accident that man perceives an analogy between physical objects and the ideas and operations of his mind. He has need of a language, and nature, by providential design, stands ready to minister to that need. The very existence of language in its second department is inspiring proof of the readiness of nature to fall under the dominion of spirit, for there words cease to be "Things" and become themselves "Powers".[64] Bushnell did not argue in this way in the book of 1858, but he might well have. And that fact suggests that the conception of nature advanced there was already present in his mind, at least in the outlines that we have presented, in 1849, with the writing of his "Dissertation on Language". The later book can therefore provide some illumination for the nature metaphysics of the earlier works on language.[65]

2. THE PURITANS AND JONATHAN EDWARDS ON NATURAL IMAGERY

An important element in the cultural history behind Bushnell's

---

[64]   Cf. Coleridge: "For if words are not THINGS, they are LIVING POWERS, by which the things of most importance to mankind are actuated, combined, and humanized." *Aids to Reflection*, p. lxi. Bushnell's failure to make mention of his language theory in *Nature and the Supernatural* is all the more intriguing in view of the great importance he had earlier assigned to the existence of language as proof of the teleology of nature. That he had not abandoned his language views by 1858, as Cross seems to suggest, is indicated by the fact that he penned "Our Gospel a Gift" at about that same time.

[65]   This conclusion is reinforced by the fact that Bushnell wrote an article in 1832 concerning which he wrote later: "This article shows the ferment out of which my Nature and Supernaturalism grew into shape thirty years after." Cheney, *Life and Letters*, 64. An article contributed to the *New Englander* in 1854 contains conceptions at one place very much like those in the 1858 work. See *Building Eras*, pp. 126-131.

idea of nature as a language that has been mentioned but now needs to be explored is the approach to natural imagery inherent in the Puritan tradition. It shall also prove of distinct value and interest to us to introduce the views of Jonathan Edwards on "The Language and Lessons of Nature."[66]

The official Puritan attitude toward language was analogous to the Lockean, Common Sense one in its profound distrust of tropes or a figured style. When Puritan preachers or writers resorted to a trope it was not supposed to be an elegant, high-blown one, but one drawn from everyday life. And even then it was to be carefully unpacked or translated into plain logical statements. The trope was merely a means to an end, which end was to be precisely elucidated at all times, and a trope which called attention to itself or that was used for its own sake, as having a stylistic beauty or symbolical value in itself, was considered nothing short of blasphemous, because it tended to lure the mind away from sound doctrine by enticing the imagination.[67] This was the explicit method of discourse which, while not prescribed as such by the formal doctrines of the sixteenth-century logician-rhetorician, Petrus Ramus, was nevertheless "made inevitable by the whole mental setting which constitutes Ramism".[68]

---

[66] This was one of the titles Edwards gave to the manuscript notes which are more generally known as "Images or Shadows of Divine Things".

[67] See Perry Miller, *The New England Mind: The Seventeenth Century* (New York: Macmillan Company, 1939), Chapter XI. See also Miller's Introduction to Edwards' *Images or Shadows of Divine Things* (New Haven: Yale University Press, 1948). I have based much of the exposition that follows on the latter.

[68] Walter Ong, *Ramus, Method, and the Decay of Dialogue* (Cambridge, Mass.: Harvard University Press, 1958), 285. Cf. also this statement of Ong: "There is little evidence from Ramus' contemporaries that anything very new and distinctive resulted immediately from Ramus' or Talon's prescriptions regarding actual style, in writing or in oral delivery. The plain style, about which so much has been written lately, emerges as ideal and actuality among their followers, particularly the Puritans or other 'enthusiastic' or 'methodistic' preachers whose formal education was controlled by a Ramistic dialectic and rhetoric evolved to the limit of its original implications." Ibid, 283. This is a modification of Miller's identification of the Puritan theory of discourse with the formal principles of Ramus. Ong has also modified Miller's statements about Ramus' logic as a reflection of the universe and showed that his conception of *exornatio* and *ornamentum* was more subtle and complicated than is implied by our English word "ornament". Ibid, 129; 277.

One of the reasons for the Puritans' finding this method congenial to their spirit was their strong reaction against aesthetic embellishment of worship in any form — architectural and liturgical as well as homiletical — as smacking of popery. An equally important reason was their suspicion of the typological method of Scriptural exegesis, which had been carried to such fabulous lengths by the scholastics of the late Middle Ages. This seemed a glaring instance of the dangers of giving unbridled play to the imagination. The Puritans stuck to what they regarded as the obvious biblical types, did not press their details very far, and sought to restrict them to one clear meaning that could be propositionally stated. As for other rhetorical and poetic elements in the Bible, they figured that these too could be reduced to plain propositions which would meet with the consensus of the faithful.

But if biblical types and figures were restricted in theory to single meanings, packed into them, as it were, by the Author of the Scriptures, tropes, a large number of which would be drawn from nature by an agrarian people hewing their livelihood from the wilderness of the new world, were placed under no such restriction. These could mean whatever the speaker or writer wanted them to mean. It was expected only that he would remain within the limits of the plain style. This attitude toward tropes was inevitable so long as they were considered to be a mere garnish designed to make plain statements digestible. For under this conception tropes were self-conscious fabrications or inventions meant to suit the needs of the moment; they did not rest on any inherent symbolical character of nature.

The Puritans were not wholly devoid of symbolical consciousness, of course. Their lives were framed in large metaphors like the covenant, theocracy, and the new Israel. Still their theory of discourse and apprehension was starkly anti-symbolical, for a symbol that can be reduced to plain statements and lose none of its essential truth, or a symbol that can be manufactured at will and that is conceived of in purely pragmatic terms, is no symbol at all.[69]

[69] The concept of "symbol" and "symbolic consciousness" I am working with here, and which Bushnell himself assumed, is very close to that sketched

Significantly, the theory did not work out in practice, and as the years wore on the Puritan consciousness underwent subtle but decisive changes. A century of preaching from the Bible made it painfully clear that biblical figures were not so easily convertible into straightforward doctrinal propositions as had been supposed. A great many of them were so rich in imaginative content that no mere statement could distill their truth. This was borne out by the embarrassing fact of manifold interpretations. The theory posed a theological crisis, for as it stood it threatened to replace Scriptural authority with anarchistic private judgment. It bred quarrels, dissensions, and divisions. So largely did types and metaphors loom on the whole horizon of the Scriptural revelation that the need for a symbolical, rather than logical, grasp of its message was becoming increasingly more apparent.

The attitude toward natural tropes also underwent significant change. As piety waned and the simple Puritan theocracy began to break up, the role of persuasion in preaching became more paramount, and the plain style gave way to greater and greater rhetorical embellishment. Imagination was beginning to supplant reason as the preacher's principal tool. And in the process, natural facts came to be viewed more and more as being significant in their own right, as having an inherent symbolical quality that needed only to be read out of them instead of fabricated from them. The Scriptures themselves assisted in this shift of attitude, for they contained certain recurrent natural tropes which carried the suggestion to an age becoming more conscious of the value of symbols that to the truly pious soul nature, like the Bible, could become the very Word and language of God.

This changing conception of natural imagery is evident in Cotton Mather's *The Christian Philosopher*. For there the method was no longer that of starting with a doctrinal statement and then casting about for some appropriate images to assist in its communication. Rather it consisted in beginning with the natural fact itself, discerning in it some analogy to spiritual truth, and then proceeding to

---

by Paul Tillich in Chapter III of his *Dynamics of Faith* (New York: Harper Torchbooks, 1958).

unravel its lessons. In addition to the factors already mentioned, the new science had a great deal to do with the rise of this new method, for it compelled a respect for natural facts that resisted a merely capricious treatment of them as ornaments and appendages to theology. They were still made to subserve theology, to be sure, but now attention was focused upon the facts themselves, which was an indication of a dawning symbolical consciousness. Mather's reaction to the new science was one of awe and wonder. He saw no incompatibility between science and faith, but was rather convinced that the natural world, in its intricacy of design, interdependence of parts, and regularly functioning plan bore witness to the wondrous providence of God. By singling out "remarkables" in the world of nature disclosed by science and interpreting their religious significance he felt that he could give glory to God. Speaking for example of the "vegetable matter" carried by water to nourish plants, Mather asserted that "the plentiful provision of this Fluid supplied to all Parts of the Earth" evidenced "that *natural Providence* that superintends over the Globe which we inhabit". And referring to the work of a Dr. Grew on plant anatomy, he enjoined: "*Gentlemen of Leisure*, consult my illustrious Doctor, pursue his *Anatomy of Plants*, ponder his numberless Discoveries, but all the while consider that rare Person as inviting you to join with him in adoring the *God of his Fathers*, and the God who has *done these excellent things*, which ought to be *known in all the earth...*"[70]

But not only was nature a vast compendium of "remarkables" pointing to the Divine Providence; it was also patterned after the Divine Mind. There was an analogy of the world and man to God. Thus Mather observed that as all "intelligent compound Beings" act in accord with the three principles of desire, object, and the sensation arising from the congruity between them, so we find a corresponding Trinity in God. His words in this connection are significant, for they show that for him nature, and the science which revealed its operations, had its chief role in pointing sym-

---

[70] Cotton Mather's *The Christian Philosopher* was published in 1721. It has been excerpted in Miller and Johnson, *The Puritans* (New York: American Book Company, 1938), 750-758. The quotations are on 752; 754.

bolically to God: "...this *Analogy* is preserved full and clean thro the *Spriritual World*, yea, and thro the *Material* also; so *universal* and *perpetual* an *Analogy* can arise from nothing but its *Pattern* and *Archetype* in the infinite God or Maker; and could we carry it up to the Source of it, we should find the Trinity of Persons in the eternal GODHEAD admirably exhibited to us". And he added another significant sentence, suggesting, if only very vaguely, that the power of the symbols outreached the power of reason: "Thus from what occurs throughout the whole Creation, *Reason* forms an imperfect Idea of this incomprehensible Mystery."[71]

Not only did Mather perceive a symbolical import in the regularities of the natural order; he also felt that specific occurrences in nature often disclosed special messages from the Deity, addressed to the person or persons involved in them. In this belief he made no break with the past. Thus the diary of Samuel Sewall tells of a visit by Mather to the former's house during a hailstorm. Mather "had just been mentioning that more ministers' Houses than others proportionably had been smitten with Lightening; enquiring what the meaning of God should be in it", when the hail stones broke the windows. Mather "told God He had broken the brittle part of our house, and prayd that we might be ready for the time when our Clay-Tabernacles should be broken".[72] As Feidelson has remarked, "Within, not superadded to, such happenings was a constitutive language...the body-house took shape and was experienced as a radical metaphor made by God."[73] Instances such as this one could be multiplied indefinitely from Puritan literature, showing that they often belied in practice the conception of natural tropes they held in theory, and that the transition to a conception such as that exemplified in Mather's *The Christian Philosopher*, John Flavel's *Husbandry Spiritualized*,[74] and other Puritan works of like character, while it was a definite break with the theory, was

---

[71]   Miller and Johnson, *The Puritans*, 757-758.
[72]   Sewell, *Diary* ... 1674-1729, in *Collections of the Massachusetts Historical Society*, 5th series, V-VII (1878-82), V, 402. Cited in Feidelson, *Symbolism*, 78.
[73]   Feidelson, *Symbolism*, 78.
[74]   Published in London in 1669. This work had wide influence in America, particularly on Mather, and was a kind of watershed between the old and new conception of natural images we have been discussing.

simply a development of elements already latent within the Puritan mind. It should be pointed out, however, that the break with the theory was hardly conscious in Mather's case, and he often exhibited far more of the spirit of the old theory in his didacticism and decomposition of natural images into elaborate and involved propositional statements than of the makings of a new one. He was nevertheless a bridge to a new attitude toward the imagery of nature which received crystaline expression in Edwards' unpublished manuscript on "Images or Shadows of Divine Things" and which came into full consciousness in the writings of Emerson and Bushnell.

Implicit in Edwards' "Images or Shadows" is a conception of natural imagery that is for the first time truly symbolical. Like Mather, Edwards would begin with the image, instead of with a doctrine to be illustrated by means of an image, but he went beyond Mather in perceiving that the truth of the genuine symbol cannot be separated from the symbol itself and still remain the same. In this way he had hit upon a theory of apprehension that could avoid the riotous extremes of "translation" to which Mather and other Puritans subjected their images. He was trying to give natural images the same sort of stability that the biblical types were thought to have in the standard Puritan theory, but his method envisioned a union of symbol and meaning, the one being expressible only in terms of the other. To the true symbol Edwards gave the name of "image" or "shadow" or "representation," and he contrasted it with a mere "signification", which corresponded to what the Puritans had before considered to be an image in that it was a natural fact which could be adapted to illustrate a truth but was not itself coordinate and integral with that truth.[75] In the following passage he does not set forth the distinction with complete clarity, but his intent is quite clear:

There are many things in the constitution of the world that are not properly shadows and images of divine things that yet are significations

---

[75] Edwards' distinction between "image" and "signification" is very much like that made by Paul Tillich between "symbol" and "sign" in his *Dynamics*, 41-42.

of them, as children's being born crying is a signification of their being born to sorrow. A man's coming into the world after the same manner as the beasts is a signification of the ignorance and brutishness of man, and his agreement in many things with the beasts.

Christ often makes use of representations of spiritual things in the constitution of the [world] for argument, as thus: the tree is known by its fruit. These things are not merely mentioned as illustrations of his meaning, but as illustrations and evidences of the truth of what he says.[76]

In the philosophy of John Locke, which he devoured in his youth, Edwards found startling confirmation of the common Puritan assumption that the world is but a blueprint of the Divine Mind.[77] For from Locke he drew the momentous conclusion that natural objects, since they function as a source of knowledge in the process of perception, must be imbued with meanings by an Intelligence lying behind them. In fact, in Edwards' early "Notes on the Mind" he thought it quite likely that the physical world exists only in the Mind of God. But whether a position of complete idealism was maintained or not, there was no doubt in his mind that "The works of God are but a kind of voice or language of God to instruct intelligent beings in things pertaining to Himself."[78] This meant that there were two levels of meaning inherent in natural objects, which required two kinds of perception for their discernment. On the one hand, there was the significance in objects grasped by the ordinary process of perception, and on the other hand, there was that level of meanings laid hold of by the regenerate soul, which Edwards conceived of as indwelt by God as a vital principle and united to him.[79] The second kind of perception was symbolical, the recognition of "images or shadows of Divine things" in everyday objects and occurrences and in the principles underlying them as those were disclosed by the new science. Because these images

---

[76]   J. Edwards, *Images or Shadows of Divine Things*, 48-49.
[77]   See Miller and Johnson, *The Puritans*, 36-39. The identification of this idea of the world as a blueprint of the Divine Mind with Ramism is not quite correct, as Ong has shown, at least if by "Ramism" one means the formal system of Ramus' logic. But the idea figured largely in the Puritan mind.
[78]   Edwards, *Images or Shadows*, 61.
[79]   See Faust and Johnson, *Jonathan Edwards: Representative Selections* (New York: American Book Company, 1935), xxxv.

and shadows were the very voice or language of God to the heart
made humble and receptive by his grace, they obviously spoke
truth in a way that "literal" or "plain" language could not. Therefore they could not be "translated" without their truths being
weakened or distorted. The truth and the image were coordinate
and integrally connected.

Edwards believed that the Scriptures led into and confirmed in
two ways his conviction of a Divinely implanted symbolical import
in natural objects. First, the typological character of so much of the
Bible showed that it was "according to God's method" to shadow
forth by inferior things "those things that are more real and excellent, spritual and divine".[80] Second, spritual things were so often
and continually compared with natural things in the Word of God.

That the things of the world are ordered [and] designed to shadow forth
spiritual things appears by the Apostle's arguing spiritual things from
them, I Cor. 15:36: Thou fool, that which thou sowest is not quickened
except it die. If the sowing of seed and its springing were not designedly
ordered to have an agreableness to the resurrection, there could be no
sort of argument in that which the Apostles alleged, either to argue the
resurrection itself or the manner of it, either its certainty or probability
or possibility.[81]

Gen. 15:5: The stars were designed by the creator to be a type of the
saints, the spiritual seed of Abraham, and the seeming multitude of them,
which is much greater than the real multitude of visible stars, was designed
as a type of the multitude of the saints.[82]

That natural things were ordered for types of spiritual things seems
evident by these texts: John 1.9, This was the true light, which lighteth
every man, that cometh into the world; and John 15.1, I am the true
vine.[83]

The principle of lower things pointing to higher could also be
discerned in the resemblances among the various ranks of being
in the world.

As it is in the analogy there is to be observed in the workes of nature,
wherein the inferiour are images of the superiour, and the analogy holds

[80] Edwards, *Images or Shadows*, 63.
[81] Edwards, *Images or Shadows*, 44.
[82] Edwards, *Images or Shadows*, 52.
[83] Edwards, *Images or Shadows*, 56.

through many ranks of beings, but becomes more and more faint and languid. Thus how many things in brutes are analogous to what is to be observed in men; in some the image is more lively, in others less, till we come to the lowest rank of brutes, in whom it is still more faint than others. But if we go from them to plants, still the analogy and similtude holds in many things and in different degrees in different plants, till we come to metals and some other inanimate things, wherein still are to be seen some faint represent[ations] of things appertaining to mankind. So it is with respect to the representations there are in the external world of things in the spiritual world.[84]

Science afforded many insights into spiritual truth for Edwards, as it had for Mather. Indeed, the deep significance of scientific facts could only be understood by the regenerate heart, so that far from there being any kind of hiatus between science and religion, it was the religious man who was best equipped to comprehend the full depth and range of the truths science disclosed.[85] The discovery of the principle of gravity by Newton was also the discovery of a potent spritual symbol.

The whole material universe is preserved by gravity or attraction, or the mutual tendency of all bodies to each other. One part of the universe is

---

[84] Edwards, *Images or Shadows*, 84-85. See also pp. 44; 46; 65. William Kirby, in the work Bushnell cited in support of his own conception of the language of nature, observed, as Edwards did, that as one ascends the scale from minerals, to plants, to animals, to man, "every where a series of references of one thing to another may be traced, so as to render it very probable that every created thing has its representative somewhere in nature". This "system of representations" indicated that "the great Instructor of man placed this world before him as an open though mystical book, in which the different objects were the letters and words of a language...". *On the Power*, II, 523-524.

[85] Francis Wayland, a Baptist minister of the nineteenth century, argued in much this same vein in his Phi Beta Kappa address on "The Philosophy of Analogy", delivered in 1831. Wayland reasoned that since God created the world, the biblical revelation of his mode of action in the spiritual sphere would shed light on his mode of action in nature. Conversely, advances in science would shed light on the truths of revelation. And if an intelligent system reflected the character of its Author, it stood to reason that those who were most successful in applying the science of analogy would be those most acquainted with God. Men with religious faith would make better scientists than infidels. For example, Newton, humble before a Creator of whose exalted greatness he was fully conscious, was able to escape the snare of a provincial, earth-centered conception of the law of gravity and to extend it far out into the solar system as a whole. For Wayland's Discourse see Joseph Blau (ed.), *American Philosophic Addresses* (New York: Columbia University Press, 1946), 347-363.

hereby made beneficial to another; the beauty, harmony, and order, regular progress, life, and motion, and in short all the well-being of the whole frame depends on it. This is a type of love or charity in the spiritual world.[86]

The invention of telescopes was "a type and forerunner of the great increase in the knowledge of heavenly things that shall be in the approaching glorious times of the Christian church".[87] The conception of the animal and the formation of his embryo was "a lively image of the manner of the formation of the new creature", and Edwards began to trace analogies between physical and spiritual birth and development.[88] The minuscule dimensions of the earth in comparison with the vastness of space seemed "to typify how that worldly things, all worldly honour and pleasure and profit, yea, the whole world and all worldly things put together, is so much lower and less than heavenly glory".[89] The Copernican discovery of heavenly motions and the invention of clocks and machines were types of the providence of God in its governance of the moral world, where there "is as it were a wheel within a wheel, the whole system is nothing else but wheels within wheels, lesser wheels within greater". The first chapter of Ezekiel confirmed the typological character of these things.[90]

Emerson and Bushnell had, in short, a conception of natural imagery that was strikingly like that of Edwards. His idea that God has given a symbolical import to the objects and occurrences of nature played a prominent part in their thought. His belief that it takes a regenerate heart to discern the meaning of these natural symbols is closely related to the conviction of Emerson that language full of metaphors drawn from nature is "at once the

---

[86] Edwards, *Images or Shadows*, 79. Bushnell put forward precisely this reading of the symbolical character of gravity in support of his position that an advancing science gives new power and precision to language: "As an example, I may say that love to God is the gravitating principle of the moral universe, and challenge anyone to express the same thought in language older than the Newtonian system." Address on "Revelation", excerpted in Bushnell, *The Spirit in Man* (New York: Charles Scribner's Sons, 1903), 357-359. See 358-359.
[87] Edwards, *Images or Shadows*, 102.
[88] Edwards, *Images*, 127-128.
[89] Edwards, *Images*, 57; see also 97.
[90] Edwards, *Images*, 85-86; 105-108; 130.

commanding certificate that he who employs it is a man in alliance with truth and God",[91] and with Bushnell's corresponding conviction that language rich in natural imagery is the expression of deep piety and conviction, while the man who speaks in abstractions reveals unwittingly that his religion has gone stale. Edwards' realization that a genuine symbol cannot be translated into plain statements and still remain the same shows him to have possessed a symbolic consciousness like that which lay behind almost everything Emerson wrote and which was the burden of Bushnell's revolt against the prevalent conception of language, with its penchant for "literal" statements. The affirmation of Edwards that the discoveries of science are at the same time the uncovering of important new symbols coincides with Emerson's view that "nature is a language, and every new fact that we learn is a new word".[92] And it is echoed in the statements in which Bushnell coupled the advance of science with the development and strengthening of language, particularly religious language, as for instance this one, which has not been previously presented:

... the day is approaching when religion will take the position of a science and command the united assent of all good men.... it will come to pass through the progress of natural science. The first order of language was built on the superficial types of nature. It reflected a flat world, not a solid orb. But now astronomy has hung up the round orb, perfect in its orbit and exact in its mute revelations. Chemistry has dissolved its particles and settled their affinities.... The whole world in short is undergoing a re-survey, in which its inner types are to be revealed.... Every one of these inner types of the world is destined, as science becomes familiar, to be wrought into moral language. And truth, lying no longer in mere superfices,[93] will beam out into a full orb of consistent, permanent

91   See above, p. 152.
92   Emerson, *Journals* III, 227. Cited by Feidelson, *Symbolism*, 32.
93   Cross' misinterpretation of this word has caused her to misunderstand Bushnell's whole point in this passage. She has stated: "Bushnell's faith in this divine language [of nature] wavered. God communicated through metaphors, but Bushnell turned to science for promise of a language in which truth, 'lying no longer in the 'mere superfices' would become 'consistent, permanent knowledge'. Like the Scottish realists and like other Americans, he anticipated the transformation of the vague realm of fancy into 'distinct and certain' knowledge by the increase of empirical data, and even suggested that until scientific investigation was complete, spiritual truths could not be fully known.

knowledge. The inner laws of nature penetrating language will impart laws to it, and it will take an orbit and obey a rule determined thereby. What I here suggest has been already accomplished to a greater extent than many suppose...[94]

Emerson or Bushnell could not have read Edwards' "Images or Shadows" since these notes remained unpublished in their time. And the theme they set forth, though it was obviously very close to their author's heart, was only vaguely implied and sometimes even deliberately veiled in his published works.[95] But Emerson and Bushnell shared in the Puritan heritage with him, and they also could sense and draw upon the practical and experiential symbolism of the Puritan consciousness for the deprecation of a methodological anti-symbolism that was continuous in principle with the Puritan theory of discourse. So rich was the strain of indigenous symbolic outlook available to the two nineteenth-century rebels that it is altogether possible that they would have come out right where they did, had they had none of the romantic currents of their day to find inspiration in. At least we know that Edwards came out essentially where they did, without benefit of anything other than the Puritan tradition and the thought of Newton and Locke. As regards their assertion of designed symbolic properties in nature, it is abundantly clear that Emerson and Bushnell were only elevating into explicit awareness a trend of thought never far from

Bushnell neither recognized nor resolved these contradictory assumptions: at times he declared that religious knowledge was given by God to the imagination in metaphors; at other times that truth was located in perceptions made exact by scientific inquiry. Though he aimed to justify transcendent faith, he shared his time's uncertainties. Suspicions of the spirit and imagination craved the certitude of factual things." *Horace Bushnell*, 101-102. This is quite inaccurate. When Bushnell stated that truth would lie no longer in mere "superfices", he meant not that it would lie no longer in symbols to be imaginatively apprehended, but that it would lie in more adequate symbols than those built on the pre-scientific "superficial types of nature". Edwards' conception of profound spiritual types disclosed by science is continuous with the conception of Bushnell set forth in this passage and sheds considerable light upon it. See note 86 of the present chapter, where it is shown that Bushnell gave exactly the same reading of the symbolism inherent in the principle of gravity as Edwards did.

[94] Bushnell, *The Spirit in Man*, 357-358.
[95] P. Miller, Introduction to *Images or Shadows*, 2.

the ken and purview of the Puritan fathers, who habitually discerned messages and symbols of the Deity in the concrete facts
and events about them. Bushnell's view of revelation as a kind of
language built up out of the matrix of history was but a fully
symbolic rendering of the old Puritan typology.

Bushnell is correctly said by historians to have made a break
with Edwardian Calvinism clean enough to mark the beginning of
a new theological era. Yet it is clear from the "Images or Shadows"
and other manuscript notes of Edwards that the founder of the
so-called Edwardian theology could have seen much of himself
reflected in what Bushnell had to say through his theory of language. He would not have been happy with the central place Bushnell
gave to the imagination in his theory, for he feared imagination
as a bewitching will-o'-the-wisp and fancied that he was reading
out of nature only what God had put there. But though he was
unaware of it or could not admit it, Edwards' notes on the symbolism of nature are imaginative in the highest degree, and there
is probably not much difference between his idea of supernatural
perception and Bushnell's faith in the restraints of a sanctified
imagination. Both men were convinced that a "nice sense of symbol" could put them in touch with the inmost secrets of nature and
its Creator.

An element in Bushnell's theory that Edwards would definitely
not have approved of was the former's allowance for multiple
meanings in natural facts, the view that each is not a type of one
spiritual sense merely but of "second, third, and thirtieth senses".
The stress Bushnell placed upon paradox, the battle of form with
form, and the easy acquiescence in conflicting creeds would no
doubt have appalled Edwards, for he was a logical reasoner of the
first water and definitely a conservative by theological temperament. In fact, he would probably have been profoundly disturbed
to see principles he had adumbrated in his unpublished notes
gathered up into a general theory of language, for he obviously
would not have wanted to press his recovery of the role of symbols so far. Fear of just this sort of thing happening may have
been a basic reason for his not wanting to publish anything clearly
setting forth the motifs of the "Images or Shadows". The fact that he

was the god-father, so to speak, for what he would surely have thought to be the *monster* begotten by Bushnell tells much about the ambivalences and dichotomies in the Puritan mind.

When Horace Bushnell is viewed in the perspective of the background we have spent four chapters in discussing — a nascent Puritan symbolism; an elevation by Edwards of that symbolism into prominence via, of all things, the philosophy of the sober and prosaic Locke; post-Kantian romanticism and American Transcendentalism; the new linguistic science and the organic philosophy of language; the destruction of easy faith in logical language at the hands of the remarkable, and until very recently, almost forgotten A. B. Johnson, by the rigorous application of that logical language's own reductionist principle; the revisions of the accepted view of language suggested by what came to be the canons of eloquence in an age of oratory; a new awareness of the need to bring poetic principles to bear upon the interpretation of the Bible — the importance of his theory of language in the history of American thought can be readily seen. This was no mere incident in American culture, hardly deserving of notice or to be lost sight of in an exaggerated emphasis upon Bushnell's *Christian Nurture* as his one notable contribution. Nor was it a passing phase in the life of Bushnell himself, to be explained away genetically in terms of his search for a sophisticated speech to replace his rude country dialect.[96] His language theory was a stroke of genius, serving not only to resolve his own personal problems of faith in plausible fashion but also to give a long-overdue fresh approach to the theological problems of New England. Bushnell's real accomplishment in synthesizing a great many divergent strains of thought and focusing them upon the theological situation in New England,

---

[96] This is the main impression one gains from those passages in which Cross discusses Bushnell's language views. Her emphasis stems from her overall method of treating the development of his thought primarily in psychological and pragmatic terms. The method is suggestive and illuminating at many points, but it does not do justice to the rich intellectual background implicit in his language theory. When this is taken into account, his status as a thinker and his place in American intellectual history looms much more importantly than it does in Cross' analysis.

in order to revive a symbolic consciousness that was part of its immediate Puritan background but that had been submerged under two successive anti-symbolical conceptions of language and discourse, has been scarcely recognized and never fully appreciated by students of American thought.[97]

---

[97]   Feidelson, treating Bushnell's language views only very briefly, has placed them in this kind of setting. A development of the intellectual background behind Bushnell's views specifically has not fallen within the purview of his book, however. But much of what he has said of Emerson applies to Bushnell. Perry Miller has also done much to prepare the way for this kind of placement of Bushnell's language theory, in the works already cited and also in the intriguing article "Jonathan Edwards to Emerson", *New England Quarterly*, XIII (1940), 589-617.

VI

LANGUAGE AND THE TRINITY: THREE VIEWS

> The theologian "must be, in the most comprehensive sense of the word, a philologist. The meaning of Scripture is controverted in every part, and he must therefore be acquainted with the art of interpreting language, an art of the very existence of which many of those, who have decided most confidently respecting the sense of the sacred writings, appear to have been wholly ignorant."
>
> Andrews Norton, "A Discourse on the Extent and Relations of Theology" (1819)

This chapter will add to what has already been said on the subject of the bearing of Bushnell's language views upon questions of theology and religion a detailed analysis and comparison of the reflections of Bushnell and those of two well-known and controversial theologians of his day on a key theological doctrine, that of the Trinity. The purpose of this will be to show how an underlying conception of language helped to govern the approach to that doctrine taken by the two theologians, and to contrast their approach with that of Bushnell, the workings of whose language theory are very much in evidence in his writings on the Trinity. This kind of concrete analysis and comparison should enable us to appreciate more fully how Bushnell's language theory served him as a theological method and how it set him apart from the methodology and consciousness that was dominant among theologians of his time.

1. THE ANTI-TRINITARIANISM OF ANDREWS NORTON

Andrews Norton dominated theological thought at the Divinity School at Cambridge for several decades and was long the leading spokesman for Unitarianism of the non-Transcendental variety. He was a master of the original sources of the Scriptures and pioneered in bringing the methods of critical scholarship from Germany to this country. Although he was greatly gifted intellectually and a man of impressive scholarly attainment, was by profession and reputation a "liberal" thinker, and was highly regarded by many of his contemporaries for his personal charm and conscientiousness, he shared nevertheless in the dogmatic outlook that was so characteristic of the theologians of his day. He came before his students, as one of them later testified, "not as one in the act of seeking after the truth, but as one who had found it".[1] And he could be, or at least give the distinct impression of being, quite cantankerous at times in pressing for his point of view. An example is when he dispatched a peremptory letter to the publishers of the *Christian Spectator* (wherein an article by N. W. Taylor highly critical of Norton had recently appeared) announcing the ultimatum that if they did not print it in the next issue "without alteration or omission", he would "take every other means in my power to give it publicity". Stung by the haughty tone and the "reproachful and menacing expressions" of the letter, as they termed it, the publishers refused to print it.[2]

Norton was acutely aware of the bearing of the problems of language upon the task of the theologian. In his Inaugural Address as the newly appointed Dexter Professor of Sacred Literature at Harvard he pointed out that

Words, as well as coins, change their value with the progress of society. By studying the character of language, the philologist and theologian will discover its intrinsic ambiguity and imperfection. He will learn, what has been but little attended to, that words regarded in themselves

---

[1] James Walker; cited in George H. Williams (ed.), *The Harvard Divinity School* (Boston: The Beacon Press, 1954), 51.
[2] H. Shelton Smith, *Changing Conceptions of Original Sin* (New York: Charles Scribner's Sons, 1955), 89-90.

alone are often inadequate to convey any one definite meaning; and that the meaning which the words themselves leave thus loose and unsettled, is to be fixed and defined by reference to extrinsic considerations.[3]

The Scriptures were a battleground of conflicting interpretations, and only he who had mastered the art of interpreting language was competent to delve into their meanings. This meant that the theologian had to be "in the most comprehensive sense of the word, a philologist".[4] Included in that "comprehensive sense" of the word was the ability to recognize and correctly interpret poetry, since the Old Testament was full of poetry and, in the New Testament, "the Oriental and popular style" which prevailed often required "no less than poetry itself, an acquaintance with all the uses of language, and with all the forms in which feeling, passion, and imagination express themselves, in order to distinguish and disengage the mere literal meaning from those images and ideas with which it is associated".[5]

Norton applied these principles with unrelenting vigor to the Scriptural texts which were alleged by the orthodox to give firm support to the doctrine of the Trinity in his influential and controversial book, *A Statement of Reasons for Not Believing the Doctrines of Trinitarians Concerning the Nature of God and Person of Christ*. There it became clear that the fact that the biblical writers were given to highly figurative and hyperbolic forms of expression was the most important of those "extrinsic considerations" of which he had spoken earlier, and only when it was introduced into the interpretation could the gross mistake of taking the Scriptural language at its face-value be avoided. Norton pointed out that in the biblical age no uniform standard had existed for differentiating the expressions of men's conceptions from those of their feelings; therefore language had naturally had a bolder and more unrestrained character, remote in form by present-day standards from its intended and proper sense. Today the modes of speech were far

---

[3] Andrews Norton, *Tracts Concerning Christianity* (Cambridge: John Bartlett, 1852), 72.
[4] Norton, *Tracts*, 71.
[5] Norton, *Tracts*, 73-74.

more "cool and exact".[6] The most characteristic error of biblical expositors, according to Norton, was their overlooking the all-important fact of this gap between ancient and contemporary ways of regarding and using language. The error went a long way toward explaining the origin of what he considered to be the outlandish and absurd doctrine of the Trinity.

But even apart from this crucial difference between the ancient and modern linguistic consciousness was the intrinsic ambiguity of all words. "If words and sentences were capable of expressing but a single meaning, no art would be required in their interpretation."[7] How to distinguish, then, between possible meanings and the actual meaning of a word or sentence, the meaning intended by its author? Only by directing

our attention to all those considerations which render it probable that one meaning was intended by the writer rather than another. Some of these considerations are, the character of the writer, his habits of thinking and feeling, his common style of expression, and that of his age or nation, his settled opinions and belief, the extent of his knowledge, the general state of things during the time in which he lived, the particular local and the temporary circumstances present to his mind while writing, the character and condition of those for whom he wrote, the opinions of others to which he had reference, the connections of the sentence, or the train of thought by which it is preceded and followed, and, finally, the manner in which he was understood by those for whom he wrote, — the consideration, the importance of which varies with circumstances.[8]

The whole technique and procedure of higher and lower criticism, as they have now come to be known, was involved, in other words, in the problem of isolating the true or intended meanings in the biblical language from the false but verbally possible ones.

When it came to the so-called "Trinitarian" passages of the Bible, it had to be admitted that the words alone of those passages would admit of a Trinitarian sense. But this was only one possible sense among others. The burden upon the advocates of Trinitarian theology was therefore "not ... proving, positively, that certain words

[6]   Norton, *A Statement of Reasons* (Boston: American Unitarian Association, 1875), 143. This is the eighth edition of the work.
[7]   Norton, *A Statement*, 147.
[8]   Norton, *A Statement*, 148-149.

will bear a Trinitarian meaning, — that is conceded; but ... proving, negatively, that it is impossible that these words should be used in any other than a Trinitarian meaning, — that they admit of but one sense, which under all circumstances, they must be intended to express. But this no man of common information will maintain."[9] Norton could make that final statement bluntly and without hesitation because to him it was a patent absurdity to say that "the same being is both God and man", and that "the Father is God, and the Son is God, and the Holy Ghost is God; and yet there are not three gods, but one God", at least if these statements were taken in anything like a literal sense.[10] And if these statements were absurd if taken in the literal or Trinitarian sense, then to say that the biblical writers meant themselves to be so understood, was nothing short of accusing them of not being in their right minds and denying them any right to the claim of Divine inspiration. And Norton dismissed out of hand the claim that what seemed absurd to one man could make good sense to another, for he believed with the Scottish philosophers that all minds are constituted alike, and that the common sense of each and every normal man is competent to distinguish absurd from meaningful propositions. The law of contradiction lay ready at hand as the logical gauge of the distinction.

But Trinitarians had defended their doctrine of the three Persons in the Godhead on the ground that its very logical absurdity showed that it outreached logic and was indeed an "incomprehensible mystery". But Norton countered that there could be no meaning conveyed in words which was not perfectly intelligible to the human understanding. In a purely Lockean passage he explained why this was so.

Words are only human instruments for the expression of human ideas; and it is impossible that they should express anything else. The meaning of words is that aggregate of ideas which men have associated with certain sounds or letters. They have no other meaning than what is given them by men; and this meaning must always be such as the human understanding is capable of conceiving; for we can associate with sounds

---

[9]   Norton, *A Statement*, 154.
[10]   Norton, *A Statement*, 169.

or letters no idea or aggregate of ideas which we have not. Ideas, therefore, with which the human understanding is conversant, are all that can be expressed by words.[11]

While it was undeniable that there *were* truths above reason or wholly out of the grasp of men's present faculties, the fact was equally undeniable that these truths could not be expressed in human language. Norton did grant that so-called "inadequate ideas" could be expressed in words — in fact, the greater portion of human ideas were inadequate — but this was something far different from an "incomprehensible" idea. "Infinity", "omniscience", "identity", "figure of twenty equal sides", and "six-hundred million inhabitants" were examples of inadequate ideas. They were inadequate because, while the understanding could grasp them perfectly, they could not be pictured distinctly to the imagination.

Norton averred that the doctrine of the Trinity, far from being an "incomprehensible mystery", was "a very intelligible, though a very absurd proposition". He termed it, in fact, just "plain nonsense".[12] Now if the literal or verbal import of the Scriptural passages marshalled in support of Trinitarianism was irrational or absurd, it was clear to Norton that this could not have been the meaning intended by their authors. This principle of exposition was obvious when applied to other books, and if any book's language were to be explained as the Bible's had been by its orthodox interpreters, "we should think that its author was regarded by his expositor as destitute of common sense; unless we ascribed this character to the expositor himself".[13] Those who claimed to believe in the doctrine of the Trinity were themselves prattling nonsense, for no man could believe an obvious contradiction in terms. What they really believed, as distinguished from what they professed, in violation of the rules of interpretation, of language, and of good sense, to believe, "could be made perfectly intelligible to another of equal capacity and information".[14]

Basic to the principles of interpretation expounded by Norton

---

[11]   Norton, *A Statement*, 162-163.
[12]   Norton, *A Statement*, 169-170.
[13]   Norton, *A Statement*, 170.
[14]   Norton, *A Statement*, 172.

was his conviction that behind all figurative modes of expression, which he emphatically took the alleged Trinitarian passages to be,[15] there was an "essential" meaning, as he termed it, which could be stated in straightforward prose, free of any semblance of obscurity or contradiction. The reason truths were not stated in this clear-cut fashion in the Bible itself was the condition of those peoples whom the Bible writers directly addressed. They habitually "clothed their conceptions in language very different from that with which we are familiar. To them, Oriental fashions of speech were vernacular. They were to be addressed through their feelings and imagination. The great body of the Jews, unaccustomed to any exercise of the understanding, had scarcely the power of apprehending a truth presented to them as a philosophical abstraction, in its naked and literal form".[16] But the present age was far more knowledgeable and advanced. Investigation, thought, and judgment could easily separate the fine metal of essential truth from its ancient figurative ore and state it with such clarity and precision that misconstruction by intelligent men would be virtually impossible.

The prominent part played by the Lockean, Common Sense conception of language in Norton's thinking should be apparent from these statements. And the extent to which he built his theology upon that conception, coupling it with the critical biblical scholarship then undergoing rapid development on the continent, is striking. The fact that he regarded a recognition of the problems of language as the key to major doctrinal issues like the doctrine of the Trinity shows that Bushnell was hardly unique in focusing upon language as a pivotal theological concern. Though they have not always been so keenly aware of the fact as Norton, Bushnell, and (as we shall see in a moment) Taylor were, the problems of language are bound to be especially crucial for theolo-

[15] Norton at one point compared the Trinitarian passages to John 6:53, where Jesus bade his followers eat his flesh and drink his blood, noting that the words of Jesus here, if interpreted literally, were as much a proof of the doctrine of Transubstantiation as the co-called Trinitarian passages were of a three-fold God. As the one was rejected by refusal to interpret literally, so should the other be. *A Statement*, 152.
[16] Norton, *A Statement*, 282.

gians, confronted as they are right at the outset with the necessity of establishing proper linguistic criteria for interpretation of the "Word". Bushnell's distinctive contribution lay, therefore, not in recognizing the importance of the problem of language for theologians, but in challenging a philosophy of language which was accepted unquestioningly by so many in his day.

From the viewpoint of Bushnell, theologians like Norton suffered from the double glaucoma of putting too much confidence in logical or so-called "literal" forms of expression and having too little comprehension of the place and significance of symbolic expression, as he himself conceived it. The polar distance between their respective conceptions of language can be brought out more clearly by the following summary of Norton's view, which we can contrast point by point with the view of Bushnell. Norton regarded the figurative language of the Bible as a rather clumsy way of putting things, necessitated by the limited mental capacities of those who lived in the remote biblical era. He felt that in the present times such language did more harm than good, because men were now so far advanced that they could do all of their thinking and speaking in a forthright logical style, and this caused them to fall all too easily into the trap of taking the Oriental metaphors, exaggerations, and indirections of the Bible in a literal way. This error could only be avoided by determining upon the essential meanings behind the biblical images and then setting the images wholly aside, stating those meanings in a plain logical language which removed all danger of misinterpretation. Far from distrusting logical language as a medium capable of giving expression to the full range of religious thought, Norton assumed that no meaning could be conveyed in words that was not perfectly intelligible to the understanding. In other words, there was no such thing as truths "beyond the grasp" of reason, which rational speech could only distort or even eclipse from view, but which more poetical forms of expression could at least suggestively convey. Whatever a man believed (if it was what he really believed) or had experienced he could state in such a manner as to make his meaning perfectly clear. Language correctly used left no penumbra of mystical vagueness; it allowed for no misleading ambiguity. The notion that language could be used in this way, urged by Norton without qualification or restraint, helps to explain that dogmatism which characterized him and others who, like him, did their thinking under the aegis of the Lockean, Common Sense conception of language. Finally, Norton's principal reason for rejecting the doctrine of the Trinity was that it contained a contradiction in terms, and such a contradiction, by violating the logical rule of consistency, made the doctrine meaningless. Men could not believe such a doctrine if they wanted to, since only what could be intelligibly stated could be believed, and since their common sense would instinctively recoil from the doctrine's absurdity.

In the view of Bushnell the biblical language abounded with images and symbols for a more significant reason than Norton thought. The Divine revelation was given to men in symbols, not because of a limited mental capacity which would yield with the passing of time to such an advance in human knowledge as would make the symbols unnecessary, even dangerous. The symbols were necessitated rather by the transcendental character of the truths themselves. Through many centuries God had prepared a symbolism and nurtured in the Jewish people a symbolic consciousness that enabled them to receive progressively more profound truths and to grasp at last the meaning of "God's last metaphor", Jesus Christ. To speak of setting this symbolism aside in favor of supposedly more adequate matter-of-fact statements was to run counter to the whole genius and power of the Scriptural language. It was to deprive the gospel of its "tonic energy", its unique capacity for opening windows to truths forever veiled to the speculative understanding. His very advocacy of such a method betrayed in Norton, Bushnell would have said, a gross misconception of the way in which symbols function. For symbol and meaning are indissolubly joined; they must be apprehended together. The method would also provoke controversy, as, indeed, it had in strife-ridden New England. For the rich import of the biblical symbols could be exhausted by no one logically consistent doctrinal paraphrase, and to think it could would only mean contending for one partially true paraphrase over another. Moreover, men would soon be led even further afield from the original truths of the symbols by their quarrels over secondary and formal elements in the paraphrases themselves. For as against Norton's easy confidence in logical statements, Bushnell was certain that they could never be rid of ambiguity and imprecision. The fact of the metaphorical character of words and grammar, joined to the variability of human experience, ever giving its own distinctive coloring to words, showed Norton's confidence to be badly misplaced.

Norton had made religion a matter of sweet reasonableness, interpreting the Bible in that same spirit, and he assumed that any man with sound faculties could correctly understand religious truth. But Bushnell could not agree that common sense is the arbiter of religious knowledge. He laid heavy emphasis upon the role of the feelings in religion and believed that only a vigorous religious experience can make the symbols of religion meaningful. He would have agreed wholeheartedly with the German pietist, Philipp Spener, that only the regenerate can qualify as theologians. It was the primacy of this experiential factor in religious knowledge that gave symbols undisputed precedence over rational formulations. Blind to the significance and working of symbols, Norton showed himself equally oblivious to the essential character of religious knowledge as something ever expanding and growing with life itself, and never to be finally settled in taut and inflexible propositions. Only symbols could be adequate to this ever deepening awareness of religious truth. Symbols lured the mind toward the infinite; formulas arrested thought at one stage in its development and fixed a short tether on the flights of imagination and feeling. Bushnell did not deny that formulas have value. But while Norton branded contradictions as anathema, Bushnell welcomed them, for he believed that only when contradictory statements are allowed to stand together can the propositional mode of language even begin to approach the multiform and transcendental character of religious truth, as contained in the biblical symbols. On this ground he could put credence in and defend the doctrine of the Trinity, although he was every bit as aware as Norton was of the logical problems it entailed.[17] This will be

---

[17]   See above, p. 103.

brought out more fully when we examine his actual thinking on that doctrine.

But first we want to consider the way in which Nathaniel W. Taylor sought to uphold Trinitarian theology against arguments like those put forward by Norton. Because of his great importance in any account of the thought of Horace Bushnell, we can offer a brief preliminary sketch of his character and temperament before going on to discuss his views on the Trinity. We will discover that, in the combination of dogmatism and yet originality and independence of thought, he was very much like Norton.

2. NATHANIEL W. TAYLOR'S ORTHODOX DEFENSE OF THE TRINITY

Taylor was the most outstanding individual in the Yale Divinity School, where Bushnell received his professional training, and where the tone was set for the thinking of most of the Calvinists of southern New England. He was also a prime target of Bushnell's attack against the "logickers", men of dogmatic and inflexible outlook who gloried in controversy and brandished the weapon of logical language against their foes with seemingly no awareness of its faults and imperfections. The intensity of Bushnell's attack must not be allowed to distort our picture of Taylor, however. For though he was without doubt one who reposed all confidence in the correctness of his own opinions, arrived at through a process of long and meticulous reasoning, and though he was indeed like a warhorse who snorts with pleasure at the sound of battle,[18] there was another side to his nature. We shall speak first of this other side and then turn to that aspect of his temperament and thought against which Bushnell so passionately rebelled.

Taylor was emphatically not a man of all head and no heart. His sermons, which he continued to preach regularly throughout his academic career, though they were "full of linked and twisted

---

[18]   Leonard Bacon, one of the contributors to a *Memorial of Nathaniel W. Taylor* published in New Haven in 1858, characterized his subject as rushing "to argument like a warhorse to battle" (p. 8). Cited in Sidney Earl Mead, *Nathaniel W. Taylor* (Chicago: The University of Chicago Press, 1942), 164.

logic", yet gave out "at every point sharp flashes of electric fire".[19]
He was especially effective as a revivalistic preacher, which he could
not have been had his style of preaching been coldly logical and
devoid of strong feeling. In the classroom his tightly-laced arguments were urged upon his students with such intensity of emotion
that he would often burst into tears.[20] One of those students, later
to be the most noted exponent of Bushnell's way of thinking,
testified of Taylor that, though on first hearing him lecture, the
tendency was to be "disgusted with his dogmatism", this impression soon gave way to admiration for his incomparable powers as
a teacher. One of the most remarkable of these powers was that
"he is ... an enthusiast, and he makes you feel. Somehow he plants
a truth within a man and it becomes life and power."[21]

Also set over against the dogmatic side of Taylor's nature was his
independence of thought, an independence which he did not fail
to pass on to his students, by precept as well as example. He fought,
it is true, "to preserve the essential principles and broad general
doctrines of a Calvinism that was already passing. But he also
fought for his right and for the right of his students to state those
doctrines and principles in their own words and to defend them
in their own way."[22] At the end of every class session he would
encourage another hour or more of discussion with the invitation, "Now, gentlemen, I'll hear you."[23] And he would magnani-
mously bid them investigate the truth for themselves and follow
it even "if it carries you over Niagara".[24] Bushnell was only one

---

[19] For a first-hand description of Taylor's preaching see the comments of
Leonard Bacon in the *Memorial of Nathaniel W. Taylor*, 6-10. The quotation
above has been cited from that work by Roland H. Bainton, *Yale and the
Ministry* (New York: Harper and Brothers, 1957), 81.
[20] S. Mead, *N. W. Taylor*, 162.
[21] Munger, in a latter to Elisha Mulford, December 26, 1856. Cited in
Benjamin W. Bacon, *Theodore Thornton Munger* (New Haven: Yale University
Press, 1913), 73.
[22] S. Mead, *N. W. Taylor*, viii.
[23] S. Mead, *N. W. Taylor*, 235.
[24] S. Mead, *N. W. Taylor*, 161. Bushnell used this same figure in advocating
decisiveness of action based on reasonableness of judgment to the students
with whom he worked as a tutor while he was studying law, prior to his entrance
into the Divinity School. This suggests that, if it was an original aphorism of

of many of Taylor's students who could say of him in gratitude in
later years, though they had departed from his views, "he taught
me one thing — that it doesn't hurt a man to think for himself".
Sidney Mead has made the apposite comment in connection with
this statement that "If Taylor did no more than that, he richly
deserves more credit than many ardent Bushnellites have accorded
him."[25]

In spite of these traits in Taylor, however, Bushnell did not miss the
mark when he sighted on his former teacher as a conspicious exem-
plar of that unyielding faith in logic and in the unassailable correctness of one's own positions which bred such bitter dissensions in
New England. For as Mead has pointed out: "Basic to the thinking
of Taylor and his fellows was the conception of fixed and eternal
'truth', to which all reasonable minds must give assent as soon as
it is made clear to them."[26] He deplored the kind of suspension of
judgment on seemingly unanswerable questions or the balancing
between opposing views, when each seems to have something to
commend its acceptance, which characterized the scholarly ob-
jectivity of his colleague, Josiah Gibbs, and which was to consti-

---

Taylor, it was quite well-known around the campus. See Cheney, *Life and
Letters*, 62.

[25] The statement of Bushnell was contained in an article by Munger in the
Congregationalist and Christian Advocate XCIII, 636. Mead cites it on p. 163
of his biography of Taylor, and his comment is on that same page. He has
insisted that a great deal of the credit that Bushnell has received as the founder
of the new liberalism in New England belongs rightfully to Taylor, since his
work, by its independence and encouragement to independent ways of thinking,
cleared the way for that liberalism. There is truth to the claim that it helped
to clear the way. But since Taylor's whole intent was to shore up the thinking
of the past, since he used the methods of the past uncritically (Mead has
admitted that he certainly was no theological pioneer; see p. viii.), and since his
urgings toward independence of thought in his students were motivated by the
conviction that infallible logic would force assent to his own views, with due
prodding from himself, it seems clear that the real break with the old attitudes
and approaches to theological questions in New England came with Bushnell,
rather than Taylor. Moreover, Taylor's system, for all its stress upon the
morality of God and responsibility of man, hardly leads naturally into the
thought of Bushnell or that of the liberals of the last quarter of the century.
Taylor was far more the conservative and doctrinaire guardian of the Edwardian
past than the precursor of the liberal future.
[26] S. Mead, *N. W. Taylor*, 159.

tute a main thread in the thinking of Bushnell. "I would rather have ten settled opinions, and nine of them wrong," Taylor loved to say, "than to be like my brother Gibbs with none of the ten settled".[27] He schooled himself to base all of his thinking on finely drawn definitions and was not open to the idea that some subjects do not lend themselves well to such precise defining. As George Park Fisher testified in a *Memorial* to the great man to which Leonard Bacon and S. W. S. Dutton also contributed, Taylor had "little respect for any thought that could not be cast into lucid propositions".[28] When these definitions were employed in strict accord with the rules of logic, he had no doubt that he was in possession of a means for establishing incontrovertible conclusions. Thus, though he did encourage his students to think for themselves, it was not with the possibility in mind that, so long as they adhered to his method, they could arrive at positions different from his own. The fact that they did still differ from him was proof enough, we might say, of the defectiveness of the method, or at least of the lack of warrant for the kind of unquestioning trust Taylor placed in it, and under its guise, in his own reasoning powers.

There was a dichotomy in the character of Taylor, then, and his positive influence upon Bushnell was probably much greater than the latter wanted to admit. The independent spirit and the emotional intensity of the man probably left their permanent stamp upon his more famous pupil. But the dichotomy was not a balanced one; logical method and dogmatism easily outweighed feeling and the tolerance of opposing points of view. Munger has shown clearly which way the scales tipped by saying that Taylor "had enough heart, but what was heart before logic based on sound principles rightly defined?"[29] Given this sense of priority, which was typical of the theologians of the day, it is hardly surprising

---

[27]   Timothy Dwight, Jr., *Memories of Yale Life and Men, 1845-1899* (New York, 1903), 265. Cited in Mead, *N. W. Taylor*, 159. For a discussion of this trait in Gibbs see Bainton, *Yale and the Ministry*, 87-88.

[28]   *Memorial to Nathaniel W. Taylor*, 32. Cited Mead, *N. W. Taylor*, 160.

[29]   *Congregationalist and Christian Advocate* XCIII, 636. Cited in Mead, *N. W. Taylor*, 160.

to find that even while Bushnell was still a student in the Divinity School he was, as an instructor put it, "t'other side".[30]

Although Taylor, like the other Edwardian theologians, is best known by church historians for his wrestlings with the problem of reconciling the sovereignty of God with the freedom of man, we have chosen to concentrate on his defense of Trinitarianism. There are several reasons for this. One is that Bushnell, in the discourses published as *God in Christ*, had a more comprehensive purpose in mind than dealing with the internal conflicts within New England Calvinism, which did center, of course, on election and free will. He was consciously trying to make use of a golden opportunity (chances to speak at Harvard, Andover, and Yale) to show how his approach to theological questions, partly through the instrumentality of a revolutionary conception of language, could heal the rifts dividing the theology of Boston from that of the rest of New England. Since this was his purpose, the doctrine of the Trinity was quite naturally the pivot-point of his effort.[31] And it is important for us to consider that effort in the context of Taylor's, as well as Norton's, approach to the Trinitarian problem. Taylor has been chosen as the representative of orthodox Trinitarianism, we might add, not so much because his treatment of the Trinity was typical — in many respects it took issue with the best known and most widely accepted treatments — but because he dealt so explicitly with arguments of the type Norton advanced and which Bushnell himself sought to contend with. Also, Taylor's thought has obvious importance for any consideration of the theology of Bushnell.

But the key role of the doctrine, as seen in terms of Bushnell's guiding purpose in the 1848 Discourses, is only one of the reasons we have chosen to focus upon it, out of other possible doctrines,

---

[30] Cheney, *Life and Letters*, 62.

[31] Of course, the doctrine of the Atonement ran a close second in importance, not only because of its prominence in discussions within Calvinism, but also because it was the conviction of the Unitarians that the Calvinistic idea of limited atonement, satisfaction theory, and original sin was grossly immoral. The Atonement, as conceived by the orthodox, hinged, however, on the doctrine of the Trinity. We shall note in a moment how closely Taylor related the two doctrines.

as a concrete demonstration of the way in which Bushnell brought his theory of language to bear upon problems in theology.[32] Another basic reason is that Norton centered his attack on the Trinity so squarely on considerations of language, and that Taylor followed suit, meeting the issue squarely on that ground. The result of this was that the conception of language which both men shared and which set the limits of theological problems for them was made more transparent in their respective writings on the Trinity than anywhere else.

Finally, it is equally true that nowhere else does the relationship between Bushnell's language theory and his theology stand out more clearly than in his writings on the Trinity. Here we get a graphic impression of the way in which his language views gave him a whole new orientation to much-controverted theological questions and enabled him to take tacks toward their solution which Norton and Taylor, so long as they adhered to the Lockean, Common Sense conception of language and method of reasoning, could hardly have conceived of and would never have entertained.

Like Norton, Taylor "applied to the Bible the test of common sense, since God cannot be guilty of absurdity".[33] This meant, among other things, that he was no more willing than Norton was to say that the doctrine of the Trinity, by its very paradoxicalness, points to a mystery incomprehensible to the human mind.

Explain the doctrine of the Trinity — this profoundest of all mysteries! What presumption! Presumption — folly — though it be, I must be permitted to profess to understand what I believe, and to hope that, guided by the oracles of God, I may lead others to understand and believe also.[34]

---

[32] Hints have been given elsewhere in this work, chiefly in the first chapter, as to how Bushnell's theory functioned as a theological method in regard to other important doctrines, but a full treatment of this subject would require another study. I have contented myself, therefore, with discussing in detail only the doctrine of the Trinity, since this provides a good feel for the direction of Bushnell's thought in applying his theory to specific doctrines, and since it provides opportunity for a rather clearcut comparison between his language views and those of Norton and Taylor.

[33] R. Bainton, *Yale and the Ministry*, 98.

[34] N. W. Taylor, *Essays, Lectures, Etc., Upon Select Topics in Revealed Theology* (New York: Clark, Austin and Smith, 1859), 1. The following passage

We have seen that Norton assumed that the supposedly Trinitarian passages in the Bible must be figurative, typifying the loose and exaggerated style of ancient peoples, because, when taken at literal or face value, they contained obvious contradictions. Taylor took issue with Norton's position at precisely this point, denying that the Trinitarian passages were at all figurative. They were, rather, straightforward statements of fact. But if they were not figurative, neither were they to be interpreted literally, since that would reduce them to absurdity.

If the passages were neither figurative nor literally true, how were they to be understood? In most of the thinking of the time these were the only conceivable alternatives. Thus Moses Stuart of Andover, in one of his widely-read Letters to William E. Channing on the Doctrine of the Trinity — Letters which set the stage for Norton's *A Statement of Reasons* — had this to say concerning the bearing of language on the Trinitarian problem:

I have one thing more to say, in relation to this whole subject [of the Nicene Creed], which I may as well say here; for, if correct, it ought to have an important bearing on modes of expression in relation to the whole matter before us. It is this, viz. the *imperfection* of language is such, that words can scarcely be employed with regard to some parts of the subject under discussion, without liability to be misunderstood. Every word is a symbol of some idea of our minds; and all our ideas are the result of sensation, consciousness, and reflection. Now the essential nature and relations of the Divine Being are not within the circle of either of these sources of ideas and words. Of course, no part of language was originally formed in reference to expressing the internal constitution (so to speak) of the Godhead. A secondary and tropical sense, therefore, in a greater or less degree, must of necessity be attached to all the words which we employ respecting the essence of the Godhead. The sober inquirer, who is fully cognizant of this, will never think of believing or

---

shows further how devoid of any "nice sense of symbol" Taylor was: "Besides, what do they mean who characterize a doctrine of *revelation* — a doctrine *revealed to faith* — a *revealed* doctrine — as a mystery? A revealed doctrine, if it is any thing, is a truth taught by divine revelation — a truth intelligibly presented to the human mind, for its apprehension and assent." Ibid. There was no such thing to his mind, in other words, as a religious truth which could not be logically rendered, if it could be known at all, which could be felt or sensed through a symbol but not explained.

denying what the mere literal sense of words thus employed would convey. He must not believe in *Tritheism*, because *Trinity* and *three persons* in the Godhead are spoken of in his creed; nor should he insist that such words necessarily infringe upon the *unity* of the Godhead: for it is only by taking the words in a *literal* sense, that he can make this out. It is here we may well say: 'The *letter* killeth, but the *Spirit* maketh alive'.[35]

Norton, schooled in the language views of Locke, Blair, and D. Stewart, had then simply to declare that, if "secondary and tropical", the Trinitarian passages were literally untrue, that they expressed only the rhetorical excesses of the biblical times. If Taylor was to controvert Norton, then, he would have to go beyond Mozes Stuart. How to do this and yet remain within the confines of the conception of language he, Stuart, and Norton held in common was a real challenge to his ingenuity.

Taylor's way of meeting the challenge was to grant that the biblical language respecting the Trinity was secondary, and therefore not to be taken literally, while at the same time denying that this necessitates its being figurative or symbolical. On the latter point he was quite emphatic, roundly asserting that the language of the sacred writers

is not characterized by the authorized obscurity of enigma, of allegory, of prophetic annunciation, or of typical or symbolical representation. It betrays no artistic plan, no dramatic or other contrivance for representing that to be real which is not real. It bears none of the peculiar marks of figurative or metaphorical language.[36]

According to him, strictly figurative speech was but one type of secondary language. Another even more prevalent type was the employment of words in a peculiar or modified, and yet wholly non-figurative sense, as that was demanded by the nature of the subject to be talked about.[37]

[35]   Moses Stuart, *Miscellanies* (Andover: Allen, Morrill, and Wardwell, 1846), 32.
[36]   N. W. Taylor, *Essays*, 92.
[37]   Another type of secondary speech of which Taylor made mention was when words, "thought at first figurative, by use lose their representative character and become in their secondary use literal terms", *Essays*, 101. This means that many words are at the same time secondary and literal, which seems to obviate the initial distinction. Bushnell denied that any words used in a secondary sense, as

This is indeed the great law of usage which has ever prevailed when new truths are to be made known in the use of ordinary terms. When such truths are to be communicated to the popular mind, the natural and common mode of communication is not to invent new, but to employ old words, in more or less of their former meaning, and to rely on the known nature of the subject, or other evidence, to determine the new and changed import of the terms employed.[38]

Elsewhere Taylor expanded this "great law of usage" into four laws governing valid changes in the meanings of words, apart from their conversion into figures: "1. That there is good and sufficient reason for the change. 2. That when a word is turned from its primary to a secondary meaning, it must be used either in a more restricted or in a more extended sense than its primary meaning. 3. That when the word is thus changed, it must admit of an obvious, definite, and consistent meaning. 4. That in the case supposed, there must be good and sufficient evidence of the new and modified meaning of the word."[39]

The language of the Trinity was a prime instance of this type of secondary use of language. So far as ordinary language was concerned, the Unitarian protest had point:

It is admitted ... that there is only one living and true God; that is, that whatever God is as a BEING, there is *one and only one* such being. Now the word *person*, as does each of the pronouns *I, thou, he,* implies in its ordinary use and application, a being — a distinct being; and the word *being* denotes or implies the existence of one substance with one nature, or with one class or set of attributes or properties. Hence to say, *in the ordinary use and meaning of these terms,* that there is *one God in three persons,* or *three persons in one God;* is a plain contradiction.[40]

But it was irresponsible and libelous for the Unitarians to aver that this ordinary-language sense of the terms of the Trinitarian formula was the sense intended by any intelligent Trinitarian.

In keeping with his laws of the usage of language, Taylor pointed out that the "fact of one God in three persons, in some peculiar

---

all second-departmental words are used, can be termed "literal", no matter how long they are so employed.

[38] N. W. Taylor, *Essays*, 4-5.
[39] N. W. Taylor, *Essays*, 119-120.
[40] N. W. Taylor, *Essays*, 3-4.

sense of the language" was the "doctrine revealed and the doctrine to be believed".[41] This was the "known nature of the subject" which determined a "new and changed import" of the key terms used in Trinitarian discourse. Thus the term "being" had to be modified from its ordinary-language meaning by *expanding* its sense to include the idea of "distinct qualification for distinct personal action" in each of the three subjects to which the personal pronouns employed in Trinitarian discourse referred. On the other hand, the ordinary-language meaning of "person" as a distinct entity had to be *restricted* so as not to obliterate the fundamental conviction that "whatever God is as a BEING, there is one and only one such being".[42] By applying his laws of usage in this way Taylor came up with one of those meticulous definitions for which he was so well known. The Scriptural doctrine of the Trinity, as explained by him, was

that God is one being, in such a modified sense of the term as to include three persons in such a modified sense of the term, that, by his tri-person-ality, or by the three persons of his Godhead, he is qualified, in a cor-responding modified sense, for three distinct, personal, divine forms of phenomenal action; or thus: God, in a modified use of the language, is one being in three persons, qualified by the three persons of his Godhead for three distinct, personal forms of phenomenal action.[43]

By way of sharp criticism of those who, like Stuart in the passage cited above, merely argued that the language of the Trinitarian formula was to be understood in a peculiar instead of literal sense, and went no further, Taylor insisted that any proposed modification of the terms of the formula had to be clearly "authorized" by laws of the usage of language plainly laid down. Only in this way could the interpretation be kept true to the meaning intended by the biblical writers themselves. To go only so far as Stuart had, merely opened the way to unchecked vagaries of subjective inter-pretation, depriving the doctrine of all dependable meaning and

---

[41] N. W. Taylor, *Essays*, 2-3. Taylor pointed out, however, that the mode of that fact remained mysterious and unrevealed. In respect to it, men were to "have no faith", i.e. hold no specific beliefs. Ibid.
[42] N. W. Taylor, *Essays*, 13-15.
[43] N. W. Taylor, *Essays*, 16.

truth. By providing such laws of usage and treating the language of the Trinity in terms of them Taylor felt sure that he had at last found the solution to a problem which had always vexed the Church.

Not only did the laws of usage permit a definitive statement of the doctrine of the Trinity, but they also provided for the detection of erroneous or "unauthorized" modifications of the terms of the Trinitarian language, of which Taylor furnished three examples. One was the assertion of the "eternal generation" of the Son by the Father and the "eternal procession" of the Holy Spirit from the Father and the Son. This form of the Trinitarian doctrine, though widely adhered to, did violence to the meaning of the anchor term "God". Christ and the Spirit could not be derived and yet still Divine or entitled to the predicate "God", because "the word God, in its primary distinctive meaning, denotes a self-existent, eternal, independent, immutable Being".[44] As understood in light of those revealed facts concerning God's nature, in other words, the term "God" could never be modified to the extent that would be required by the association of it in any way with the terms "generation" or "procession". Another version of the doctrine of the Trinity, holding that "the three persons of the Godhead are three distinct divine minds or agents, each being a complete subsistence", was obviously destructive of the monotheistic meaning of the term "God" in the Scriptures. A third, asserting "a three-fold distinction in the Godhead denoted by the personal pronouns, without describing affirmatively at all what this three-fold distinction or tri-personality is", left the mind in obscurity and invited heretical ideas, because it did not avail itself fully of the known facts of revelation in order to specify just those modifications in the terms of the Trinitarian formula its sound interpretation required.[45]

Taylor took up two additional topics in his discussion of the Trinity that deserve brief notice. First, he sought to show that the "nature of the subject renders it impossible that the human mind should know on *a priori* ground, that the doctrine of the Trinity,

[44]   N. W. Taylor, *Essays*, 120-121.
[45]   N. W. Taylor, *Essays*, 119-126.

as now explained, involves a contradiction".[46] This was as against the logic of the Unitarians. Second, he tried to demonstrate that the orthodox conception of God was required by his "Moral Government" conception of the Atonement. This conception Taylor took to comprise a major aspect of the "known nature" of the Scriptural revelation which forever precluded, to his mind, the idea that the persons of the Trinity are merely figures of speech, modes, or the "dramatis personae" of God's dramatic self-disclosure. This was as against Sabellianism, which, as he would have it, "contradicts the whole tenor of the Word of God".[47]

The Unitarian case was based on the assumption, Taylor declared, "that it is impossible in the nature of things, that, in any mode of conceiving of a being, or the mode of his subsistence, such a one as the doctrine of the Trinity affirms should be conceived to exist; and that of course the existence of such a being is impossible, and cannot be taught even by a revelation from God".[48] But he was quick to point out that this assumption, far from being self-evident as regarded God, was just "the ordinary conception of the mode of a being's subsistence — a merely phenomenal conception".[49] And it stood to reason, or it was at least within the realm of possibility, that the mode of God's

subsistence and the constituent elements of his being should differ, at least in some respects, from those of creatures; and that, should it become necessary for the purposes of his goodness and mercy, to reveal this difference to any extent to the human mind through the medium of human language, it would become necessary also to change the terms used from the meaning they had acquired in their ordinary application.[50]

In this case, of course, there could be no *a priori* ground for declaring against the possibility of a Trinitarian God, nor could arguments from the ordinary uses of language apply at all to the problem.

It is significant that Taylor spoke of God's revealing himself "though the medium of human language", for this seems to suggest

46 N. W. Taylor, *Essays*, 46.
47 N. W. Taylor, *Essays*, 40.
48 N. W. Taylor, *Essays*, 4.
49 N. W. Taylor, *Essays*, 7.
50 N. W. Taylor, *Essays*, 41.

that the primary data of revelation are propositions, not events. And much of Taylor's reasoning does seem to ground itself on this unconscious assumption, which he would no doubt have repudiated, had it been put before him in just that bald way. But to strive to render the data of revelation into logical formulas and a close-knit rational system is a perfectly reasonable procedure, given this assumption as to its nature. The appeal to feeling or the symbolical sense would be almost entirely out of place.

Did the Unitarian then declare that, given the limitations of his knowledge and experience, he could not even conceive of such a being and could therefore not believe in the doctrine of the Trinity even if God had revealed himself in such a manner? Taylor's reply was that, if the Unitarian was admitted to have ordinary intellectual capacities and could "form the ordinary complex conception of a being's subsistence", he could also,

having the ordinary power of abstracting and compounding ideas — modify and change his ordinary conception of this process, and so form either of the supposed conceptions of the mode of the divine subsistence. If he can conceive of a substance to which one self-active nature pertains, he can conceive of a substance to which two or three self-active natures pertain.[51]

Since this was precisely the Lockean and Common Sense epistemology, the Unitarians could hardly accuse Taylor of having failed to meet them on their own ground!

Taylor went on to argue that if there was no presumption from *a priori* reasoning *against* the doctrine of the Trinity, there was plenty of presumption *for* it, based on the reasoning that

God is administering a perfect Moral Government over men under an economy of grace, with the design to reform, to pardon and reward sinful beings; that the accomplishment of this design renders necessary the two great provisions of an adequate Atonement for sin and an adequate reclaiming influence from its power; and that the mode of divine subsistence in the Trinity furnishes the most, if not the only satisfactory explanation of the adequacy of these provisions, which by the human mind is conceivable.[52]

[51] N. W. Taylor, *Essays*, 41.
[52] N. W. Taylor, *Essays*, 64.

Taylor's thinking was that God could not establish his right to reign over the creatures created in his image (and hence, presumably, possessed of his own sense of morality) unless he could prove his moral perfection or benevolence. But such proof could not be forthcoming unless God could show his utter disapprobation of disobedience to his righteous will, either by inflicting the highest possible degree of punishment on every transgressor — hence, every human being — or else by making an equivalent manifestation of his disapprobation by the expedient of an Atonement. The question then was, could such a proof of his supreme abhorrence of sin equivalent to that which would be furnished by the infliction of the full legal penalty on every member of the human race, be satisfactorily provided by the Atonement of Christ, except in view of his Divine Personality and inherence in a Trinity in the Godhead? Taylor was certain that it could not.

The alternate view to this satisfaction theory of the Atonement[53] in terms of which Taylor was working which came most readily to mind was the moral influence theory. Under that theory it was perfectly conceivable that a Christ who was only a creature of God could symbolize the infinite love of a holy God by suffering on behalf of sinful human beings, though being himself innocent of all sin. As against this view Taylor had the criticism to make that it was inconceivable that "the temporary sufferings of one who is merely a creature, however intense these sufferings, and however exalted in rank the creature who endures them, and still less, that any sufferings or evil endured by a mere man, should furnish the requisite manifestation and proof of God's supreme abhorrence of sin..."[54] Moreover, the "single naked act of putting to death a perfectly holy being" could have no direct tendency to reclaim sinful creatures, since "the act considered simply in itself or aside from its relations to other ends, can be viewed only as an act of

---

[53]   The difference from the classical satisfaction theory, however, was important. Where that had laid stress merely on the need of God to satisfy the demands of his own justice, Taylor emphasized that the failure of God to fulfill his moral law would abnegate his right to reign as Moral Governor over his creatures.
[54]   N. W. Taylor, *Essays*, 77.
[55]   N. Taylor, *Essays*, 75.

palpable injustice and cruelty, fitted to dishonor its author, and to increase the alienation and disloyalty of every rebel".[55] Finally, the death of this kind of Christ could not have even an indirect salutary effect upon the sinner, as though, by dying a martyr's death, he could show his own intense desire for the sinner's reformation, for Christ did not have, according to Taylor, the martyr's option of recanting his convictions. Also unlike martyrs, he died, not in triumph, but forsaken by God and abandoned to the terrors of death without alleviation.

The upshot of Taylor's arguments was that so long as God was conceived as a Moral Governor, which nearly every page of the Scriptures revealed him to be, only the Deity of Christ, and hence, the doctrine of the Trinity, could be the adequate ground for an Atonement that could truly vindicate his morality before his creatures, as well as express his mercy to them. Given the Trinity lying behind the sufferings of Christ, the "great crisis" in the universe caused by the fact of human sin could be met and resolved.

Law is magnified and made honorable. The pillars of eternal justice stand unshaken, and the splendor of its throne is untarnished, while mercy lavishes all its riches on a guilty world. Thus we see the most impressive spectacle, the highest achievement of infinite goodness and grace, the fullest expression of God in the Atonement of Christ. No similar event can we suppose has occurred on the theater of the universe, or will ever again occur in a coming eternity. It has formed an epoch in the moral administration of the Deity, and given birth to a new order of things throughout his moral creation.[56]

The doctrine of the Trinity, then, struck to the very heart of the gospel. Nothing, as we can now see, would be so important to Taylor as to release it from the charge of self-contradiction and yet preserve its truth, which he considered so vital to the Christian faith. And here everything depended on arriving at correct rules for interpreting the language of the doctrine's formulation. Overtly expressed considerations of the nature of language figured very prominently in his analysis and proposed resolution of the problem, just as they had for Norton.

But as was also the case with Norton, even more fundamental

---

[56] N. W. Taylor, *Essays*, 87.

to our understanding of Taylor's approach to the Trinity and more crucial, of course, to our discussion here, are the ways in which the Lockean, Common Sense conception of language operated as the assumptional ground of his thinking. There are several points, which can now be noted, at which it is evident that the prevailing conception of language entered rather decisively into Taylor's treatment of the doctrine of the Trinity. And we can also make some contrasts at these points with Bushnell's theory of language, before launching into a direct examination of his own writings on the doctrine of the Trinity.

Taylor took it for granted that figurative language is characterized by "obscurity", that it customarily represents "that to be real which is not real", and that by its vague suggestiveness, it serves as an invitation to heresy. Against it he strongly favored language which could "admit of an obvious, definite, and consistent meaning" and which could be shown to function in strict accord with clear-cut rules of usage. Behind him, as he makes such statements, we can see lurking the ghosts of Locke, Blair, and Stewart, still incanting their solemn warnings about the untrustworthiness of the imagination and the tendency of figurative speech to seduce it in order to overpower the reason.

Out of this disparagement of figurative language came Taylor's unalterable conviction that doctrines revealed in the Bible could not be couched in figurative language. He had no patience with those who wanted to leave room within the doctrine of the Trinity, for instance, for the symbolic imagination to brood upon the mystery of God. If the doctrine was revealed, it was revealed to the understanding, not the imagination, and it could be handled with complete competence by a careful methodology and precise definitions. Taylor insisted that the Scripture writers were not poets or literary artists. Their language was "the language of plain men in practical life writing or speaking for the instruction of plain men — the language of common life consisting of common words in common forms of combination; language, the meaning of which, in all these respects, is fitted to the apprehension of the most ordinary capacity..."[57] One did not have to be a cultivated

[57]   N. W. Taylor, *Essays*, 92.

aesthete, in other words, in order to understand what the biblical writers were talking about. Nor, presumably, did one have to participate in their kind of experiences.

The fact that Taylor believed that revelation, in order to be intelligible and reliable, had to be conveyed in non-figurative language by the biblical writers meant for one thing that he had no doubt of the capacity of non-figurative language to communicate truths from God. He felt no need for a symbolical transmission of the revelation, as though the truths to be revealed transcended the limitations of straightforward prose and required symbols which could lure the mind beyond the confines of the finite into the mystery of the infinite. For another thing it meant that, though the Scriptural language was not precisely logical (a fact which Taylor readily admitted), it was entirely amenable to being rendered into logical form. This, in fact, was the task of the theologian — to set forth the Scriptural truths in language which left their correct interpretations unambiguous and unmistakable. Taylor's easy assumtion that this could be done shows him to have shared heartily in that confidence in the powers of logical language which characterized the adherents of the prevailing language view.

Wrong interpretations had crept in. Taylor believed, not only because of sinful presumption, but also because men had grown careless in their thinking and had let go of their common sense. That interpretations other than his own might contain some truth did not enter his mind. His was no organic conception of truth. He was confident that his conclusions were arrived at in the only valid manner, that common sense was entirely on his side. In a brief characterization of common sense that furnishes an important clue to his own cocksureness and to the dogmatic attitudes of the day, he had this to say:

What is common sense? It is the competent, unperverted reason of the human mind, whose decisions, in the interpretations of the Scriptures, are to be relied upon as infallible. Men must know *some things* beyond the possibility of mistake, or there is an end to all knowledge and faith... If there are no judgments or decisions of the human mind which are entitled to unhesitating confidence, then is universal skepticism authorized.[58]

[58]   N. W. Taylor, *Essays*, 221.

Taylor's faith in common sense as the criterion of truth and that of his contemporaries was seemingly unshaken by the brute fact of so many sincere thinkers being unable to arrive at a consensus on vital religious questions, and yet each upholding his own position as the only possible one in its name. One only concluded from this, evidently, that the others still needed to be shown the light. If they yet resisted the truth, stated in perspicuous arguments, it could only be because perversity was clouding their reason. Implicit in this unquestioning trust in common sense was a confidence in logical language. There was no thought of the seductions of form in words or of their ambiguities, nor was consideration given to the possible bearing of differences in temperament and experience, as these might be reflected in the use and reaction to language. All of these difficulties, it was believed, could be cleared away by the rules of inference brought to bear on precisely defined terms. Even matters outside of the range of human experience could be knowingly discussed and described, through the simple expedient of abstracting and compounding ideas and modifying terms to suit them.

The contrasts with Bushnell's theory of language are obvious. Bushnell exalted figurative speech above logical, believing that it is more appropriate to religion as something to be felt and experienced, rather than merely reasoned out; that it confronts man with the mystery of the infinite; that by its frank tolerance of contradiction it shows religious truth to outreach logic and the understanding and opens the way to an organic comprehension of differences in interpretation. Far from distrusting the imagination, Bushnell considered it to be the instrument of a higher order of knowledge than the reason could afford.

Fully conscious of the primacy of events as the media of revelation, Bushnell insisted that a new kind of symbolical language had been built up out of them in much the same manner as the second department of ordinary language is built up out of the first. The events and experiences which constitute the *material* of revelation become, in his view, powerful metaphors containing the *meaning* of revelation. Therefore, to treat the data of revelation propositionally and logically, rather than figuratively and symbolically, and to ignore their grounding in the experiences of the Jewish race and their corresponding principal reference to the spiritual experiences of the believer today, is grossly to misinterpret their true character. It was this fundamental misconception which had created a theological situation in New England so "indisputably mournful", where theologians wrestled futilely with problems that were, in the final analysis, so "mournfully indisputable".[59]

Bushnell was also representative of a growing number who drew quite a different conclusion than Taylor did from the fact of so many different positions being maintained in the name of common sense. The conclusion was that common sense was not as dependable a test of truth as had been supposed and that man's reason and his logic were not so infallible or utterly competent to treat of religious questions as had been generally assumed. To experience and feel the truth, and to *do* the truth, was perhaps more important after all than to try to say the final word about it. Bushnell concentrated especially on showing how language, the medium of human communication and thought, both reflects and compounds the inherent limitations of human perspective and understanding.

3. HORACE BUSHNELL'S SYMBOLICAL VIEW OF THE TRINITY

Where Norton had deemed the Trinitarian passages in the Scriptures figurative and had dismissed them on that account, and where Taylor had considered his task to be that of demonstrating that the passages were not figurative, nor yet to be taken literally, and hence, neither fanciful, obscure, nor self-contradictory, Bushnell frankly acknowledged their figurative and paradoxical character and sought to show that, in the very nature of the case, this was the only kind of language in which a revelation of the infinite God to finite man could be made.

Considered as he is existing in himself, apart from figures and symbols, what could man say of God? Only that he is "the Absolute Being — the Infinite — the I am that I am, giving no sign that He is, other than that He is".[60] The Unitarians had complained

---

[59]   Bushnell, *Christ in Theology*, vi.
[60]   Bushnell, *God in Christ*, 139.

that the doctrine of the Trinity was figurative, and therefore not true. But to ascribe *personality* to God, as they readily did, was also to speak of him in a figurative way. For could God be said to reason, as persons do? No, since this would imply a want of knowledge prior to the deducing process in his mind. Could he be said to remember? Hardly, since this would imply calling up what was out of mind, and nothing could be out of the mind of God. Nor could God be said to have emotions, or to believe, or to inquire or think, as finite persons do.[61] So far as the character of the language used was concerned, therefore, "we do exactly the same thing ... when we say that God is a person, that we do when we say that He is three persons, and there is really no difficulty in one case that does not exist in another".[62] Similarly, to speak of God as "Father" was to make use of figurative language, and in this respect the Unitarians were quite as much at fault — if the mere use of figurative language be thought a fault — as those who wanted also to call him "Son" and "Spirit". The designation "Father" implied, after all "a conception as truly finite and a humanization every way as difficult to reason, as the other — a finite-infinite as absurd and contradictory, and involving ... precisely the same charge of idolatry that is laid against the worship of the Son, or the Word made flesh".[63] In fact, just "To name God, or even to speak of Him is, in one view, to raise a difficulty; for in so doing we are always seeking to represent the infinite by the finite; that is, by terms whose symbols and significances are relative only — subject to finite conditions and measures."[64] Figurative speech could not be avoided, therefore, and the choice was not between literal or figurative language in speaking of God but only between more or less adequate collocations of figures.

[61]   Bushnell, *God in Christ*, 38-139.
[62]   Bushnell, "The Christian Trinity a Practical Truth", *Building Eras*, 106-149. See p. 115. This article was contributed to the *New Englander* in November, 1854, and is the most concise presentation of Bushnell's conception of the Trinity available, particularly as that presupposed his theory of language.
[63]   Bushnell, *Christ in Theology*, 168. Bushnell also felt that the fact that "Father" is a consistent designation of God only after the coming of Christ was a fatal objection to the Unitarians' having any right to the use of the term. It presupposed Trinitarianism. See *God in Christ*, 167.
[64]   Bushnell, *God in Christ*, 156.

Bushnell was convinced that the greater adequacy lay with the figurative language of the Trinity. There were several reasons for this. One was that the Trinity was sanctioned by the authority of the Scriptures and could not be dismissed in the manner the Unitarians had dismissed it. "That there is, in the scriptures, a three-foldness, which contains the real matter of a trinity, is to me undeniable, and ... it must be of the highest consequence to religion, that this trinity be admitted..."[65] A second reason was that some such paradoxical representation as the Trinity of three persons was precisely what God's mode of self-disclosure might have been expected to be, given his infinite nature, on the one hand, and the limitations of human comprehension, on the other. In himself God was the One, the Infinite, the Absolute, as we have already seen. But he could not reveal himself to men in that way, since they possessed no capacity of laying hold of the Absolute by direct inspection. The only absolute knowledge they had related to the few necessary ideas of space, cause, truth, right, and the axioms of mathematical science. And these were but simple ideas, having their reality in men's minds, while God considered as the Absolute was wholly outside of the mind of man. As regarded all else than these simple ideas, men were obliged to get their knowledge "under the law of action and reaction — through finites that are relative to each other, through antagonisms, contrasts, comparisons, interactions, counteractions".[66] Obviously, then,

the One must appear in the manifold; the Absolute in the conditional; Spirit in form; the Motionless in motion; the Infinite in the finite. He must distribute Himself, He must let forth His nature in sounds, colors, forms, works, definite objects and signs. It must be to us as if Brama were waking up; as if Jehovah, the Infinite I Am, the Absolute, were dividing off Himself into innumerable activities that shall dramatize His immensity, and bring Him within the molds of language and discursive thought. And in whatever thing He appears, or is revealed, there will be something that misrepresents, as well as something that represents Him. The revealing process, that which makes Him appear, will envelop itself in clouds of formal contradiction — that is, of diction which is contrary,

---

65   Bushnell, *God in Christ*, 174.
66   Bushnell, *God in Christ*, 141.

in some way, to the truth, and which, taken simply as diction, is continually setting forms against each other. [67]

Far from being untrue or unbelievable because of its paradoxical and self-contradictory character, therefore, the doctrine of the Trinity commended itself to faith because it presented, by its formal repugnances, "a Being infinite, undiscovered, undiscoverable, therefore true". A more logical presentation of God might seem to give sight of his "last boundaries ... and hold Him clear of a question", but its very perspicuity would be proof that "He is not God any longer, we have lost the conception of God."[68]

Bushnell's theory of language is very much in evidence here. He deliberately related the appearance of the infinite God in the finite moulds of human understanding to the "relation of form to truth in every term of language".[69] And he said it specifically of the two natures in Christ, but could have spoken in the same fashion of the Trinity, that

if we insist ... on understanding the composition of the person of Jesus, and the relations of the infinite to the finite in his person, we can create as much of difficulty as we please; though scarcely more than we could, if we pleased to investigate, in the same manner, the interior relations of words or the types of words to thoughts; for we can as easily perceive how Jesus is constructed for the expression of God, as how a straight line (*rectus, right*) becomes a symbol of virtue. There is a point of mystery and even of contradiction in both — a something transcendent, which no investigation will ever reach.[70]

In the same place he pointed out that what was true of language in general was true many times over of words applied to God: they "have their truth or falsity in what they express, what they put others on thinking of God, not in their measures or boundaries, under the laws of space and time. Their reality is in what they signify, not in what they are".[71]

But if the paradoxical character of a conception of three persons in one Godhead was no proof of its falsity, but rather an impressive

---

[67] Bushnell, *God in Christ*, 139-140.
[68] Bushnell, *God in Christ*, 145.
[69] Bushnell, *Christ in Theology*, 117; 126.
[70] Bushnell, *God in Christ*, 156-157.
[71] Bushnell, *God in Christ*, 156.

credential of its authenticity as a finite representation of the infinite God, the question still remained of why it, rather than some other multiform symbol, could be said to best disclose God to man. And here Bushnell, in what can be called a third major reason urged in support of the doctrine, laid stress on what he called the "practical truth" or "practical uses" of the Trinity. He wanted it fully understood, however, that he was speaking only of the Trinity of the Scriptures, and not of the various conceptions of the Trinity held by the orthodox Trinitarians of New England. Those he professed himself entirely unable to accept, for reasons which shall become clear further on.

The Trinity served two purposes of an intensely practical nature for religious faith and life, as no other representation of God could. In the first place, it saved the practical infinity of God without sacrificing his religious availability, or his warmth and love as a person. Second, it was "the instrument and co-efficient of a supernatural grace or redemptive economy",[72] that is, it provided a conception of God which accorded well with the gospel's message of salvation by faith in the work of Jesus Christ. We can look at each of these purposes in turn.

Bushnell declared that pantheism sacrificed the personality of God for the sake of guarding his infinity, while Unitarianism sacrificed his infinity for the sake of upholding a consistent and uncomplicated view of his personality. The Trinity, however, avoided both one-sided extremes. The God of the pantheist was absolute enough, but was also aloof and unapproachable, the "vast impersonal abysm, or platitude" of the Brahmins or the "unconscious principle of an eternal Cosmos" of the modern pantheists.[73] The God of the Unitarians, conversely, was so emphatically personal that there was a continual tendency to reduce him to anthropomorphic proportions. "It could not be otherwise. How is it possible to keep up the figure of a one personality, and be always seeing God under that figure, without finally dragging him down by the force of its finite associations, and subjecting him practically

---

[72] Bushnell, "The Christian Trinity a Practical Truth", *Building Eras*, 125.
[73] Bushnell, *Christ in Theology*, 137.

to its measures?"[74] Here was a classic example of the way in which the form element in words, if left unchecked by the conflicting forms of other representations, tended to eclipse their meanings, which were "out of form".

Bushnell believed that the Unitarians were "conscious of a certain decay of impression, a dimunition of tonic force in the idea of God", because they had abandoned the symbol of the Trinity. There was something in the "Trinitarian feeling" that they sensed was not theirs. They dimly perceived that the Trinitarian God "is more a God, higher in majesty, and heavier on the soul's feeling". This unconscious awareness of the need for something more transcendent and forceful in their conception of God was what was causing "poets, essayists, and nominally Christian teachers" brought up in their doctrine to "begin to be heard speaking in a heathenish and mock-classic way of 'the gods'". They did it because there somehow seemed to be "more rhetorical power" in the plural designation than in the mere unity-of-person God.[75] That plurality was a natural way of giving expression to the majesty and magnitude of God, considered as the Absolute, could be readily seen in the Old Testament designation of him as *Elohim*.[76]

In contrast to Norton and Taylor, who professed themselves unable to believe anything they could not understand, Bushnell regarded it as a great part of the value of the Trinitarian revelation of God that it was incomprehensible to the mind, that it set him forth "under a veil of mystery; for, as nothing that is infinite can be definite, so mystery is a necessary dynamic of expression for the infinite".[77] The sense of the infinity of God was preserved better by the Trinitarian conception, in fact, than it was by the pantheistic. By the "cross relations of a threefold grammatic personality," the mind was "thrown into a maze of sublimity," and the believer made to feel, even if he could not comprehend, the vastness of God.[78] The three persons were "set before the mind

[74] Bushnell, "The Christian Trinity a Practical Truth", *Building Eras*, 121.
[75] Bushnell, *Building Eras*, 120-121. The allusion was, of course, to the Transcendentalists, particularly Emerson and Thoreau.
[76] Bushnell, *Building Eras*, 125.
[77] Bushnell, *Christ in Theology*, 118.
[78] Bushnell, "The Christian Trinity a Practical Truth", *Building Eras*, 122.

at the outset as a holy paradox, that only gives the truth in so great power of expression that it defies all attempts at logic or definition". And if the paradox could not be reasoned out, it was all to the better, because "it stops the clatter of our speculative mill-work and speaks to us as God's great majesty should, leaving us to adore in silence".[79] Even the centuries of controversy over the riddle of the Trinity, despite their production of much that was barren and unprofitable in the way of speculation, had had the beneficial result at least of not allowing the world to rest any longer in a conception of God "so easy to thought, and, in fact, so nearly finite" as Jewish monotheism. During these centuries mankind had been conducted to "a new sense of the possibilities included in God and the mystery of infinite being".[80]

The Trinity, in short, was to be symbolically, rather than rationally apprehended. It was addressed to feeling and imagination, which Bushnell saw, in contradistinction to the Lockean, Common Sense view of them, as "good interpreters and proper inlets of knowledge".[81] It could be "as little subjected to mere logic as a poem or a painting..."[82] To bring the techniques of logical analysis to bear upon the mere forms of the language of the doctrine of the Trinity, as if that were the only way in which it could be interpreted, was to overlook the major role of words "taken as instruments and powers of expression".[83] It was to betray as great a degree of boorishness and aesthetic insensitivity as would be seen in "a man standing before that most beautiful and wondrous work of art, the 'Beatified Spirit' of Guido, and there commencing a quarrel with the artist, that he should be so absurd as to think of making a beatified spirit out of mere linseed ochres, and oxides! Would it not be more dignified to let the pigments go and take the expression of the canvass?" Still there was the New England "tribe of sophisters" whose theory of language permitted them to approach a painting in no other way and to whom a poem would be "ill

[79] Bushnell, *Building Eras*, 147.
[80] Bushnell, *Christ in Theology*, 123.
[81] Bushnell, *Christ in Theology*, 120-121.
[82] Bushnell, *Christ in Theology*, 197.
[83] Bushnell, *Christ in Theology*, 208.

... if it does not stand well in the predicaments".[84] It was no wonder that they failed entirely to perceive the symbolic import and power of the Trinity.

But if the Trinity, viewed in this symbolical way, preserved a more profound sense of the infinity of God than even pantheism could, it also more effectively presented the liveliness and warmth of his personality than Unitarianism could.

... it is by setting ourselves before this personal history of the Father in heaven, and the Son on earth, both as representatives standing out before the Absolute Being, watching the relative history they unfold in finite forms, their acting and interacting, and discovering what is expressed thereby, — cleared of all the repugnant and contradictory matter that is attributable to the vehicle, in distinction from the truth — it is thus that we ascend, as by a resultant of the two forces, into a lively realization, and a free, spiritual embrace of God, as our Friend, Redeemer, Peace, and Portion. A mere philosophic unity, it will be seen at a glance, is cold and dead in comparison — altogether insufficient to support the Christian uses of the soul.[85]

It has already been noted that, for Bushnell, the second practical purpose served by the Trinity was its provision of a conception of God which could fit in with the redemptive scheme of the gospel. That scheme depended, by his analysis, upon a view of the economy of God as comprehending the two factors of nature and the supernatural, since that economy must encompass both the idea of the consequences of moral deterioration and death following inevitably upon sin, considered as a cause, and the idea of Divine intervention from the realm of freedom to arrest those consequences and redeem mankind. If only the single term *God* were available in speaking of this redemptive scheme, however — and the point depends upon Bushnell's immanental-transcendental view of God as being somehow included within nature as well as standing above it — "then we must speak of God as dealing with God, contending with the causations of God, the grace-force of God delivering from the nature-force of God".[86] Considered from the standpoint of the practical needs of the religious life, this was an awkward and

---

[84]   Bushnell, *God in Christ*, 159.
[85]   Bushnell, *God in Christ*, 170-171.
[86]   Bushnell, "The Christian Trinity a Practical Truth", *Building Eras*, 128.

highly confusing state of affairs. But the Trinitarian conception of God resolved the problem easily, as Bushnell pointed out in the following passage:

First, we have the term Father, which sets Him before us as the king of nature, the author and ground of all existent things and causes. Next, we have the Son and the Spirit, which represent the supernatural, the Son coming into nature from above nature, incarnate in the person of Jesus, by a method not in the compass of nature, erecting a kingdom in the world that is not of the world; the Spirit coming in the power of the Son, to complete, by an inward supernatural working, what the Son began by the address he made without to human thought, and the forces he imported into nature by his doctrine, his works, his life and his death.[87]

Mention has already been made of the fact that Bushnell regarded the Logos as "the power of self-representation in God," by which he "is able to represent Himself outwardly, in the forms of things."[88] And we have noted that he considered the appearance of the infinite God within the finite categories of human understanding to be analogous to the relation of meaning to form in language. He also, on the basis of a familiar passage in the Epistle to the Philippians,[89] liked to speak of the Logos as "the Form of God", and in one place he described how the Logos had first "bodied Him forth in the creation and government of the world", and then later had made "another outgoing from the Absolute into the human, to reside in the human as being of it; thus to communicate God to the world, and thus to ingenerate in the world Goodness and Life as from Him".[90] Although God had been previously known as Creator and Ruler and hence, in effect, as the first person of the Trinity, it was not until the appearance of Christ that he came to be actually known as a Father relative to a Son: "As Christ himself appears in the finite, he calls out into the finite with him, if I may so speak, another representative of the Absolute, one that is conceived to reside in the heavens, as he himself is seen to walk upon the earth."[91] Finally, the third person of the Trinity, the

[87] Bushnell, *Building Eras*, 130.
[88] See above, Chapter II, note 88.
[89] Philippians 2:6: "Who, being in the form of God, thought it not robbery to be equal with God." (King James version).
[90] Bushnell, *God in Christ*, 168.
[91] Bushnell, *God in Christ*, 169.

Holy Spirit, had come onto the scene, making his advent under physical signs just as the Logos had earlier been embodied in the creation and incarnated in the flesh.[92] In view of the manifest correlations between these statements and Bushnell's theory of language, it is not at all surprising to find him declaring simply that the "Trinity may be regarded as language for God...".[93]

And like all language, with its admixture of meanings and forms, there was "a sense in which the representation is true, and a sense in which it is not true, and exactly where the line is to be drawn, we cannot often tell more exactly, than simply to say that we speak in a figure".[94] Because the Trinity was to be viewed as a language, Bushnell wanted it to be clearly understood that its persons

are given to me for the sake of their external expression, not for the internal investigation of their contents. If I use them rationally or wisely, then, I shall use them according to their object. I must not intrude upon their interior nature, either by assertion or denial. They must have their reality to me in what they express when taken as the wording forth of God.[95]

What we have already said about Bushnell's stress upon the symbolical and "practical" character of the doctrine gives reinforcement to this point. To subject the Trinity to logical analysis, as though its truth were to be found in some kind of adjustment of its forms, was to miss its real meaning and to deprive it of its life and power. The doctrine was to be understood, then, not as an ontological "solution" of the inner nature of God, but only as the *instrument* whereby he accomodates his inconceivable vastness to the limited forms of human thought and discourse, the means by which he communicates himself to men and is met, experienced, and known by them. This view of the Trinity Bushnell labeled an "Instrumental Trinity".[96]

There was one important additional reason for Bushnell's arguing that the Trinity had to be instrumentally, and not ontological-

[92]   Bushnell, *God in Christ*, 171-172.
[93]   Bushnell, "The Christian Trinity a Practical Truth", *Building Eras*, 112.
[94]   Bushnell, *Building Eras*, 112-113.
[95]   Bushnell, *God in Christ*, 175.
[96]   Bushnell, *God in Christ*, 175; also *Christ in Theology*, 163-165.

ly, conceived. And that was his belief that God cannot be ultimately tri-personal; he must be "a proper individual being, included under one simple consciousness". He cited this as "a radical assumption which must not be violated".[97] But this belief is inconsistent, despite his arguments to the contrary, with his root conviction that God as the Absolute, the unrevealed, is completely unknown to man. It has no defense against the point of Taylor's that nothing can be said to be self-evident regarding the nature of God, since the mode of his subsistence and the constituent elements of his being may differ profoundly from our own.[98] But if he did lapse from his own overall position in this respect, Bushnell upheld it in all, or nearly all, others.[99] In keeping with his plea for a reverent agnosticism on the question of the essence of Deity, he strongly stated his refusal "to investigate, as being, to us, impossible subjects", the contents of the persons of the Trinity; "their relations to each other; their root of connection, taken as external, with the one substance; their precise mode of being the one substance".[100] These questions were to be met with the "true simplicity ... which takes the practical at its face, uses instruments as instruments, however complex and mysterious (for what is more so than a man's own body,) and refuses to be cheated of the uses of life, by an over-curious questioning of that which God has given for its uses".[101]

Clearly reflected in Bushnell's approach to the Trinity, at many major points, is the influence of an article by Friedrich Schleiermacher written in defense of Sabellianism, which Moses Stuart had translated and commented upon extensively in two successive issues of the *Biblical Repository*, in 1835.[102] Bushnell went so far as to admit the coincidence of many of the ideas in the article with views he himself was advancing with respect to the Trinity, but he

---

[97] Bushnell, *Christ in Theology*, 142.
[98] See above, p. 200.
[99] Another exception, however, is Bushnell's arguing for the eternity of the three persons, considered as God's perpetual mode of self-disclosure. This will be discussed in a moment.
[100] Bushnell, *Christ in Theology*, 142.
[101] Bushnell, *God in Christ*, 179-180.
[102] Schleiermacher's article was originally published in the *Theologische Zeitschrift* in 1822 (dritt. Heft, 295 ff.).

hastened to add, with characteristic independence, that the work had only "confirmed me in results to which I had come by my own private struggles".[103] In a statement suggesting Bushnell's Instrumental Trinity, Schleiermacher had declared: "To Sabellius and his friends, no doubt, it seemed very important to maintain, that *Trinity was not essential to Godhead as in itself considered, but only in reference to created beings and on their account.*"[104] And the following summary of Schleiermacher's position, as offered by Stuart, shows how closely his view of the Trinity did accord with that of Bushnell, at least on the points of the prior unity of God; his hiddeness or "absoluteness" apart from the modes of his self-disclosure; the Trinity as an accomodation, through successive revelational events, of that unity and absoluteness to the level of human cognition and experience; and the fallacy of ascribing personality in any literal sense to God as he is in essence.

The sum of Schleiermacher's opinion ... is, that the Unity is *God concealed*, and the Trinity is *God revealed*. The Unity or *Monas*, as he supposes, is God *in se ipso*, i.e., simply and in and by himself considered, immutable, self-existent, eternal, and possessed of all possible perfection and excellence. But as to the Trinity, the Father is God as revealed in the works of creation, providence, and legislation; the Son is God in human flesh, the divine Logos incarnate; the Holy Ghost is God the Sanctifier, who renovates the hearts of sinners, and dwells in the hearts of believers. The *personality* of the Godhead consists in these *developments*, made in time, and made to intelligent and rational beings. Strictly considered, personality is not in his view eternal; and from the nature of the case (as thus viewed) it could not be, because it consists in developments of the Godhead to intelligent beings; and those developments could not be made, before those beings had existence. [105]

In the comments made by Stuart himself there can also be recognized important correlations to the view of Bushnell. For example, in one place he set up a series of queries which foreshadow Bushnell's call for a halt to speculation when it comes to the interior mystery

[103]   Bushnell, *God in Christ*, 112.
[104]   F. Schleiermacher "On the Discrepancy Between the Sabellian and Athanasian Method of Representing the Doctrine of the Trinity", trans. Moses Stuart, *Biblical Repository* V (1835), 265-353; VI (1835), 1-116. See VI, 52.
[105]   Schleiermacher, *Biblical Repository* V, 316-317.

of the Godhead and his plea for a simple acceptance of the puzzlement of the Trinitarian symbolism, as preserving a sense of the vastness and total-otherness of God.

Why have so many men, who allow in theory that the mystery of the Trinity is inscrutable, practically neglected what they have urged upon others, and undertaken to give us graphic and specific views of it, and to settle with precision the relation of the persons in the Godhead? Why did they not content themselves with adopting the simple biblical declaration, and leave the subject there if it be truly inscrutable? How can the man who believes really and truly, that in many respects the *modus existendi* of the Godhead is altogether inscrutable, when the reads many things that have been written on this subject, refrain from the conviction and feeling, that those persons are usually most prone to exclaim *mystery! mystery!* on every occasion where close inquiry is urged, who take the greatest liberties of all in defining, or attempting to define, the mysteries of the Godhead by metaphysical propositions?[106]

Stuart showed himself even more plainly to be moving in an orbit of thought later to be occupied by Bushnell when he attributed much of the mystery that surrounds the interior nature of God to the limitations of human language and warned of the wholly erroneous inferences that can result when these limitations are not kept in view.

In a word, it is only when we come adequately to learn the imperfection of human language, and the difficulties which attend communications by it respecting distinctions in the Godhead, that we shall be satisfied how inconclusive all reasoning must be, which is founded on deductions drawn from the language of Scripture, when we interpret that language just as if it had relation to finite intelligences who are altogether distinct and separate beings. What cannot be proved, if we are to take liberties such as these? Surely the Anthropomorphites are not to be confuted, when such a position is taken.[107]

And finally, Stuart, in another foreshadowing of Bushnell, stated that the names "Father", "Son", and "Holy Ghost" have only a *relative* sense, as within the context of the redemptive economy and the processes of God's self-disclosure to his creatures. The overlooking of this simple fact had produced errors and difficulties

---

[106] Schleiermacher, *Biblical Repository* V, 306-307.
[107] Schleiermacher, *Biblical Repository* VI, 88

in theology which he considered to be "beyond the bounds of computation".[108]

When these lines of influence have been duly recorded, however, we must not allow ourselves to lose sight for a moment of the remarkable achievement that was uniquely Bushnell's, in not only establishing his Trinitarian views on this kind of reasoning, but also on the basis of a theory of language whose main outlines he considered to be normative for any kind of communication to or among creatures of a finite world. Here he went far beyond Schleiermacher, Stuart, or any one else of his time, pitching the entire subject on wholly fresh ground. It is much to his credit that, in the process, he succeeded in showing that the real value of the Trinitarian formula is symbolic and that he provided a rather trenchant explication, when his thought is fully understood, of what symbolic apprehension is and of the major role it plays in the religious life.

Deeply influenced though he undoubtedly was by the Schleiermacher-Stuart article, Bushnell nevertheless took issue with it at some points, most notably in regard to the approaches it had made to the question of the eternality of the Trinity. Schleiermacher had categorically disallowed any eternal character for the Trinity, holding that it, as well as the personality of God, were but transient manifestations to creatures dwelling in finite time. Stuart, on the other hand, had been unwilling to move that far afield from orthodoxy, though he was much impressed by much of what Schleiermacher had said in defense of Sabellianism. He accordingly argued for same kind of "foundation" in the Divine nature itself, in the *Monas*, for the Trinitarian manifestation. To suppose otherwise, as he thought, would be to speak of having an effect without an adequate cause. Of course, if it were asked how this modification or property or distinction could be described, as it existed originally in the Godhead, there were no data available by which such a description could be made out.[109] To Bushnell, Stuart's tactic seemed like verbally defending one's orthodoxy

---

[108] Schleiermacher, *Biblical Repository* VI, 110. See *Christ in Theology*, 184, for Bushnell's comments on the relative character of the term "Father".
[109] Schleiermacher, *Biblical Repository* VI, 94-96.

although one had already denied it in theory. And he charged that neither Schleiermacher nor Stuart had a right to go behind the revelation God had given of himself to discuss how he might be in his essence. The Trinity, it had to be continually borne in mind, was given "for use and not for theory".[110]

Not only did the modalism of Sabellius and of his modern champion, Schleiermacher, attempt the impossible by probing behind the revealed facts concerning God, but it also gave a view of the three persons which, Bushnell complained, made them nothing more than "an occasional matter, a voluntary expedient", "a matter only of words, and not in any proper sense an eternal fact". Such a view was "painful, and quite ... remote from all our most earnest convictions...".[111] He therefore felt the need of somehow establishing the eternality of the Trinity without committing the error of Stuart and going beyond it as the instrument of revelation. Because he felt that need, he was reluctant to have himself regarded as a "modalist", preferring to call his view of the Trinity an "instrumental" view. But if the Trinity, like the personality of God, was to be conceived of as an analogical, figurative, or symbolical representation of his infinite and unknowable nature to finite minds, how could its eternality be established? Bushnell's answer was to point out that it was as much in the nature of God to reveal himself as to create or to be. And since the symbol of the Trinity was the primary mode of his self-manifestation, it had to be considered as grounded in the eternal nature of God.[112] Or as he put the matter in another place,

if God has been eternally revealed, or revealing himself to created minds, it is likely always to have been and always to be as the Father, Son, and Holy Spirit. Consequently, it may always be in this manner that we shall get our impressions of God, and have our communion with Him. As an accomodation to all finite minds in the universe, it may be the purpose of Jehovah to be known by this divine Formula forever.[113]

Bushnell linked his defense of the eternality of the Trinity with

[110]   Bushnell, *Christ in Theology*, 147; 119-120.
[111]   Bushnell, "The Christian Trinity a Practical Truth", *Building Eras*, 132;134.
[112]   Bushnell, *Christ in Theology*, 146.
[113]   Bushnell, *God in Christ*, 177.

the Nicene conception of "eternal generation", a conception that had been largely set aside by the theologians of New England, because it seemed to imply a subordinate status for the Son.[114] In this way he sought to demonstrate the continuity of his own view with the traditional thinking of the Church and to turn the tables against the heresy-hunters who had brought him under severe fire following the publication of *God in Christ*. In *Christ in Theology* Bushnell confessed, with respect to the Nicene Creed, that at the time of writing *God in Christ*, he "had not sufficiently conceived its import, or the title it has to respect as a Christian document". But now he had come to the realization that, by pursuing his own method of analysis, he seemed "only to have reproduced, in a different form, what is really the substantial import of that doctrine".[115] This held true, however, only so long as it was recognized that "the scheme of trinity it affirms was itself true to its authors, not so much as a rigid definition ... but had its meaning or verity more as a combination of symbols offered to the imagination".[116]

When symbolically perceived, it could be seen at once that "the eternal generation is not a matter collateral to the conception of trinity, but fundamental to it".[117] For what it implied was a "trinity of act", a Trinity that "is eternal, because it pertains to the eternal necessary going on of the life or conscious spirit of God; and, in that sense, it is immanent".[118] Such a Trinity, with its correlate assertion of the simplicity and strict unity of God, and its denial of a Trinity in the divine essence, rather than act, was little different than Bushnell's own Instrumental or revelational Trinity. There the "act" in question was more specifically the act of God's eternal self-expression, but otherwise, the views melded into one another without difficulty.

Despite the ingenuity of Bushnell's argument for the eternality of the Trinity within the framework of his conception of it as purely expressive, there is a serious flaw in his reasoning that needs

[114]   Cf. Taylor, for example, on this point. See above, p. 199.
[115]   Bushnell, *Christ in Theology*, 177.
[116]   Bushnell, *Christ in Theology*, 183.
[117]   Bushnell, *Christ in Theology*, 178.
[118]   Bushnell, *Christ in Theology*, 176.

to be pointed out. In the first place, he spoke of God's eternally revealing himself to created minds. But if those minds all originated at some point in time, as the word "created" requires, then there must have been a time prior to their creation when there were no finite minds for God to reveal himself to, and, hence, a time when there was no Trinity. Secondly, Bushnell too easily assumed that creatures dwelling in the after-life will be under the same limitations of finitude as they are in this life. But it is quite conceivable that there they would no longer need a Trinitarian revelation of God, either because they could now at last "see him as he is",[119] or because they might now be capable of viewing him under some higher or wholly different order of symbolism. In saying that God "is datelessly and eternally becoming three, or by a certain inward necessity being accomodated in his action to the categories of finite apprehension, adjusted to that as that to the receiving of his mystery",[120] Bushnell was actually encroaching upon the mystery of the *eschaton*, a mystery that lies as much beyond present human knowledge as does the Divine essence itself. Interestingly enough, he took note of this fact in *God in Christ*, but not in his later works. For there he entered the reservation upon his argument for the eternality of the Trinity which he took to be implied by the declaration of Paul: "When all things shall be subdued unto him, then shall the Son also himself be subjected unto him that did put all things under him, that God may be all in all."[121] And he stated his unwillingness to "go into a discussion of these very remarkable words", for he did "not care to open God's secrets before the time".[122] The reservation seems to have been forgotten in *Christ in Theology*, however, perhaps because Bushnell's desire to defend his orthodoxy against his attackers was now the thing uppermost in his mind, and such a reservation would have detracted from the strength of his case. There is no trace of the reservation in his other principal work on the Trinity, "The Christian Trinity a Practical Truth".

[119]   I John 3:2.
[120]   Bushnell, "The Christian Trinity a Practical Truth", *Building Eras*, 135
[121]   I Corinthians 15:28.
[122]   Bushnell, *God in Christ*, 177.

Bushnell was merciless in his attack upon the orthodox defenders of the Trinity in New England, who had been, to his mind, both presumptuous and wholly ignorant of the nature of language and symbolism in insisting that the three persons belong "not to the *machina Dei*, by which God is revealed, but to the very *esse*, the substantial being of God, or the interior contents of His being".[123] This was to uphold the truth of Trinitarianism at the price of asserting what no man can assert, namely, a knowledge of what God is in himself. It was to forget the gulf of mystery which separates God from man. But still the debates went on in New England, as to whether the three persons were three sets of attributes in a common substance; or whether they were merely a "threefold distinction" in the Godhead, on the analogy of the soul, the life-principle, and the body, united in one person called a man; or whether they were three distinct personalities, dwelling together in a kind of social unity.[124] These acrimonious debates and the hopeless perplexities they engendered in the minds of believers were proof of the complete futility of trying to prepare "a psychology of His infinite Spirit in the tiny molds of our discursive understanding".[125]

Lacking the symbolical sense, the New England theologians had rejected out of hand the "church doctrine" (as Bushnell called it) of eternal generation. But if they had had the imagination to penetrate beneath the offending *form* of the language of that doctrine, i.e. the physical meaning and implications of the term "generation", to its symbolical import, they would have seen at once that the Church's traditional belief was in a Trinity grounded in the necessary *activity* of God. And they would have realized that this view of the Trinity automatically branded as a "fatal heresy" any attempt to find a trinity of persons in the Divine essence, substance, or nature.[126] But the theologians of New England seemed constitutionally unable to come to such insights, and Bushnell attributed the fact in part to their preoccupation and tedious grapplings with "a few speculative questions related to the will

123   Bushnell, *God in Christ*, 130.
124   Bushnell, *God in Christ*, 130-135.
125   Bushnell, *Christ in Theology*, 121.
126   Bushnell, *Christ in Theology*, 171-172; 175.

and responsibility". So introspective and unimaginative had their approach to theology become thereby, that they were in the habit of neglecting "many great subjects of revelation, which did not come within the range of their speculative method...".[127]

Busied thus about their own metaphysical center, they fall into a raw logical habit, as much more confident, as it was more incompetent, to some of the highest subjects of revelation. They were *thinking out* a gospel, and could not so well receive one offered to their faith and their imaginative power — phosphorescing bravely enough, but unable to stand in the shining body of the sun and shine with it.[128]

The prevailing conception of language lent itself admirably, of course, to this "raw logical habit", and it made for just the kind of blindness toward the place and value of symbolism of which Bushnell was speaking.

Before taking leave of Bushnell's reflections on the Trinity, it is important for us to make note of the fact that here, as well as in his views on language, there are strong Kantian overtones.[129] This serves as one additional factor tying together his language theory and his theology. The polarity between the Absolute, unknowable God and the God revealed through forms intelligible to the human mind is strongly suggestive of Kant's conception of a noumenal world mediated through the forms or categories of the mind. And we have seen already how Bushnell consciously linked his Absolute God with those mental and spritual truths which are "out of form" and took the doctrine of the Trinity to be a kind of language which symbolically indicates by its forms, as all language must, those truths which it cannot literally convey. Bushnell's language theory operates, in other words, in terms of the Kantian scheme of noumena and phenomena. That is its fundamental orientation, just as it is the fundamental orientation for his interpretation of the doctrine of the Trinity. Bushnell's stress on the "practical truth" of the

---

[127]   Bushnell, *Christ in Theology*, 170.
[128]   Bushnell, *Christ in Theology*, 171.
[129]   I do not intend here to catalogue all of the Kantian elements in Bushnell's theory of language, but only to point up those which correlate with his conception of the Trinity. For additional Kantian elements in his language theory see the discussion of S. T. Coleridge, pp. 96-107 above.

Trinity, as over against its ontological implications, sounds very much like Kant's founding of religious truth in the "practical" rather than "pure" reason. Bushnell's overall deprecation of logical language, in favor of expressive or symbolical language, for the uses of religion also dovetails into Kantianism at this point. Finally, Bushnell drew up a list of eight classes of "antinomies" into which he felt the Scripture passages relating to the Trinity naturally fell. Unitarianism and each of the orthodox interpretations of the Trinity held in New England were nothing else than a fixing upon one or two of these classes of antinomies and then trying to force the others into accord with them.[130] This is strongly reminiscent of Kant's demonstration that the pure reason cannot yield a metaphysical system because it is always running into an impasse of antinomies. Bushnell asserted that his Instrumental Trinity could easily take the antinomies in stride, because it showed that such antinomies were just what might be expected, given an accomodation of the infinite God to the limited categories of human thought, and because it could affirm the antinomies as pointing symbolically to a truth which outreached and yet comprehended them all. The correlation with Bushnell's theory of language, in its anticipation of paradoxes and its organic approach to contradictory statements, is readily apparent.

We have sought to make clear in this chapter the marked and decisive differences in approach to the doctrine of the Trinity (and, by implication, to theology as a whole) Bushnell's language views enabled him to make. Because he took the Trinity to be a kind of "language" by means of which God communicates himself to man, he could escape the problem of it as an ontological puzzle, and could thus set himself apart from the debates going on in New England which revolved about the attempt in some way to "solve" the puzzle. Conceived of as a language, within the context of Bushnell's theory of language, the paradoxical character of the Trinity gave no offense, but testified to its authenticity as a revelation of the Absolute God. For like the poet or man of genius who, in his use of language, must multiply repugnant figures in order

---

[130]   Bushnell, *Christ in Theology*, 155-164.

to open up perspective upon surpassing truths, so the Trinity presented contradictory forms to the mind which symbolized both the mystery and grandeur of God and also his warmth and availability as a person, and the saga of his redemptive love. But though the forms of representation within the doctrine of the Trinity were thus admirably adapted to the practical uses of religion, it was as erroneous to equate them directly with the truth they were given to portray as it would be to equate the truths of the second department of language with the physical images by which they were suggestively or metaphorically indicated.

What Bushnell's language theory did, in short, was to make it possible for him to recover a sense of the doctrine of the Trinity as a *symbol*,[131] whose truth was to be found, not in what it stated, but in what it stood for or represented. This was to say that it was neither to be regarded as a straightforward, factual proposition about the ontological structure of God, as Taylor believed, nor yet as a mere bit of hyperbolic fancy, as Norton wanted to maintain. Because it was a symbol, it could never be "translated" into equivalent logical statements. But that did not imply that it was meaningless; it only meant that its meaning was of a different order than that which could come under the definitions and rules of logic. It was a meaning that had to be participated in emotionally and imaginatively to be understood, a meaning that could not be abstracted from the concreteness of the religious life and worship, as that stretched from the earliest biblical times right down to the present day. It was a meaning that had always to be contemplated through and by means of its symbol, never apart from it, for the simple reason that no equivalent expressions of the meaning could be found. Still it was a meaning that was not to be confused with the mere outward characteristics of the symbol itself — any more, we might say, than the meaning of an Englishman's patriotism can be reduced to the outward regalia of a coronation in Westminster Abbey by which it may be profoundly stirred. The doc-

131 Feidelson has suggested that Arianism reduces to an attempt to take literally the symbolism of the Sonship of Christ. Athanasius, on the other hand, sought to preserve a symbolic sense of its meaning by comparing it to the light radiating from the sun. Feidelson, *Symbolism*, 66-67.

trine of the Trinity in itself was a mere earthen vessel, but when rightly apprehended, it would be found to contain the transcendent power which comes from on high.

ATTACKS ON THE LANGUAGE THEORY

> Never was book more open to attack from every
> quarter — never was book more avowedly liable
> to all sorts of misapprehensions and logical mis-
> construction — than this book of Dr. Bushnell.
>
> Leonard Bacon, "Review
> of *God in Christ*" (1849)

In order to make it all the more plain why it can be said without exaggeration that Bushnell's "entrance into the company of New England theologians with such a theory was like Copernicus appearing among the Ptolemaists",[1] we will devote this final chapter to a discussion of attacks upon that theory which appeared in the religious periodicals and elsewhere as a part of the shocked reaction to *God in Christ*. For nowhere does the variance between the reigning conception of language and that held by Bushnell stand out more vividly than in these attacks. We shall want to assess their fairness and validity and, by that means, to come to some final judgments on the historical and enduring philosophical importance of Horace Bushnell's theory of language.

The attacks can be boiled down to a few basic criticisms, which we can discuss in turn.

1. WORDS IN THE SECOND DEPARTMENT OF LANGUAGE NOT ALL SENSIBLY DERIVED

Some critics of *God in Christ* took issue with the very basis of

---

[1] T. Munger, *Horace Bushnell*, 109.

Bushnell's theory of language by claiming that he was entirely mistaken in assuming that all words designating things of the intellect or spirit had their origin in sensible experience. Thus Enoch Pond, a professor in the theological seminary at Bangor, Maine, while he recognized the truth of Bushnell's assertion that there is a sensible root in many words of every language, yet insisted that there was not sufficient proof that this was the case with all words. In fact, there seemed to be much evidence to the contrary. What external acts, he wanted to know, were ever denoted by such simple, everyday words as *smell, taste, feel, think, peace,* and *please*? So far as it could be discovered philologically, these words were of "purely internal application" and had no sensible origin at all. Moreover, there was no reason to suppose that all words were sensibly derived, even on a theoretical or hypothetical basis.

The sensation of hunger, for example, is a reality, and one with which man, in the early stages of his existence, would be likely to become as soon acquainted as any external object whatever; and why should he not as early give it a name? Why should he wait till names had been applied to external things, and then borrow one of these, to use it metaphorically, so setting forth the important fact that he was hungry?[2]

But a reviewer who went into much greater detail in attacking Bushnell at this point was David Lord, in an article of seventy pages which dealt exclusively with the "Preliminary Dissertation on Language".[3] Lord pointed out for one thing that Bushnell was in the wrong in saying that figures are never used in the designation and description of physical things but are confined to spiritual things. A word like *fly,* for example, though literally applicable to the movement of a bird or insect through the air by its wings, could be applied figuratively to a cloud, a fast locomotive, or any rapidly moving thing. Poetry, as Lord showed by profuse illustration, was full of this kind of metaphorical designation of sensible

---

[2]   Enoch Pond, "Review of Dr. Bushnell's 'God in Christ'" (Bangor, Me.: E. F. Duren, 1849), 4.
[3]   David Lord, "Review of Bushnell's 'Dissertation on Language'", *The Theological and Literary Journal*, II (1849-50), 61-131. A review of the three discourses in *God in Christ* is also contained in this volume and was also written by Lord. See 173 ff.

objects. But not only was Bushnell mistaken in this assumption; he had also failed to notice that words naming attributes, affections, and acts of the mind were frequently used in application to physical objects, thus precisely reversing his theory of the sensible origin of all words. Young's lines were but one instance from a legion of passages in literature and oratory which would bear the point out:

The breeze that *mourns* the summer's close
With *melancholy wail*.[4]

The fact that these obvious exceptions to his theory of language had apparently completely escaped Bushnell's notice was indication for Lord that in place of a careful examination, he had "cast but a superficial glance at his subject".[5]

But Lord also ventured the more basic criticism, as Pond did, that there was no sound theoretical basis for saying that spritual subjects must be designated universally by figures. In the first place, changes in the countenance could register the most subtle of emotions. And as

these emotions and dispositions of the mind thus become known through the eye, as perfectly as the changes of the countenance, and the gestures by which they are indicated, it is thence as possible and easy to designate them by arbitrary or literal names, as it is to apply such words to those modifications themselves of the features and body, or to any other objects or appearances that are perceived by the senses. The names of the principal affections, accordingly, are perfectly literal, and formed as independently of analogies as the names of the objects in the material world.[6]

Then, too since the mind was directly conscious of its thoughts and emotions, it could as easily designate them by arbitrary and literal names as it could the objects it perceived through the senses. Proof of this was the fact that such words as *mind, soul,* and *thought* were available in language to denote the whole intellectual nature and its perceptive acts, and that all man's emotions and passions,

4 Lord, Review, 69.
5 Lord, Review, 71.
6 Lord, Review, 76.

and every form in which they were exercised, could be indicated by some such literal word as *love, hate, fear, rejoice, grieve,* or *mourn.*

A third reason put forward by Lord in support of his view that mental and spritual objects could be as easily designated by literal as by figurative language was that it was impossible to give to these objects metaphorical names "without *such a knowledge of their nature as to render it equally practicable to give them literal denominatives*".[7] This was undoubtedly true, since the figurative name had to be founded on analogy, and in order for an analogy to be drawn, the nature of both that from which it was drawn and that to which it was to be applied had to be understood at least to the extent that the analogy itself could be discerned. But this meant that the nature of the latter had to be apprehended with clarity enough for the mind to give it a literal name, if it so chose. The following statement made by Lord in this connection reveals quite clearly that in the background of his thinking was the Lockean, Common Sense conception of the nature of figurative speech:

There is not a proposition which our language is capable of expressing, more indubitably, without an exception, than that all the terms of our speech that are used by us metaphorically, are also used by us in their literal meaning; as the literal use is necessary in order to the possibility of a tropical one.[8]

The presence of this bias in Lord is borne out further by his assertion that Bushnell had proceeded throughout his language theory on a wholly erroneous view, namely, "that tropical expressions are, from their nature, extremely obscure and equivocal, and instead of illustrating a writer's meaning, render it uncertain...".[9] Had he been possessed of a better understanding of the laws of figurative language, he would have seen that "the subject of a metaphorical affirmation is always denoted by a literal term",[10] and, therefore, it was clearly understood before the figurative expression was applied to it. Now it is true that Locke, Stewart, and others of their ilk distrusted tropes and held them to be "ex-

---

[7]   Lord, Review, 77.
[8]   Lord, Review, 96
[9]   Lord, Review, 128.
[10] Lord, Review, 128-129.

tremely obscure and equivocal". But this was only when they were used without the preliminary precaution of making sure that the meaning to be figuratively stated could be set forth in clear logical form. In their view, the figure was not to add or give meaning in itself, just as it was not for Lord. It was intended merely to ornament and illustrate the meaning, making it more graceful, palatable, or forceful than a literal statement could. A figure which was supposed to "suggestively convey" (to use Bushnell's expression) a meaning which could not be put in logical form was a figure which, in reality, only obscured meaning — a figure poorly chosen and wrongly used. Instead of an instrument of enlightenment, it was an implement of confusion. Once again, the possibility of truth being communicated symbolically, instead of literally, was left wholly out of mind.

A fourth and final argument against Bushnell's contention for the sensible origin of words was that there was a large group of what Lord called "affiliated" terms employed in the description of mental and spritual things which were formed, in his view, entirely apart from analogies in the physical world. This was the entire group of abstract nouns, adjectives, and adverbs, which were derived from common nouns or verbs and used to denote qualities and powers of the mind. An illustration of the type of words meant was the derivatives of the word *love*: *loveliness*, *lovableness*, *lovingness*, *lover*, *lovely*, *lovable*, *loveless*, *lovelorn*, and *lovingly*. All terms such as these had "the ground of their use in our consciousness, not in anything external to us".[11]

Such, then, were the kinds of arguments set in array against the assumption, so crucial to the entire language theory of Bushnell, that all words used to denote data of the mind or spirit were originally physical in their meaning and reference. What response can be made to them?

First, Pond's point must be well taken that only an exhaustive philological investigation into the history of nearly every word in every language of the world could prove conclusively Bushnell's contention that all mental and spiritual words are of sensible origin.

---

[11] Lord, Review, 79.

This kind of investigation is, in effect, impossible, not only because of its staggering proportions, but also because the origin of so many words has been long since lost in the mists of time. Attempts to recover these origins generally require as much speculation and hypothesis as is involved in Bushnell's theory of the sensible origin of words,; witness a work like Horne Tooke's *Diversions of Purley*, for example. Linguists today steer clear of any such sweeping and all-inclusive statement about the origin of words as that of Bushnell, and with good reason.

Secondly, there do definitely seem to be some words which, as Lord pointed out, reverse Bushnell's theory of the sensible origin of all words, in that they are primarily designative of the states and acts of the mind, and only secondarily denominative of physical things. The naturalness of the movement of thought in this direction is clearly seen in poetry and literature, where it has been dubbed "the pathetic fallacy". Of course, it is still undetermined whether such words were, in fact, originally physical in origin, then applied to the mind and spirit, and then again, having acquired their mental and spiritual meaning, applied to physical phenomena. But this is a point which Bushnell should have discussed, since it does have important bearing on his whole theory of language. Like Locke, he seems not to have noticed it.[12]

Thirdly, Lord was certainly correct in saying that a physical name can be applied metaphorically to some other physical object or event than that which it primarily signifies. There can be, therefore, figurative speech in the first, as well as the second, department of language. The point is an interesting one, but it is minor and does not affect the applications of Bushnell's theory of language. He himself readily admitted that he was only an amateur on the subject of language, and that he was not attempting a theory that would be technically sound at every small point. This admission, coupled with the minor nature of this particular point, makes both exaggerated and unfair Lord's charge that Bushnell showed himself to be utterly incompetent and inattentive to his subject by failing to take notice of it.

[12]   See Chapter III, Note 114, above.

We come in the fourth place to a very fundamental point. And that is the assertion by both Pond and Lord that there is no theoretical (as opposed to philological) reason why all words should be thought to be sensibly derived. Lord argued in the first instance that names could as easily be given directly to the inner states which gestures and facial expressions registered[13] as to the physical expressions themselves. Bushnell, on the other hand, believed that it was the physical expressions which were actually named, and that because these names were taken as signs of the inner data, they had a kind of secondary or metaphorical sense. But Lord had already made the important admission that, in this case at least, there had to be something in the physical world to mediate the data in question. And it is much more likely, on a purely theoretical plane of argument, that the gesture or expression was not at the very outset distinguished from that which it expressed, but that, in naming the one, the other was named also. Bushnell's argument is therefore the sounder one. Then too, the very fact that gestures and expressions can so well communicate the inner world of thought — a fact hardly less mysterious and marvelous than the existence of language itself — gives some support, at least for the purposes of theory, to Bushnell's insistence upon an unanalyzable correlation between the physical and mental realms which makes analogical reference from one to the other possible and therefore explains how language in the second department, based on sensible images, could have come into being.

But Lord argued, in the second instance, (as Pond also did), that the mind can directly perceive its own operations and can therefore name them directly, without having to have recourse to the roundabout way of first finding a suitable physical image. If language were purely a matter of solipsistic, internal discourse, this point would have weight. But language is a social phenomenon, and neither Pond nor Lord perceived or faced up to the question of how there could have been mutual agreement on a term to be used for an internal state of the soul if the term had not already designated an external object which could intervene as a sign. The

---

[13]   This was in reference to Bushnell's point in this same connection. See above, pp. 17-18.

existence of this problem gave a strong theoretical basis for Bushnell's insistence upon the sensible origin of words. There may be other ways of meeting the problem, but he at least recognized it and tried to deal with it, while Lord and Pond evaded it entirely.

Fifthly, there is Lord's assertion that, in order for an analogy to be perceived, and thence, a metaphor to be used, the nature of both that from which the analogy is drawn and that to which it is applied must be known. This implies that the second can be named literally, as well as figuratively. But the problem of why we consider one thing to be an apt metaphor or symbol of another and can agree that it is such is much more complex than Lord's remarks would lead us to believe. The fact is that there are many cases where a figurative expression or the use of sensible images seems to be the only intelligible way of treating of a subject, and where no literal statement begins to do it justice. This important fact was not recognized in the prevailing conception of language, and that was, as Bushnell saw, its most glaring fault. The theory of figurative or symbolical speech as merely ornamentative or illustrative of that which can be lucidly stated in literal propositions is simply not an adequate account of the way in which analogies, metaphors, and symbols do operate in actual experience. We frequently resort to them, not as mere ornaments or empty rhetorical devices, but as ways of bringing into focus insights which more straightforward forms of expression simply cannot capture or convey. This point having been established, it is readily apparent that Lord's analysis of the nature of analogy and of figurative discourse is not sufficiently astute to give weight to his argument that since whatever can be figuratively apprehended can and must also be capable of being rendered into literal statements, there is no theoretical ground for Bushnell's contention for the sensible origin of all words.

Finally, there is Lord's point about the "affiliated" terms, which constitutes another philological argument against the sensible origin of words. Bushnell would hardly allow that the so-called "affiliated" terms are "all in their primary sense absolutely literal",[14]

---

[14] Lord, Review, 79.

for the simple reason that their "primary sense", as he regarded it, implied the original meaning of their roots. Thus, so long as it could be argued that the root element in the word "love", in Lord's illustration, was sensible in its origin, it could not be said that such words as "lovable", "lover", "lovingly", and the like were arrived at *independently* of sensible analogies.

We can summarize our discussion in this section by saying that Bushnell's claim for the sensible origin of all words cannot be conclusively proved or disproved on philological grounds. It is made somewhat questionable by the existence of a good many words which are metaphors of the mind applied to material things, instead of the other way around, but there is a way in which this criticism can be met and the claim still upheld, as we have shown. As a hypothesis, which tries to take into account the vital problem of how mutual understanding of a term applied to the interior data of the mind and spirit could have been achieved, his claim has plausibility. And that plausibility was not detracted from in the least by the theoretical arguments which his critics held up against him. To say this is not to conclude that Bushnell's claim is unquestionably true. It is only to say that is is a legitimate conjecture. Of course, one may well choose not to conjecture along these lines, and that has been the choice of most linguists and philosophers of language today.

2. MOST WORDS, THOUGH ONCE FIGURATIVE, ARE NO LONGER SO; AND THE AMBIGUITIES WITH WHICH THEY ARE CHARGED IN BUSHNELL'S THEORY EITHER DO NOT EXIST, OR THEY ARE EASILY REMOVED BY THE LINGUISTIC CONTEXTS IN WHICH THEY ARE USED.

Another type of criticism directed at Bushnell's theory of language was that most of the words we use have lost their figurative meanings and now stand as plain words directly indicating the objects they represent. Correlate to this assertion was the protest that words have nothing like the ambiguity Bushnell accused them of having, and even where such ambiguity does exist, there are ample provisions within the patterns of the usage of language for removing it.

Thus, according to Lord, "There certainly is no impossibility that a word that is employed metaphorically should lose its tropical use, and acquire a literal sense". The moment a word was employed without conscious reference to sensible analogies, it was employed literally, and there were "thousands and millions of instances in which that takes place".[15]

But Lord not only denied the figurative character of words in the second department of language; he also denied categorically that they have the ambiguity Bushnell had represented them to have.

There is no such ambiguity, ... or deceptiveness, as Dr. Bushnell represents, in the meaning of terms. Instead, every word has an individual and specific office assigned to it, as clearly and absolutely as the letters of the alphabet, or the vocal sounds which they are employed to represent.[16]

The difficulty with him is not at all, as he represents, that there are no words that are adequate to convey the thoughts with which his mind teems, but instead, that he has not the thoughts which it is the office of the words he uses to convey.[17]

Orestes Brownson, who after a life of many shifting allegiances and points of view had finally found a home within the Roman Catholic fold, wrote a lengthy review of *God in Christ* in which he concentrated almost exclusively on Bushnell's language views. The article was entitled, in caustic reference to Bushnell's organic approach to creedal differences, "Bushnellism: Or Orthodoxy and Heresy Identical". In this article Brownson, like Lord, insisted that the sensible figures in words are lost sight of with use. But even when, after etymological study, perhaps, the figure was borne in mind, it did not detract from the accuracy of a word's meaning. Rather, it reinforced that meaning in the mind of the word's user. The material sense of the word *attend*, for example, served "to intensify the spiritual meaning, for *bending* to a thing indicates resolution and earnestness".[18] Moreover, careful deter-

---

[15] Lord, Review, 94. Chauncey Goodrich also made the point in one of his articles in the *New York Evangelist*, written under the pen name "Omicron". See his article in the *New York Evangelist*, XX. 13, 49.

[16] Lord, Review, 111.

[17] Lord, Review, 114.

[18] *Brownson's Quarterly Review*, n.s. III (1849), 505.

mination of the meanings of words by speakers and writers could easily eliminate their possible ambiguities.

As against Bushnell's point that there is a kind of infinite regress in the meanings of words, deriving from their past history, the contexts in which they are used, their associations and relations, and the temperament and experience of him who uses them, the critics insisted that language was admirably suited to overcome just this difficulty. In language properly used, said Lord, there was "the limitation of each word, in each instance of its use, to the denomination of some one individual thing; and appropriation of a different term to every different genus, species, kind, individual, form, office, relation, quality, and degree that is the subject of affirmation".[19] Goodrich pointed out that terms were generally "hemmed in and restricted by qualifying adjuncts, so as to admit of only one sense and application".[20] And Charles Hodge complained that

The fallacy of Dr. Bushnell's reasoning on this subject, is so transparent, that we can hardly give him credit for sincerity. Because by words a man cannot express everything that is in his mind, the inference is that he can express nothing surely; because each particular word may be figurative and inadequate, it is argued that no number or combination of words, no variety of illustrations, nor diversity in the mode of setting forth the same truth, can convey it certainly to other minds. He confounds, moreover, knowing everything that may be known of a given subject, with understanding any definite proposition respecting it.[21]

Thus, while Hodge saw "nothing either new or objectionable" in Bushnell's general theory of language, he felt that he had carried his principles to such an "extravagant length" that they were made productive of "absurdity and evil". The fault, though one of degree, rather than kind, was no less malicious.[22]

---

[19] Lord, Review, 115.
[20] C. A. Goodrich, *New York Evangelist*, XX. 13, 49.
[21] C. Hodge, "Review of *God in Christ*", *Princeton Review*, n.s. XXI (1849), 266-267.
[22] C. Hodge, Review, 265. Critics like Lord and Pond could not agree that there was nothing objectionable in Bushnell's general theory of language. As far as its newness was concerned, Brownson recognized in it "an old acquaintance". But the remark was meant to be disparaging, for now that his Transcendentalist phase was behind him, he could speak of such a theory as "the one very generally resorted to by unbelievers". *Brownson's Quarterly Review*, III (1849), 497.

Turning now to our own appraisal of these points, the following things can be said. Bushnell did not deny that the root meanings of words are unknown by the vast majority of the users of language and that, therefore, most words do not have for them a sense which is consciously figurative. But while the critics we have been discussing reasoned that as soon as words designating thoughts and emotions cease to be consciously entertained as figurative they must be said to have become literal, Bushnell's argument was that, whether consciously figurative or not, words in the second department of language are nonetheless figurative in fact. And it is precisely when their true character is forgotten or overlooked, when it is assumed that they can have a directly significative or "literal" application to the objects and events of the mental and spiritual world, that the most characteristic errors in the uses of language occur. In pointing out that failure to recognize a metaphor as such does not somehow automatically transform it into literal language, Bushnell was right and his critics wrong.

But there is another, more cogent, criticism of Bushnell's theory that can be made than this one which assumes a gradual "fading" of original conscious metaphors into literal speech. Such a criticism would take issue with this assumption itself. It is by no means self-evident that men would first have named the physical things around them and then subsequently decided to use these thing-words as metaphors with which to express facts of the inner life. This model of the origin of language presupposes a clear understanding on the part of primitive man of the distinction between his "inner" world of thought and consciousness and the "outer" world of physical objects, and it also presupposes a conscious awareness of what a metaphor is as distinguished from literal speech. But surely both distinctions are ones themselves made possible only by a relatively sophisticated stage in the development of language. It is far more likely that in naming sensible objects and events in the context of some experience men also quite simultaneously named the emotions and thoughts connected with that experience. In this case there would be no deliberate act of extending a thing-language metaphorically so as to apply it to the mind and feelings, nor would there be any gap of time in which a thing-language was entertained solely as thing-language. Still, the mediation of things would make agreement possible, avoiding problems of "private language", and it would help to account for the sensible roots in so many words. But with such a model it would no longer be meaningful or appropriate to speak of all words concerning mental phenomena as having originally been regarded as or consciously employed as "metaphors".[23] It is noteworthy that this model for the origins of the so-called "second department" of language accords much more closely with the organic theory of the development of language, to the extent that that theory makes thought and self-consciousness dependent on language; while the "faded metaphor" one taken for granted by Bushnell and his critics is more suggestive of the mechanical invention theory, in that it must assume a pre-linguistic clarity of self-consciousness. Since, as has been shown, Bushnell was in other ways much more sympathetic with the organic theory than he was with the mechanical invention theory, there is a disturbing incoherence in his thought.

But even granting the untenability of the "faded metaphor" model, are words concerning mental phenomena metaphors nonetheless? That is, now that language has advanced to the stage where we know the difference between metaphor and literal designation, are we entitled to regard all words having to do with faculties and operations of the mind as metaphors? It is difficult to see how we could be said to be so entitled. For to speak meaningfully of "metaphorical" designations for mental phenomena, we ought to be able to specify, at least in principle, what it would mean to speak "non-metaphorically" or "literally" about those phenomena. But what could it mean literally to designate mental phenomena in Bushnell's theory? Obviously, such a designation is impossible. And if it is impossible, then there is no kind of speech about the mind and emotions to be contrasted with the metaphorical, and this vitiates the distinction on which the meaningfulness of the term "metaphorical" must turn.

[23] For a somewhat more extended critique of the "faded metaphor" hypothesis see Owen Barfield, *Saving the Appearances: A Study in Idolatry* (New York: Harcourt, Brace and World, Inc., A Harbinger Book, n.d.), Chapters XVII and XVIII and passim.

Bushnell's thoughts on language would perhaps have been more successful had he restricted himself to religious language and not tried to offer a general theory of language. For he does succeed in getting at the crucial role played by symbolic consciousness in religious thinking and speaking, and he does offer enlightening comments on differences between the kind of response appropriate to religious symbols and suggestions and that appropriate to prosaic statements.[24] D.G.C. Macnabb, in commenting on the philosophy of David Hume, has noted that Hume made a number of important philosophical discoveries in spite of the inadequacies of his doctrine of impressions and ideas, and in spite of Hume's conviction that these discoveries were intimately dependent upon that doctrine.[25] Similarly, Bushnell arrived at lasting insights concerning religious language despite the precariousness of his view concerning the metaphorical character of all second-department words, and despite his certainty that these insights were inseparable from that view. The principle illustrated in both cases is a kind of philosophical serendipity.

A second argument of the critics which we can deal with in this section is the contention that there are ample resources within the patterns of accepted linguistic usage to compensate for and eliminate whatever deficiencies individual words may have. Goodrich insisted that "qualifying adjuncts" can cause a word to have "only one sense and application". It is certainly true that qualifiers can reduce vagueness and ambiguity, but it is doubtful that they can eliminate it entirely, since the qualifiers are themselves words, with their own degree of vagueness and ambiguity, and since meanings have a tendency to change with changing contexts. Lord's version of this criticism seems to assume that a speaker's wishes are the only factor to be considered when it comes to defining words, that he can define them entirely as it suits his own purpose, without

---

[24] For a discussion of the fundamental role played by nonpropositional, symbolically conveyed "suggestions" in the logic of religious discourse, see William Christian, *Meaning and Truth in Religion* (Princeton, New Jersey: Princeton University Press, 1964), Chapter VI and passim.

[25] David Hume, *A Treatise of Human Nature:* Book I: *Of the Understanding*, edited with an introduction by D.G.C. Macnabb (New York: The World Publishing Company, Meridian Books, 1962), 21.

having to be concerned with the meanings they have in public discourse. But of course if a speaker's definitions are too narrow or too individualized, he will find that he fails to communicate his meaning altogether, so far removed are his definitions from the public uses of his terms. At the very least, the ordinary meanings of his precisely defined words will continually be creeping into his hearers' reactions to them, blurring or obscuring his nice distinctions. Brownson's argument that discovering the figurative root of a word does not detract from the precision of our understanding of its meaning, but rather reinforces that precision, could be interpreted in a different way than he has interpreted it. It could turn out that we resort to the figure precisely because of our inability to get clear about a word's meaning by means of an abstract definition. The definition fails to make the concept clear, so we turn to an image and find that it does a job that the definition could not.[26]

Hodge's criticism of Bushnell sounds almost like a paraphrase of what Bushnell had himself already insisted upon. For Bushnell regarded a "variety of illustrations" and a "diversity in the mode of setting forth the same truth" to be just the resource which language does provide for rendering meanings explicit. Of course, Bushnell went farther than Hodge would have wanted to go, in saying that the multiplication of illustrations and modes of presentation should often be pressed beyond the point of formal contradictions, just as in poetry and much literature. Also, he would not have endorsed Hodge's statement that such a tactic is guaranteed to convey truth "certainly" to other minds, because he believed that there is required in those minds something which language cannot convey, namely, a level of experience and a capacity for imaginative insight that is able to recognize and perceive the truths that words can only suggest.

[26] Cf. on this point Henri Bergson's insistence that certain images have the advantage over abstract definitions that they keep us "in the concrete". For example, "no image can replace the intuition of duration, but many diverse images, borrowed from very different orders of things, may, by the convergence of their action, direct consciousness to the precise point where there is a certain intuition to be seized". Bergson, *An Introduction to Metaphysics*, trans. T. E. Hulme (New York: The Liberal Arts Press, 1950), 27.

Finally, Bushnell was not the skeptic about the capacities of language that Hodge and the other critics made him out to be. The numerous reservations he entered upon the uses of words, and most notably, his contention that words in the second department are figurative, were meant as a caveat against uncritical reliance upon them, and especially, upon the logical inferences that might be falsely drawn from their forms. When language was used with a proper caution, and poetry, rather than logic, was recognized as its true norm, then it was, by his account, as reliable and serviceable a tool as could be desired. There was a crucial advantage in the very imperfections of language, in fact, for by its limitations it focused attention upon the primacy of concrete experience and personal reflection over purely mechanical modes of reasoning and transmitting ideas. If language was found thus to coincide perfectly with the needs of man, this was but testimony to the power, wisdom, and goodness of Him who had set its foundations in nature and mind.

3. BUSHNELL'S DOCTRINE OF THE LOGOS IN NATURE AND MIND UNFOUNDED AND INCONSISTENT WITH HIS OTHER VIEWS

But Bushnell's metaphysics of nature was not at all well received by his critics. Pond registered his disagreement in no uncertain terms, clinching his disapprobation of the logos theory with the inference, all too true, as we have shown, that it could be linked with Swedenborg's principle of correspondence. The theory, complained Pond,

is *essentially unfounded*. Beyond question, there is a sufficient resemblance or analogy between certain external and internal objects, to lay a foundation for the use of metaphors, comparisons, and other figures of speech. No one has ever doubted this. But to say that there is a universal and divinely instituted correspondence between the worlds of matter and mind; that every object in external nature is a type of something in the soul; and that the soul is so constituted as to perceive the resemblance and base upon it a language of thought — this is carrying the matter quite too far. We could as soon accept the Swedenborgian doctrine of correspondences.[27]

[27] E. Pond, Review, 3-4.

But not only was the theory unfounded, it made the rest of Bushnell's language theory a colossal *non sequitur*. For if the theory were true, "What room is there for doubt or mistake?... Who can impute any want of definiteness and certainty here, without impeaching the wisdom and goodness of the Creator?"[28] The conclusion and the premises had no affinity and could never stand together.

Lord's criticism, as before, went into much greater detail than Pond's. One point in his criticism was that Bushnell was mistaken in thinking that there was some kind of incomprehensible mystery about how relationships of analogy could be founded between sensible and mental things. Had he never considered what the import of analogy in rhetoric was? Had he never attempted to analyze a simile or metaphor, in order to ascertain the principle underlying it? Apparently not, for if he had, he would have discovered how simple and readily intelligible that principle really was. A great part of his difficulty, Lord believed, had been created by Bushnell's false assumption that there were no "analogies except as subsist between physical forms — lines, curves, circles, angles, dimensions and colors..."[29] He had of course been unable to understand how such a geometric analogy could pertain to most things in the mind and spirit. But that there were many other kinds of analogy could be demonstrated by a consideration, say, of Isaiah 55 : 10-11, where it is said that the Word of God shall *bear fruit*. Here the resemblance was not at all geometrical but "between the *efficacy* of two causes, *which is the relation in which they are compared...*"[30] There was nothing plainer in the nature of human thought and language "than that every figure of speech, whatever its species may be, is founded on a resemblance either of nature, condition, agency, or effects, that subsists between that from which it is drawn and that which it is employed to illustrate,

---

28   E. Pond, Review, 7.
29   Lord, Review, 84.
30   Lord, Review, 85. Lord also charged Bushnell with speaking of words themselves as having a form, shape, or sensible quality. The idea, or so he contended, was "clearly embodied in his expressions". Ibid, 101. But Bushnell obviously meant, in the passage cited by Lord (p. 41 of *God in Christ*) not that words themselves, but the physical objects to which their roots referred, had such form, shape, or sensible quality.

and owes to that correspondence its whole use".[31] If the whole matter was no great mystery, then, but could be simply analyzed and explained, then there was no call for an imposing metaphysical principle such as Bushnell's logos of nature and mind. On the other hand even if it were granted, purely for argument's sake, that the nature of correspondence or analogy on which Bushnell had based his language theory were absolutely unknown and undiscoverable, there could then be no possibility of proving that it was true anyway.

Lord criticized Bushnell's metaphysical position on a second score by contending that his plea for some mysterious correspondence or analogy, whereby words were arrived at for the second department of language, was in flat contradiction to his other statement that such words are "generally determined arbitrarily". If they were determined arbitrarily, then analogy could not be the ground of their determination; if they were determined not by man but by God, then there could be, as we noted above, no proof that they were founded on analogy. Lord's triumphant conclusion was that "Whichever view he takes..., his system fails".[32]

Thirdly, in the philosophy of Kant and Coleridge, in whose terms Bushnell was obviously working, there were, in fact, no external forms whatever.

Instead, the whole series of the apparent objects of our sense perceptions are mere forms and products of the understanding, and exist only in the mind that perceives them. There is no room, therefore, for an analogy between them as external things, and the thoughts and acts of the mind, as they are themselves mere mental phenomena. It is, in truth, on that scheme only by a metaphor that they are called *external*; and accordingly, instead of a derivation of all words of thought and spirit, as he represents, from physical things, all names of physical things are in reality only names of the phenomena of the mind![33]

How, Lord demanded to know, could so obvious a result of his own philosophy have been so completely overlooked by Bushnell?

Fourthly, in view of the fact that some words primarily designative of mental things can come to stand as metaphors for the denomination and expression of physical things, Lord held that

[31] Lord, Review, 86.
[32] Lord, Review, 93.
[33] Lord, Review, 93.

Bushnell would have to argue not only for a logos in physical things, fitting them to be taken up as figures in the second department of language, but also for a logos in mental and spiritual things which would permit them to be applied figuratively to the physical realm. This seemed to demonstrate the capriciousness of the logos theory.

The first reply we can make to these criticisms is to point out that Pond's contention that any lack of precision in language would impugn the wisdom and goodness of God, if language had been provided for by the Deity in the way Bushnell had declared, operates on the Lockean, Common Sense assumption that language at its best is language which has the unfailing accuracy of algebraic calculations. Bushnell denied the assumption and insisted that language in its present form best serves the true interests of man, as we indicated just a while ago.

In the second place, Lord's assertion that the nature of analogy is not mysterious but readily analyzable, and that, therefore, there was no need for Bushnell's metaphysics of the logos, can be met in several ways. For one thing, Lord has not encountered the question of whether or not it is possible to speak of mental and spiritual phenomena without recourse to analogies. The implication of Bushnell's language theory clearly is that it is not. If it is not, secondly, then the mystery for us will not lie in giving verbal explanations of an analogy like the one, *to bear fruit*, cited. For at every step our verbal explanations themselves are analogous. Analogies seem obvious and susceptible of easy analysis because this is, in fact, the only way we have of talking about what is within us. We have no literal statements for saying just what it is that we mean by an expression such as *to bear fruit*. To say it means *to produce* is only to resort to a different metaphor, that of *leading forth* something. To speak of *effecting a result* is to call upon still another, that of *making* (in the physical sense of *fabricating* or *manufacturing* something) a thing *spring up* as a consequence. Even to explain the analogy between mentally and physically bearing fruit as a *resemblance* between the *efficacy of two causes* is, in etymological or ultimate linguistic terms, to talk of there being a *sameness of form, or outward appearance* between one kind of *making a falling* and another. The implication of all of this, thirdly, is that there must be some kind of correspondence, continuity, or relationship between the material and mental spheres which can allow such analogies to be meaningful, and not only meaningful, but universally recognizable in their meaning. Thus Lord's arguments have not really met those of Bushnell.

In the third place, Lord has charged Bushnell with speaking as if geometrical analogies alone are brought into play in language. He did tend to stress those, it is true, as in his favorite illustration, *rectus, straight, right*. But this was only, perhaps, because they illustrate so well the mystery of analogical relationships. Another word which he discussed and we have taken note of was *gressus, walk with measured tread, congress*. The analogy here is not geometrical but dynamic. And the number of such illustrations he offered could be multiplied extensively. Moreover, in stating why thoughts, ideas, and mental states could be termed "formless", he said not only that they had no "geometric form", but also that they had "no sensible qualities whatever".[34] This latter characterization includes, we can take it, qualities of action and movement which the senses can perceive.

Fourthly, the fact that Bushnell held the ground of analogy to be ultimately inexplicable does not disprove or in any way detract from the plausibility of his theory of the logos. For that theory is meant to *underline* the mystery of the analogy between mind and matter, not to eliminate it. Bushnell is saying that even though we cannot understand how it operates, there is such an analogous relationship. Therefore, he reasons, the Creator must have provided for it when he laid the foundations of the world. This is an attempt to explain its origin, not its nature.

Fifthly, Lord misconstrued Bushnell's statement that words are "generally determined arbitrarily". For Bushnell meant this only in respect to the words of the first department of language, words as they initially arose. The whole import of his logos theory was to discount the allegation of Locke that words of the second department of language are given "by a perfectly arbitrary im-

[34] See above, p. 24, text and note 24.

position", for this seemed to imply that there is no analogy whatever between the images in words and the thoughts and feelings they come to represent.[35]

Sixthly, Lord's point about the Kantian bent of Bushnell's philosophy confuses the consciousness which accompanies perception of an external world and whatever ultimate explanation may be given for that consciousness. Kant, like Locke, held that sensation sets in motion the train of experience out of which all knowledge develops. And despite the fact that he held that the world as we know it is the result of the imposition of inherent categories of our minds upon whatever it is that is "out there", he assumed throughout his analysis that this is the only world we can ever know. We can make no judgments whatever on the unmediated *das ding an sich.* Bushnell's theory of language is not inconsistent with this Kantian analysis because it proceeds throughout on the plane of the world as we experience it, of the world that the first framers of language found themselves obliged to think and speak within.

Seventhly, in respect to Lord's contention that, given the application of metaphors of the mind to physical phenomena, Bushnell would be forced to argue for a logos in the things of the mind and the spirit also, we can say this. Bushnell would insist that the problem of initial communication required that process work only one way at first — from external to internal. But once words were possessed for inner states and operations of the mind they could then, because of their already analogous character, be employed to designate physical things. Bushnell contended, after all, for a logos in nature *and mind* as the only adequate explanation of how this initial communication could occur, and a reversal of the direction of the analogy at a subsequent time does not invalidate his theory. In fact, it reinforces it, because it further illustrates the continuity between the worlds of matter and spirit.

The criticisms we have discussed in this section make it abundantly clear that those who attacked Bushnell's language theory were so initially prejudiced against it and anxious to refute it that

[35] See above, p. 21.

they could not meet it at its own depth. In fact, they often misconstrued and distorted its simplest features. Instead of being given a fair hearing and having its many important insights recognized and dealt with, the theory was met with clichès and oversimplified arguments, responses that were frequently more emotional and rhetorical in character than careful and well-founded. This was due in part to the unassailable confidence the critics had in the prevailing Lockean, Common Sense conception of language. Steeped as they and the vast majority of their readers were in this conception, it was refutation enough to show, with proper rhetorical force, how completely Bushnell's theory of language failed to measure up to the view which held sway. But the emotional and half-cocked character of so many of the responses of the critics stemmed also from another source. And that was the deep-seated anxiety they felt when any of the assumptions of the generally accepted view of language were called into question. As we shall see in the next section, they thought that such a theory as Bushnell's, should it be allowed to go unrefuted, and should it ever begin to take hold in men's minds, would bring their whole world toppling down. And in this they were not far wrong, for the theory of language was, as we can see now with the hindsight of history, one of the unmistakable signs of the end of an era — the demise of the old Edwardian theology and the dawn of a new Trinitarian liberalism, with all the implications that had for the culture of New England.

4. BUSHNELL'S THEORY OF LANGUAGE CONTRADICTS "ALL THE FACTS OF CONSCIOUSNESS AND OBSERVATION ON WHICH NOT ONLY THEOLOGY, BUT THE WHOLE FABRIC OF SOCIAL LIFE IS FOUNDED".[36]

Bushnell's critics painted in the darkest terms the disintegration that would come about in the Church and in society if his language views were allowed to gain a foothold in the general consciousness. Hodge declared that the implication of the language theory was

---

[36]   Lord, Review, 127.

that "no dependence" could be placed on speech as the medium of human converse, with the result for religion that "there can be no such thing as a scientific theology; no definite doctrinal propositions; creeds and catechisms are not to be trusted; no author can be properly judged by his words; ... as creeds mean nothing or anything" any and all of them can be subscribed to.[37] The effect of all of this was "shocking", both for religion and for the life of society.

It undermines all confidence even in the ordinary transactions of life. There can, on this plan, be no treaties between nations, no binding contracts between individuals; for 'the chemistry' which can make all creeds alike, will soon get what results it pleases out of any form of words that can be framed. This doctrine supposes there can be no revelation from God to men, except to the imagination and to the feelings, none to the reason.[38]

Such were the manifest absurdities required by Bushnell's theory; a theory which, in its religious implications, flew in the face of the self-evident fact that "there are certain doctrines so settled by the faith of the Church, that they are no longer open questions. They are finally adjudged and determined. If men set aside the Bible, and choose to speak or write as philosophers, then of course the way is open for them, to teach what they please. But for Christians, who acknowledge the Scriptures as their rule of faith, there are doctrines which they are bound to take as settled beyond all rational or innocent dispute."[39]

Goodrich spoke in the same dire vein when he declared that "if one-tenth part of what Dr. Bushnell has said about the vagueness of language were true, society would long since have been thrown into inextricable confusion, by the misunderstanding of men as to the use of terms".[40] And Brownson complained that Bushnell had introduced an impossible relativism into religious truth.

Unity of language or of mind is not to be looked for or desired; the only possible unity is the unity of love, the unity of sentiment, and all who have the sentiment have the unity of the spirit, and really and truly

[37] C. Hodge, Review, 266.
[38] C. Hodge, Review, 266.
[39] C. Hodge, Review, 296.
[40] C. A. Goodrich in the New York Evangelist, XX. 13, 49.

worship God, whether they conceive of him as 'Jehovah', 'Jove', or 'Lord', or manifest it outwardly in the forms approved by the Protestant, the Catholic, the Gentoo, the Chinese, the Thibetian, or by the ancient Phoenicians, Greeks, or Romans.[41]

A basic part of Bushnell's trouble, according to Brownson, was that he had made the mistake of confusing dogma with speculation, and experience and intuition with faith. Although it is clear-cut Roman Catholic doctrine, it is rather striking to observe how closely, at least in spirit, the following statement of Brownson resembles Hodge's claim that some doctrines are "settled beyond all rational or innocent dispute".

Does (Bushnell) need to be told that the dogma is the *revelatum*, the revealed truth, and essentially non-speculative, preceding theological speculation as its postulate? The dogma is enjoined or imposed by authority, and demands simple assent; speculation is an operation of the discursive reason, assuming the dogmas as its postulates or axioms, and its results are conclusions depending on the authority of the logical process which demonstrates them; the dogma is accepted on the veracity of God, whose word it is, immediately or mediately spoken or transmitted to us.[42]

And by calling for immediate intuition of religious truth Bushnell was actually calling for a certainty that was the negation of faith, which latter Brownson characterized as submission and assent to doctrines which, though they could not be comprehended, were yet to be believed in as authoritatively revealed.

Pond joined the chorus of voices pointing out the chaotic consequences of the theory of language by observing that, with Bushnell's views as to language's severe limitations, "we should despair utterly, not only of expressing our theological opinions, but of telling when we were hungry of thirsty, or making known our simplest personal wants".[43]

It may seem a small matter to some, to cast doubt upon the settled significance of language, and destroy confidence in it, in its applications to the subject of religion; but it must be remembered that there is no

---

41   O. Brownson, Review, 508-509.
42   O. Brownson, Review, 511.
43   E. Pond, Review, 11

stopping place here. The foundations of human intercourse, and with them of society, are disturbed, and a mischief is perpetrated for which there is no remedy. It may seem a light thing to say that a system of theology cannot be taught in words; but if theology cannot be taught in words, no more can psychology, morality, or anything else. If a creed or a catechism cannot be understood, no more can the Bible; no more can Dr. Bushnell's discourses; no more can the household words of common life. In short, if, to save or destroy a creed, the foundations of language must be broken up, then we are all afloat together. We have come to another tower of Babel, and as the tongues are again confounded, it is time that the earth were again divided.[44]

Pond pointed specifically to Bushnell's views on the Trinity to show how, to his mind, the Hartford minister's language views had led him to obscure all distinctions between truth and error. For Bushnell had failed entirely to preserve the real difference between Unitarianism and Trinitarianism, a difference which Pond saw as follows.

The Unitarian believes in one God in *one* person, while the Trinitarian believes in one God in *three* persons. And these three must be, not *fictitious, dramatic, representative* persons, like the characters in a romance, or a play, but *real*, substantial, *eternal distinctions*, in the one undivided essence of the Godhead. So the Church has always understood the subject. So it is understood by the most intelligent Christians, on both sides, at the present day. So the matter *must* be understood; or there is no real, valid distinction between the Trinitarian and the Unitarian — none which is at all worth contending for — none which does not lie in mere words, and fancies, and figures of speech.[45]

The Fairfield West Association, which sought unsuccessfully to have Bushnell brought to trial for heresy, criticized him "for advocating that interpreters of our faith should accept what they may from the Bible through sensibility, taste, and imagination, and then construct their theology out of consciousness This they maintained would make theology as variable as the experience of different men and of the same men at different times. It would require theology to be continually in the process of formation and reforma-

[44]   E. Pond, Review, 13-14.
[45]   E. Pond, Review, 29-30.

tion and would make heresy impossible".[46] Much the same complaint was registered in the pages of the *Christian Observatory*, although it was pressed even farther there and with a greater degree of emotional indignation. Noting that if a book of the same character as *God in Christ* had been written by a member of the medical or legal profession in connection with the subjects of "his department of science", his *sanity* would have been called into question, the reviewer went on to say:

The wildest assaults are made on the most stable facts of revelation; propositions are laid down with great confidence and an air of defiance, which, if received, would subvert every school of theology in evangelical Christendom, confute our books of practical piety, — the Pilgrim's Progress, the Force of Truth, and our practical commentaries on the Bible; make it necessary to give new instructions to Christian missionaries around the globe; and in short, confound all Christian churches with the discovery that they are fundamentally wrong. [47]

David Lord did not fail to add his voice to that of his colleagues in waging this particular assault on Bushnell. The theory of language, so he claimed, "exhibits the whole revelation which God has made, as nothing else than a stupendous deception — a vast complication of false shows, so intrinsically and necessarily treacherous, that to attempt to pierce the disguise and discover the truth, is only to advance into an inextricable labyrinth — to sail on to a shoreless ocean of darkness and uncertainty".[48] What was true of the revelation was even more true of the theology that might be founded upon it.

Not only are definitions and doctrinal creeds defective and unequal to a just expression of the truth, but they are positively false and deceptive; they are absolute and consummate misrepresentations, and misrepresentations that cannot be corrected or counteracted by explanations, retractions, or modifying statements, and that must, thence, of necessity, lead

---

[46] Heininger, Harold R., *The Theological Technique of a Mediating Theologian — Horace Bushnell* (Chicago: University of Chicago Libraries, 1935), 181. This is in pamphlet form and is part of a doctoral dissertation distributed privately by the University of Chicago libraries.

[47] "God in Christ", *The Christian Observatory* III (1849), 245.

[48] Lord, Review, 120-121.

to delusion, precisely in proportion as they command assent. The use of them, therefore, is not only inexpedient, but criminal, and ought to be discontinued.[49]

But the whole situation could be stated in still stronger terms. If the theory of language were true, then "The whole material and social universe, as well as God and his Government, is ... swept from existence, *and nothing left to any individual but what is in his own consciousness!*"[50] Bushnell showed himself, by his advocacy of such a theory, to be a more powerful influence for godlessness than even the infidels and apostles of atheism.

But despite these portentous implications of the language theory, it could be easily refuted. And the critics could join as one man in Lord's confident assertion that "common sense will maintain its dominion..."[51] The "delusive and atheistic" German rationalism which informed Bushnell's thought, with its absurd denial of even an external world, would gain no grip on the minds of those "who have not become the victims of a fanatical delusion, or surrendered themselves to the sway of a violent hostility to the truth".[52]

The contention that Bushnell's language theory undermines confidence in even the ordinary transactions of life, making social existence an impossibility, can be dealt with first. We have already noted that Bushnell was nothing like the complete skeptic about the capacities of language his critics made him out to be.[53] And neither does his language theory lead to the absurd conclusions they drew from it. In fact, we might say that no more powerful proof could be offered in support of the view that language does tend to mislead the mind than the inferences the critics of Bushnell founded upon the surface impressions of his words. For these critics had failed entirely to do what Bushnell pled for, as Frank H. Foster has said in another connection, in responding to any one's language. They had not "used *his* words suggestively and themselves burrowed down by original thinking into his true

---

[49] Lord, Review, 120.
[50] Lord, Review, 121.
[51] Lord, Review, 127. The term "common sense" is revealing.
[52] Lord, Review, 130; 127.
[53] See above, p. 244.

meaning". Had they done this, they would have discerned that "No man was ever more anxious to promote correct thinking and clear views than Bushnell. It was *because* he was so earnest for the *substance* of thought that he exposed and ridiculed the abuse of its *form* as though that were substance".[54] It is one thing to condemn language as such, and quite another to deplore its misuse. But Bushnell's critics were unable to make the obvious distinction.

They were unable to make the distinction, in large measure, because they could see no middle ground between the position that language can be made to state with utter precision whatever truth it is desired to convey and the view that it can express no truth at all. It was either the Lockean, Common Sense conception of language, which had so long dominated their thinking, or intellectual and moral chaos. It was out of this false dichotomy that they were led to assume that, if Bushnell's theory were at all correct, one could no longer make an intelligible request for a glass of water or a bite of food. This was, of course, a *reductio ad absurdum* and a ridiculous parody of Bushnell's view, one of which he was totally undeserving. It is ironic that Hodge should have accused Bushnell of the error of extremism, when that error was so flagrantly committed by himself and his fellow critics in their attack upon Bushnell at this point.

But Bushnell was at variance with his critics not only on the level of assumptions about the nature and capacities of language. He also differed profoundly from them in his conception of theology. In fact, in both cases the one difference reinforced and contributed to the other. And it is from the perspective of these two fundamental differences that we must view, in the second place, the ominous conclusions Bushnell's critics drew for religion from his views on language.

The commonly held conception of theology was that it is a set of formulas which make their appeal primarily to the intellect. Theology is made up of propositions and demonstrations of logic which

---

[54]   Frank H. Foster, *A Genetic History of the New England Theology* (Chicago: The University of Chicago Press, 1907), 407.

state and deduce facts. Some of these facts are beyond dispute and serve as the basis for arriving at others. Whatever appeal theological statements may have to the feelings or the imagination is entirely secondary; they are meant primarily for the mind. Implicit in this conception of theology was an unquestioned confidence in the capacities of language to express and convey the facts in question. Revelation also was given propositionally, or at least, it could be readily rendered into propositions. To cast doubt upon the capacities of language, therefore, seemed tantamount to denying the possibility, not only of theology as it was conceived at the time, but also of revelation itself. It was to lay an axe at the very roots of religion.

With Bushnell, however, theology was quite differently conceived. Foster has spoken of his "quite original and characteristic emphasis on *the religious life* as the source and guiding principle in theology".[55] And Amos Cheesborough, a personal friend of Bushnell and one of the few men who came to his defense following upon the publication of *God in Christ*, characterized his conception of theology in these apt words: "Christian doctrine was to him no longer a conclusion from a process of reasoning, but it was *formulated Christian experience*. It must be, not a speculation, not a piece of well-reasoned framework which nicely fits into a theological system, but something to *live by* — something firstly, secondly, always vitally practical for the uses of the soul."[56] This emphasis reflected many current influences, of course — revivalism,[57] pietism, and romanticism, to name three of the most important ones. It also reflected important autobiographical elements, such as Bushnell's struggle between heart and head at the time of his Yale conversion

---

[55] Foster, *A Genetic History*, 408.

[56] In *Bushnell Centenary* (Hartford: Hartford Press, 1902), 47. This is a series of papers and addresses commemorative of Bushnell, which constituted the official Minutes of the General Association of Connecticut at its One-Hundred and Ninety-Third Annual Meeting.

[57] Timothy L. Smith has observed that "An important by-product of revivalism's triumph over Calvinism was that American theology stood increasingly upon the practical, empirical foundation of Christian experience." *Revivalism and Social Reform in Mid-Nineteenth Century America* (New York, 1957), 92. Bushnell's conversion of 1831 occurred in connection with a revival.

— a struggle which eventuated, significantly enough, in his discovery of the two-departmental character of language[58] — and a moving mystical experience which came to him in the same year *God in Christ* was written.[59] Then too, the fact that Bushnell was a pastor instead of a professional theologian has important bearing on his conception of theology, as Foster has shown: "As a preacher he was daily engaged in the task of developing the religious life of his people. He needed truth for his work, and needed to find those elements in it, and those forms of expressing it, which were best adapted to promote the religious life, and therefore he was compelled in his thinking to approach theology on the experiential side."[60] His experience as a pastor tended, moreover, to make him more of a "practical psychologist" than the somewhat cloistered professors in the seminaries, and to cause him to see a human being as an emotional and intellectual unit.

He realized that people are not all head. They have hearts. He realized that men build up emotional loyalties around objects and terms of religious devotion. While much of his ministry was engaged in helping Christians reexamine these terms, hoary with age, and fraught with accumulated associations which were precious, and while under his guidance the objects of religious devotion were subjected to scrutiny and reinterpretation, he did not make the mistake of supposing that religious living is simply a matter of building a satisfactory intellectual formulation of the meaning of the Christian religion. He seems to have sensed the fact that we are 'behaving' beings as well as thinking beings.[61]

And by striking this characteristic emphasis upon religious experience as the ground and final norm of theological formulations, he did produce a message that was eminently preachable, not only for his own justly renowned pulpit deliverances, but one which largely inspired the even more widely acclaimed ministries of Henry

---

[58]   See above, pp. 97-100; 103-104.
[59]   See Cheney, *Life and Letters*, 192-193. At the end of his "Preliminary Dissertation" Bushnell admitted that there was a mystic strain in his view of the sources of meaning in religious language and that it could also be detected in the ideas concerning Christian life and doctrine that were to follow in his three Discourses. See *God in Christ*, 94-96.
[60]   Foster, *A Genetic History*, 408.
[61]   Heininger, *The Theological Technique*, 176.

Ward Beecher and Phillips Brooks, through whom it reached Christian people in every part of the nation.[62]

Religious truth for Bushnell, then, was not so much a matter of formulas and definitions as of an immediate apprehension of God within. This fundamental difference of ground and approach between him and his opponents cannot be emphasized too strongly, for it explains almost everything of the great divide between an old theology and the new. And it explains what is more nearly germane to our pupose here: why Bushnell was not at all troubled by the implications of his view of language for religion, in the way that his critics were — why for them it was a hole in the dyke setting up a universal cry of alarm, while for him it was a set of wings with which to soar.

Turning now to some of the more specific arguments against the language theory which were set forth within the general category of criticism we are discussing in this section, we can take account, as a third point in our analysis, of the contention of Hodge and others that there is a settled and final character to orthodox formulations of basic Christian teaching, and that these formulations demand simple assent. On the basis of this contention it was maintained that Bushnell's theory of language, as applied to theology, would lead to a reckless questioning of the solidity and finality of the orthodox formulations, making theology more a matter of personal, than churchly, concern, and necessitating a periodic reexamination and reinterpretation of Christian truth on the part of each successive generation.

But is it true that even the most basic Christian doctrines are "so settled by the faith of the Church, that they are no longer open questions"? We are bound to ask what Church is being talked about. Certainly it cannot be the Church of actual history, for there we find Catholic contending with Protestant on fundamental doctrines; Armenian disputing with Calvinist; Unitarian taking issue with Trinitarian; and even, within the fold of so-called New England "orthodoxy", at least three basically different conceptions of the

---

[62] William W. Sweet, *The Story of Religion in America* (New York: Harper and Brothers, 1950), 342.

Trinity being contended for, to say nothing of the different points of view taken with respect to equally fundamental doctrines.[63]

To say that there are some doctrines settled beyond dispute is as much a contradiction of our experience as to make the linguistic claim, to which it is closely allied in its dogmatic defiance of fact, that such terms as *sin, faith,* and *forgiveness,* which touch such profound levels of experience and temperament in most persons,[64] can be made plain words directly indicating the objects they represent — that is, terms to which no disagreement or ambiguity will attach. Not only do the terms vary widely in meaning; for some people they are virtual semantic blackouts, having little or no meaning at all. The most diligent effort has to be expended by preachers and teachers of religion to give meanings to them. But even the most artful and concise expositions of their meanings can do nothing more than comprise under single terms a great variety of individual differences. And this is to make no mention of the appeals to the imagination necessitated by the reference in such words to transcendent conceptions concerning God and his relation to man.

So far as the implication of a need for periodic reinterpretation of Christian teaching is concerned, Bushnell did insist that every doctrinal formula should be reinvestigated every fifty years. Symbols once fresh and alive with significance had a way of becoming dulled and stereotyped with usage and would have to be replaced or reinvigorated at stated periods. Far from regarding any creedal statements as the last word, he was convinced, as we have already seen,[65] that all creeds are only "proximate representations" of truth lying beyond the reach of fully adequate statement and should not therefore be allowed to become laws over belief or guardians

---

[63]   For a statement of Bushnell in this same connection see the closing paragraph of his Preface to *Christ in Theology.*

[64]   William James' distinction between the "healthy-minded, who need to be born only once" and "sick souls, who must be twice-born in order to be happy" suggests how profoundly differences in temperament can affect the meanings assigned to the above words. See *Varieties of Religious Experience* (New York: The Modern Library, 1929), Lectures IV through VIII; also, p. 163.

[65]   See above, p. 34.

of "purity".[66] Bushnell would find himself very much in accord
with the conviction of Alfred North Whitehead that dogmas are
necessary as "clarifying modes of external expression", but "a
dogma which fails to evoke any response in immediate apprehension stifles the religious life". Dogmas are at best "bits of truth"
which are "in effect untrue when carried over beyond the proper
scope of their utility".[67] The corollary of this is that all dogmas
which, despite their resistance to being comprised under a single
coherent system of theology, do elicit a personal religious response,
have meaning and are at least approximately true. And this response is a more important test of their validity than the official
sanction they may or may not receive. Of course, these assertions
make Bushnell no less blameworthy in the eyes of his conservative
critics. Whether one takes them as criticism or praise depends on
one's theological point of view. If he tends toward the liberal side,
the assertions will seem to have real merit. They also help to coun-
teract, as we shall see in a moment, the criticism that Bushnell's
theological views reduce to solipsism.

A fourth criticism with which we can deal is that Bushnell advocated the construction of theology out of the consciousness of
the individual, thereby negating its objective and social character.
The criticism was stated explicitly by Lord and the Fairfield West
Association, but it underlay much of what the other critics were
saying. The first thing that needs to be said here is that there is a
definite element of truth in the criticism. Foster has observed that
Bushnell not only based his approach to theology upon religious
experience, but

He seems to have gone a step farther and to have said to himself, not
only that truth must contribute to life, but also that nothing was truth
which did not thus contribute — a step leading easily to the further and
quite false position that the theologian's personal view of the religious
life, limited though it may be by defects of temperament and character,
is to be made the measure of universal truth. Thus this movement of

---

[66] Bushnell, *God in Christ*, 80-81.
[67] A. N. Whitehead, *Religion in the Making* (New York: The Macmillan
Company, 1926), 137, 145.

Bushnell's mind had elements of danger in it from the beginning; but it also contained the promise of fresh and valuable results.[68]

Bushnell himself fully recognized the danger and sought to provide safeguards against it in his theory of language in three ways.

We have already seen that Bushnell recognized that the individual's religious consciousness "is always a mixed and never a pure state", that is, that it fluctuates between sensuality and spirituality, truth and falsity, faith and disbelief.[69] It therefore clearly cannot serve as the sole criterion of religious truth. Other criteria must also be introduced. And one of those, surprisingly enough, was speculative activity, always to be subordinated, of course, to feeling and imagination, but nevertheless, having its role to play. The following passage from *Christ in Theology* is given in full, because it brings out an emphasis in Bushnell's thinking that is often overlooked and because it represents the reply he would make to our question raised some time ago as to what checks his theory of language provides against "a wild or weak sentimentalism".[70]

... considering that Christian character is imperfect, liable to the instigation of passion, to be overheated in the flesh and think it the inspiration of God, Christian theology and speculative activity are needed as providing checks and balances for the religious life to save it from visionary flights, erratic fancies, and wild hallucinations. ... The intellectual life needs to be kept in high action, else, under pretense of living in the Spirit, we are soon found living in our fancies and our passions — just as the kite rises gracefully and keeps in equipoise on the upper air, only in virtue of a pull upon the cord below; and if it be maintained that the cord only pulls downward, and not upward, it does yet hold the bosom of the paper voyager to the breeze, without which it would soon be pitching in disorderly motions to the ground. It appears, in other words, that we have two distinct methods of knowledge, a lower method in the life of nature, and a higher, in the life of faith. Therefore, we are not to set them in mutual opposition, as has generally been done heretofore, by the rationalists on one side, and the mystics on the other; but we are to assume that a healthy working of our religious nature is that which justifies, uses, exercises, all. Regarding the realm of reason, and the realm of faith, as our two Houses of Assembly, we are to consider nothing as enacted

---

[68] Foster, *A Genetic History*, 408.
[69] See above, p. 44.
[70] See above, p. 119. The response does not really answer the question, however, as shall presently be pointed out.

into a law, which has not been able to pass both houses. For if a man will reduce all religious truth to the molds and measures of the natural understanding, receiving nothing by faith, which transcends the measures of the understanding, he acts, in fact, upon the assumption that he has no heart; and as he cannot perceive, by the understanding, what is perceivable only by the faith of the heart, he ignores all living truth, and becomes a sceptic or a rationalist. If, on the other hand, what power of reason or science he had is wholly disallowed and renounced, so as to operate a check no longer on the contemplations of faith, or assist in framing into order the announcements of feeling, then faith and feeling are become a land of dreams, and the man who began as a Christian, ends as a mystic. Faith must learn to be the light of nature, nature to apply her cautions and constraining judgments. The heart and the head must be as two that walk together, never so truly agreed as when they agree to help each other.[71]

It was, Bushnell maintained, one of the chief problems of Christianity to settle the relationship between speculation and faith, reason and imagination. In fact, this could even be called the real burden of the whole past history of the Christian Church.[72]

Despite the great beauty of this passage, and although it undoubtedly sets forth a vital truth, it must still be said that it is not at all clear how the speculative reason can enter positively into Bushnell's theory of language in the way he urged. For on the level of language, how can the speculative reason manifest itself, except through logic? And do Bushnell's tireless castigations of logic leave it with any positive role? Logic fastens upon the form element in words, he tells us, instead of treating them in their proper role as metaphors. It comes at language as though it could "literally convey" truth rather than merely "suggest" it. It creates illusory worlds of thought that correspond to nothing in reality and in experience. Bushnell himself stated that in *God in Christ* he had resorted to logic "principally as a negative ... instrument, and as *ad hominem* to the disciples of logic".[73] If the speculative reason can operate apart from logic, or if it can somehow avoid the pitfalls of logic, Bushnell's theory of language has not shown us

---

[71]   Bushnell, *Christ in Theology*, 315-316.
[72]   Bushnell, *Christ in Theology*, 316-317.
[73]   Letter to Cyrus Bartol, dated March 20, 1849. See T. Munger, *Horace Bushnell*, 139-140.

how. Because there is this weakness in his general theory, his contention for the role of speculative activity in checking the excesses of mere imaginative flights of fancy and in giving some socially corroborative character to a theology based on religious experience is left without sufficient theoretical support.

The second safeguard Bushnell sought to provide against pure individualism in theology was his view that, though the Bible was to be imaginatively received and interpreted, its symbols were rooted in historical fact, and were therefore objective. Moreover, God had chosen to approach man, or to come into his knowledge, "not under terms of logic and notionally, but under laws of expression. To this trinity is brought down; to this, atonement. They meet us poetically, aesthetically, to pour their contents into us through feeling and imagination; to deposit their contents, not in our reason, but in our faith, — by faith to be experimented or known experimentally..."[74] It therefore stood to reason that God himself, incarnated in the consciousness and life of the Church, would guard the interpretation of the revelational symbols and insure that they were correctly apprehended.

But, as has been pointed out by a recent writer, the problem in the appeal to the collective consciousness of the Christian Church as the criterion of religious truth is the brute fact of profound differences on basic convictions among Christians. How are we to tell who are the "genuine" Christians?[75] And this was where Bushnell's third safeguard came in. His was not just a religious version of the customary reliance upon "common sense", i.e. the consensus of intelligent men on basic questions,[76] because he stressed not agreement so much as organic comprehension of differences. It was only by taking into account the insights afforded by all creeds

---

[74] Munger, *Horace Bushnell*, 139-140.
[75] Daniel D. Williams, *The Andover Liberals* (New York: Kings Crown Press, 1941), 89-90.
[76] It is significant that J. D. Morell, a writer much admired by Bushnell, found the term "common sense" most appropriate as the designation for his conception of religious ideas as centered in the progressively developing religious consciousness. See his *The Philosophical Tendencies of the Age* (London: Robert Theobald, n.d. — prior to 1849, however), Lecture IV. This demonstrates a line of continuity between the Common Sense Philosophy and the new stress on the group consciousness of the Church.

and dogmatic formulations that one was placed in a position to arrive at truth for himself. Thus, while the final judgment of validity for his own life lay with the individual, he was to utilize as many other corporate and individual expressions of the faith as he could in coming to the theology that seemed most satisfactory for him. The consciousness of so many other positions differing from his own would also serve to deliver him from the dogmatic belief that he held the corner on Christian truth, once he had arrived at his theology.

It was for this purpose, in fact, that so many denominations and sects were to be found in Christendom. While Bushnell did not deny the desirability of having the Christian body "coalesce more perfectly and draw itself towards a more comprehensive and catholic polity",[77] he nevertheless felt that it was by Providential design that there was a diversity of communions. He stated that he regarded them, on the whole,

not as divisions, but as distributions rather; for it is one of the highest problems of divine government in the church, as in all other forms of society, how to effect the most complete and happy distribution, — such a distribution as will meet all wants and conditions, content the longings, pacify the diversities, and edify the common growth of all. Thus it may be said that the present distribution of the church, abating what is due to causes that are criminal, makes it more completely one ...[78]

He followed the declaration with an analogy drawn between the diversified Church and an army, subdivided into companies and batallions, each with its own peculiar function entering into the work of the whole.

But Bushnell considered the "distributions" of the Church to be not only Providential but inevitable, given three facts. And here we can see quite clearly how his ecumenical ideal of "Christian Comprehensiveness" operated in terms of ideas which figured prominently in his theory of language. There was first the *incom-prehensibility* of theological subjects. Years or even centuries of

---

[77] Bushnell, "Christian Comprehensiveness", *Building Eras*, 386-459. See p. 388. This article was first published in the *New Englander*, in the same year Bushnell wrote *God in Christ*. The affinities between the two works are many.
[78] Bushnell, *Building Eras*, 387.

debate were required to bring out the many approaches, each containing some truth, which could be taken with regard to them. A thinker who would look through the eyes of all of the advocates of partial views, however, could come to a perspective upon those subjects that was broader and more comprehensive than any of the single positions.[79] Second, the different *temperaments* of advocates of various views was a definite factor in their taking different positions. "For example, the Pelagian doctrine of will or self-supporting virtue, and the Quaker doctrine of quietism, may arise, in no small degree, from varieties of personal temperament".[80] Finally, there was the nature of *language*.

Language can not convey truth whole, or by a literal embodiment. It can only show it on one side, or by a figure. Hence a great many shadows, or figures, are necessary to represent every truth; and hence again there will seem to be a kind of necessary conflict between the statements in which a truth is expressed. One statement will set forth a given truth or subject-matter under one figure, and a second under another, and a third possibly under yet another.[81]

Such, then, were the safeguards Bushnell set up against the charge of an anarchistic individualism[82] in his theology, as that was made to rest upon his theory of language, with its assignment of primacy to personal experience and imaginative insight. With the exception of the first one, which we have shown to be without sufficient theoretical ground, he can be said to have made provisions for meeting the problem which are both original and highly

[79]   It is notable that much of contemporary ecumenical discussion in the realms of faith and order has taken this approach.
[80]   Bushnell, *Building Eras*, 394. The writer of an article in the *Biblical Repository* entitled "Theological Systems Modified by Mental Peculiarities", also cited Pelagius as an illustration of the point, saying that his and Augustine's respective systems were already present in germ "in their peculiar constitutions and individual experience". 3rd s. V (1849), 317-321; see p. 317.
[81]   Bushnell, *Building Eras*, 394-395.
[82]   It has no bearing on the point, but it is somewhat humorous to note that, following on the publication of *Christian Nurture*, with its stress on the church as an organic power, "The *Christian Observatory* warned that Bushnell's organic church would undermine personal responsibility by an enervating collectivism, while the *Christian Review* damned it as 'downright socialism'". B. Cross, *Horace Bushnell*, 70.

suggestive. If he did not solve the thorny problem of the relation of the individual to the group once and for all, it must be borne in mind that this is a problem, after all, which admits of no one final and conclusive solution. But he at least recognized it clearly and tackled it with a degree of insight which his critics ignored.

We can take up next the charge that, since the only unity Bushnell called for was a unity of love and sentiment, he has introduced an impossible relativism into religion, destroying all valid distinctions between the Christian and the heathen, the Protestant and Catholic, the Unitarian and the Trinitarian. The charge was made, as we have seen, by Brownson and Pond, and it is clearly implied in the lament of the Fairfield West Association that, with Bushnell's language views, detection of heresy would no longer be possible.

With regard to the non-Christian religions, Bushnell would undoubtedly answer that an authentic experience of God can only be mediated through those symbols he has provided for his self-revelation. What he would say about the everlasting destiny of the adherent of another religion in light of this belief is not clear, but his answer does at least provide for a definite distinction between Christianity and the other religions of the world and states a basis for the supremacy of Christianity among them.

As for the difference between Roman Catholic and Protestant, it can be said quite emphatically that he made a clear-cut distinction in his own mind. For in 1843 he, along with Beecher and some other Connecticut clergymen, founded the "Protestant League", the aims of which were to defend religious liberty, foster Protestant unity, and overthrow the papacy. Bushnell addressed large audiences on the subject in New York and Boston, and during a stay in Europe he wrote an open letter to the Pope that was widely circulated, in which he demanded religious liberty for Catholics.[83] We can gather from this letter that his chief quarrel with Roman Catholicism, and, therefore, the major distinction he would draw between it and Protestantism, was that it authoritatively suppresses free religious inquiry, thence making impossible that "Christian comprehensiveness" he held to be so absolutely essential to the

[83] B. Cross, *Horace Bushnell*, 81-82.

discovery and maintenance of the full-orbed truths of Christianity. He would also complain, no doubt, that in Catholic theology the head was made to subjugate the heart. In sum, then, he would say that a theory of language which gives primacy to personal experience and individual insight, and which approaches statements organically, clarifies, rather than eclipses, the essential differences between Protestantism and Catholicism.

As for the difference between Unitarians and Trinitarians, he would say that the line of demarcation was clearly drawn by his theory of language, although it had not been held intact by the "orthodox" Trinitarians of New England. For the theory showed that the Divine revelation was meant to be symbolically received, rather than reasoned out by the mechanical and deadening methods of logic. This was, in fact, the only way out of the Unitarian cul-de-sac, for if the orthodox chose to defend their view with logic, they would be forced finally to concede the whole match to the Unitarians, who made a much more competent use of constructive logic to expose the inconsistences and logical absurdities inherent in their opponents' defense of their systems.[84] The theory of language showed the way, on the other hand, to a recapturing of the meanings of the Christian symbols in all of their pristine power.

Enoch Pond felt, of course, like many others,[85] that the symbolic approach was no solution. It reduced the Trinity, for instance, to a fiction, to "mere words, and fancies, and figures of speech". Clearly implied in this statement is the Lockean, Common Sense distrust of figures, the very blindness to symbols as vehicles of truth of which Bushnell so constantly complained. But Bushnell did feel, evidently, that the call for some kind of eternal distinction in the Godhead as the ground for the Trinitarian manifestation had some point. For he attempted later to show, as we have seen, that God eternally reveals himself and is thus eternally a Trinity.

---

[84] Bushnell, *God in Christ*, 106-111. See also above, p. 40.
[85] Pond unfairly charged that Bushnell had "refuted" the doctrine of the Trinity; Hodge and Leonard Bacon, contending against it on the same ground as Pond, stated that he had "rejected" it and "explained it away". The symbolically true, as opposed to the "really" true, had no place in their thinking. See Hodge, Review, 271-273; Bacon, "Review of *God in Christ*", *New Englander*, VII (1849), 325.

This deference to his critics was not needed, however, and is itself open to serious question, as has been pointed out.[86] He spoke more convincingly when he said that what God is like in himself it is not given for man to know. What can be known is the mode in which he has chosen to reveal himself. And Bushnell built a strong case for the view that, when the Trinity is symbolically received, it can be shown to have certain explicit practical values for the religious life.

When viewed from the perspective of his fundamentally different approach to theology and to the meaning and interpretation of symbols, then, much of the criticism that we have made the subject of this section loses its force, and comes to be seen as the pitting of one assumptional ground, with the conclusions drawn from it, against another. Here arguments pro or con can hold little sway until the assumptions themselves are brought into the open and subjected to critical discussion. Bushnell's ideas seemed so self-evidently wrong and even calamitous to his critics, because they blithely attacked his views from the ground of their own assumptions, not taking the trouble to recognize that his thought called for a re-examination of just those kinds of assumptions. Had they been willing to focus the discussion on this deeper level their criticisms might have been less cocksure and emotional, and more penetrating and fair.

We did cite in this section one important weakness in Bushnell's theory, and that was that it makes no clear provision for a positive role for logical reasoning. It is no surprise that Bushnell's critics should have branded him as inconsistent, since, while assailing logic, he yet made such frequent use of it in his own writings.[87] This was, of course, inevitable, for there is some logic (or illogic) involved in almost everything we say. Bushnell did recognize the fact and wanted to insist upon the positive role logic must have in language. And despite the inconsistency with his theory of

---

[86]   See above, pp. 221-223.
[87]   See Lord, Review 127; Brownson, Review, 500, 516; Pond, Review, 12-13. It might also be pointed out that Bushnell's critics accused him of using his theory of language as a kind of smoke screen, into which he could retreat when attacked and when not himself taking the logical offensive against his foes.

language as it stands, his overall intent was abundantly clear. He was calling for a shifting away from abstract to imaginative forms of expression, for an awareness of the limitations of logical language, for a recognition of the dimension of symbolic truth, particularly in religious language. And his own style, so rich with metaphorical allusion and poetic feeling, best illustrates his meaning. If his language theory was not theoretically complete, it was filled with important insights and was at least, we might say, contextually or "organically" valid, in view of the excessive logomachy which marked his time and the stark anti-symbolism of the prevailing conception of language.

5. BUSHNELL IN ERROR IN SETTING FEELINGS OVER THE REASON: "THE ILLUMINATED INTELLECT INFORMS AND CONTROLS THE AFFECTIONS"[88]

A strong implication behind most of the criticisms leveled at Bushnell's theory of language was the conviction that the intellect is prior to the feelings and hence, logic takes precedence over poetry. This conviction was, as we have already seen, the major premise, so to speak, of the Lockean, Common Sense theory of language. Two critics by whom the conviction was stated in just this form were Hodge and Brownson. But it also underlay the assertion of Pond and Bacon that the Trinity and the Atonement must be doctrines which the mind can accept as literal facts, and not just symbolical representations.[89]

---

[88]   C. Hodge, Review, 274.

[89]   Bacon declared that the most serious defect of Bushnell's view of the Atonement was that he "does not seem to recognize the life and death of Christ in this world as having any other than the most incidental relations to the universal government of God. ... In the whole range of theology as a human science, there is nothing grander or more impressive than the theory, the fairest distinction of New England theology — the theory which undertakes to solve the speculative difficulties in regard to forgiveness through Christ's death, by illustrations and arguments drawn from the nature of a moral government. ... The mission of Christ into this world had a high relation to the glory of God in other worlds and to other orders in the creation." Bushnell saw, it was true, the need for God to vindicate his moral purpose and his law, "But the defect of all this is that the necessity thus recognized is a necessity existing in us, and not in

Hodge traced Bushnell's views on language back to that "philosophical mysticism", which he attributed to Neander[90] and
Schleiermacher, by which doctrine was evolved "scientifically"
out of feeling. "Instead of making the objective in religion control
the subjective, it does the reverse. It admits no doctrines but such
as are assumed to be the intellectual expressions of Christian
feeling."[91] By Bushnell this approach had been reduced to a "mere
poetic sentimentalism".[92] In opposition to it Hodge urged recognition of the fact that

The whole healthful power of the things of God over the feelings, depends
upon their being true to the intellect. If we are affected by the revelation
of God as a father, it is because he is a father, and not the picture of one.
If we have peace through faith in the blood of Christ, it is because he is
a propitiation for our sins in reality, and not in artistic form merely. The
Bible is not a cunningly devised fable — a work of fiction, addressed to
the imagination.[93]

Few persons will believe that the life and death of Christ was a mere
liturgical service, a chant and a dirge, to move "the world's mind;" a
pageant with a moral.[94]

---

the exigencies of God's universal government." "Review of *God in Christ*",
New Englander, VII (1849), 325-326. Neither Bacon nor Taylor seemed to
recognize that the whole idea of moral government is analogical and symbolical
in the highest degree, and its entire rationale is the representation of himself
God must impart to his creatures, whether in this or other worlds.
[90]   Bushnell reacted to Neander's *The Planting and Training of the Church*
(trans. J. E. Ryland, Philadelphia: James M. Campbell and Company, 3rd ed.,
1844) with enthusiasm. He mentions the German Church historian in his writings
on language on pp. 94-95 and 114 of *God in Christ* and p. 24 of *Christ in Theology*.
[91]   Hodge, Review, 274. According to a recent work on Schleiermacher's
theological method, this is a misleading oversimplification of his thought,
although it is one which has been a basic assumption in interpretation of his
theology throughout the nineteenth century and up to the present day. Instead
of the usual popular dichotomy between "subjective" and "objective", Schleiermacher substituted the categories of "inner" and "outer", the new alternative
resting "on the supposition that there can be no radical separation of self from
the world, but only an appreciation of one's inner free agency within the world".
T. N. Tice, *Schleiermacher's Theological Method* (Princeton Theological
Seminary Th. D. dissertation, 1961), III.B.1. Bushnell did retain, however, the
usual subjective-objective distinction.
[92]   Hodge, Review, 277.
[93]   Hodge, Review, 269.
[94]   Hodge, Review, 264.

The jaundiced view which a genuinely Christian theology would have to take toward the Bushnellian type of mysticism, with its subordination of rationality to feeling, stemmed in Hodge's mind from the connection of that theology with the Scriptures, the Word of God.

After regeneration, all the operations of the Spirit are in connexion with the Word; and the effects of his influence are always rational — i.e. they involve an intellectual apprehension of the truth, revealed in the scriptures. The whole inward life, thus induced, is therefore dependent on the written word and conformed to it. It is no vague ecstasy of feeling, or spiritual inebriation, in which all vision is lost, of which the Spirit of truth is the author, but a form of life in which the illuminated intellect informs and controls the affections.[95]

Brownson's criticism of Bushnell at this point was far more radical than Hodge's, in that it dwelt not just on the primacy of the rational in theology but also on the paramount role it had in the very origins of human knowledge and speech. The world of the senses was manifold and various in character; it could obviously, therefore, only be given coherence by the reason. The dictum of the ancients, upon which the Lockean psychology, as well as Bushnell's language theory, had been based, was: *nihil est in intellectu, quod non fuerit in sensu.* But this had to be met with the philosopher Leibniz' crucial exception, *nisi ipse intellectus.* And beyond that, the truth had to be added that the intellect could not be constituted without the existence of an "intelligible world, which is objective, above the human intellect, and independent of it".[96] This Platonic realm of intelligibility was the true "logos", the source and reference of all knowledge. Language had also to be viewed as primarily adapted to the intelligible, for

God has evidently placed the intelligible above the sensible, and our great concernment in life is chiefly with truths which pertain to the super-sensible order, that is, moral, political and religious truths. It is these truths that, in the commerce of life, it is chiefly necessary to communicate from one to another, and around which all serious conversation does and must turn. To suppose that God had given us a language for sensibles,

95   Hodge, Review, 273-274.
96   Brownson, Review, 502.

and not for these, is to suppose that he has taken care of what is comparatively trifling, and neglected to provide for matters of grave importance, which would be to suppose him to act from folly, not from wisdom.[97]

Bushnell had made much of the confusion and errors which can arise from language, but Brownson insisted that the difficulties in communication did not lay in language as such, but in the fact that the natural human race, deriving from Adam, had lost its original unity in the intelligible. There was no longer, at least in its original strength, a common reason, on which the common significations of language depended. This was the import of the Tower of Babel story. Language had originally been a gift from God to man, perfectly adapted to his intellectual needs. But with the severance of man's primordial unity, language had come to reflect the disjointed human intellect.

The antidote to this sad state of affairs was not at all, as Bushnell had suggested, the poetic and imaginative use of language. It was rather the restoration of the pristine unity of mankind through spiritual conversion to the elected society of the Roman Catholic Church. In Brownson's eyes, Bushnell was no prophet or seer, as he seemed to regard himself, but one "mentally and morally in a chaotic state". To one who had himself once been in just such a state, he was "an object of tender interest", to be pitied even while his ridiculous antics were being chuckled at. The brethren of the true Church should pray for his conversion.[98]

So far as the specific relation of Bushnell's theory of language to theology was concerned, it seemed to Brownson, in the first place, that it eliminated the possibility of a revelation from God to man. For such a revelation would have to be communicated somehow to the uninspired by the inspired, and how could this be done except through the medium of language? But Bushnell had held that "language is not a medium of thought from mind to mind, and can only by its symbols suggest to the mind addressed the truth it already possesses, or that lies intuitively perceptible or apprehensible

97 Brownson, Review, 502-503.
98 Brownson, Review, 516-517.

before it".[99] Revelation was therefore possible only to those whom God directly or immediately inspires. To all others, as Thomas Paine had said, "revelation is mere hearsay". This was not orthodox Christianity; it was sheer Quakerism.

Secondly, in declaring that Christian truth is not addressed primarily to the intellect, and that it is distorted when put in formal statements, Bushnell had run counter to the plain fact that the intellect was the only faculty for the apprehension of the truth. Without it, the will was blind, for one could hardly obey what he had not first rationally apprehended. Moreover, truth had always to be presented to the mind in some more or less distinct and definite form. The more distinct the propositions in which it was stated, the more readily would it be received and the less likely it was that the mind would fall into error. Far from creating confusion, then, such statements worked to reduce it. "How else", Brownson demanded to know, "will you teach Christian truth, except by means of formal statements? What else is every sermon that is preached, every book that is written, with a view to induce men to believe and practice the Christian religion? No teaching, no instruction is possible without formal statements to the understanding."[100] To disclaim against all intellectual education, and to call for "only moral education, the education of the feelings, of the moral affections and sentiments", as Bushnell had done through his theory of language, was to become a party to "the cant of the day". It was to act as though there were some way in which such education could be imparted without the principal address being made to the intellect.[101]

By way of critical response to these statements we can note, first, that Hodge seemed not to have taken into account the great stress Bushnell laid, in the spirit of the "negative theology" of past Christian thought, upon the Absoluteness of God, his total difference from man. For Bushnell it was the fact of his being totally outside the forms of human contemplation that necessitated his being talked about in figurative speech, just as it was the formless-

99   Brownson, Review, 510.
100   Brownson, Review, 515.
101   Brownson, Review, 515.

ness of second-departmental truths in language that required their being designated with sensible metaphors. Not only did Hodge overlook this important emphasis in the thought of Bushnell, he also got into a rather ridiculous position by pleading that certain biblical conceptions must be "literally" true. What does it mean, for example, to say that God is literally a father? Does he procreate as well as create? The thought is, of course, absurd. Further, does the blood of Jesus propitiate the wrath of God in a literal way, as the animal sacrifice in crude religions is thought to please the nostrils of the deity and, hopefully, curry his favors? If this is the kind of thing that must be believed in for the Bible to be "literally" true, and something other than a "fiction" and a "fable", then it does not deserve belief. And to call Bushnell's conception of the Atonement, which we have unfortunately not had space to study, "a pageant with a moral", is hardly to do justice to those significant considerations of the demands of morality, the conditions of revelation, and the crucial role symbols must play within revelation, which Bushnell so carefully laid down.

Secondly, Hodge's contention that theology must be primarily rational because of its connection with the Word begs the whole question of whether the biblical revelation is primarily symbolical or propositional in character. Thirdly, the Lockean, Common Sense peremptory dismissal of the truth-value of symbolic speech is very much in evidence in Hodge's statements, for he did not think that symbols such as Bushnell found in the Bible could do any more than induce a kind of emotional stupor, "a vague ecstasy of feeling", which must countermand the ministrations of the Spirit of truth. Such a conception of language cuts truth entirely too thin, for it reduces all great literature and the whole symbolism of life to a desultory play of feeling, a superficially pretty, but practically useless, appliqué. With such a view there is obviously something seriously wrong.

In the fourth place, the argument of Brownson that it would be absurd to suppose that God has given us a language for the sensible things in life but not for the supersensible truths of morality, political life, and religion, implies that in Bushnell's language theory God has made no provision for the designation of such truths. The implication is false, of course, for by his theory of the logos Bushnell meant to show how God has provided for a language which can best meet all the needs of man — mental, moral, and spiritual, as well as sensible. What Brownson was really saying was that a metaphorical language with the imperfections Bushnell assigned to it could hardly be said to best provide for the moral and intellectual needs of mankind.

And that belief grew out of his assumption that the intellect is the only faculty for the apprehension of truth, and that truth is always best expressed when put in formal (that is, presumably, plain and non-figurative) language. In this belief he stood squarely on the side of the prevailing conception of language. Bushnell differed from this view by way of basic assumption, for he felt that the imagination is also a "proper inlet" of truth. In fact, he assumed that certainty can only be had in an immediate imaginative grasping of the truth; the truth of language, by contrast, was only "mediate".[102] And since he also thought it to be an observed fact that all words in the second department of language must function metaphorically, rather than literally, he thought that poetic or imaginative forms of speech reveal most clearly how language does, in fact, work. Abstract and formal language was the most "mediate" language of all, for it was farthest removed from the intuitional apprehension of truth, and it tended to obscure the true nature and functioning of language. Also, to press for primacy of this language of formal statements was to shut the mind off entirely from the fact that symbolic speech is far and away the most adequate and, indeed, the most commonplace way of giving expression to the transcendent truths of religion.

Bushnell was certainly right in calling attention to the fact that there are certain kinds of truth which only poetic or symbolic language can meaningfully express. His opponents were wrong to so severely deprecate the role of imaginative language, and their assumption was ill-founded that only a plain style with long-drawn defintions can dependably convey truth in all of its nuances and

---

[102] See Bushnell's sermon "The Immediate Knowledge of God", *Sermons on Living Subjects* (New York: Charles Scribner's Sons, 1903), 119.

types. Any theory must be judged by the degree with which it takes into account all of the pertinent facts of our experience, and by that test the assertions of Brownson restricting truth to formal statements and the prevailing language theory's assumptions along that same line fall far short.

Now it is evident, in making this judgment, that we are using the word "truth" in a specific way that needs to be clarified. Recent analytic theory has made a distinction between "the scientific use of language" and "the emotive use of language". The first kind of speech, it has been said, conveys *information* and can therefore be either true or false. The second kind is meant to arouse in the hearer a certain response, to create in him a certain state of mind. Here the question of truth or falsity does not arise.[103] Obviously, we are not using "truth" in this narrow sense. It is our contention rather that, in the totality of his being, mental and emotional, man stands in such a relationship to his universe (and, Bushnell would say, to its Author) that there are certain verities, or "facts", if you will, about his situation of which he can become aware only through profound existential response, and never by way of disinterested intellectual judgment. This being the case, it is evident that only such language as is able to elicit the appropriate responses can express the "truth" about those verities or facts. And since coldly scientific statements can rarely evoke a response from our whole being, there is an order of truth which they cannot communicate. This is, of course, a religious or an "existential" rendering of truth. It carries with it the implication that poetry, for example, can do far more than just stir up vague emotions inside of us. It can also shed significant light on our existence and deal effectively with some of the most crucial and perplexing problems with which it confronts us. Surely the self-awareness that we gain through the language of religion and of great literature is as much, if not infinitely more, entitled to the word "truth" as the information which ordinary factual or theoretical statements can convey.

---

[103] See L. S. Stebbing, *A Modern Introduction to Logic* (London: Methuen and Company, Ltd., 1933), II, 3: "The Two Uses of Language". The terminological distinction between "scientific" and "emotive" language was first suggested by I. A. Richards in his *The Principles of Literary Criticism*, Chapter XXXIV.

This, then, is the orbit of thinking in which Bushnell's theory of language, in opposition to the prevailing view of language, moves. And it would seem to have a highly germane contribution to make to the problem of the nature of religious language and of religious truth.

Fifthly, Brownson was quite obviously speaking from assumptions which were alien to the thought of Bushnell when he posited a Platonic realm of essences immediately apprehendable by the intellect and directly nameable by words, when he sided with the Divine-gift theory of the origin of language, and when he saw the imperfections of language as but a reflection of that severed intellectual unity which only communion within the Roman Catholic Church could heal. A critical treatment of these points would be futile, since Bushnell's arguments can have effect only with those who assume, as did the champions of the Lockean, Common Sense conception of language, that it is the data of sensation with which the reflective faculties of the mind must deal and that the majority, at least, of our words are sensibly derived.

Sixthly, Brownson's argument that Bushnell's language theory eliminates the possibility of a revelation from God to man can be dealt with. Brownson assumed that revelation consists in communication of knowledge from the inspired to the uninspired. To hold otherwise was "Quakerism". But is it not also long-standing Christian theology? Calvin held, as Augustine had before him, that "the illumination of the Spirit is the true source of understanding in the intellect".[104] And many passages in the Bible, as especially the following one, would seem to give support to the view.

Now we have received not the spirit of the world, but the Spirit which is from God, that we might understand the gifts bestowed on us by God. And we impart this in words not taught by human wisdom but taught by the Spirit, interpreting spiritual truths to those who possess the Spirit.[105]

Revelation, by this view, is not mere information "mediately" imparted. The Bible becomes revelation for any given indivdual when

---

[104] John Calvin, *Institutes* III, ii, 36.
[105] I Corinthians 2:12-13.

he is moved by the immediate agency of the Divine Spirit working within him to make the appropriate responses to the language of the Scriptures. The mediate gains import and significance only in terms of the immediate. And the truth of the Scriptures is not simply information requiring mental assent. It is truth requiring a total response of the human personality, truth which can be grasped only through such a response. It is truth of the order of which we spoke above. Bushnell's language theory coincides exactly with this conception of revelation.[106]

Apart from the historical and Scriptural precedence for this conception of revelation, the observation can be made that, even with Brownson's view that the *revelata* are to be believed in as authoritatively given, instead of on the basis of personal inspiration, it is obvious that the terminology and the symbolism of the revelational data can have no meaning or significance apart from experience within the cultus. One never receives the alleged revelation in a vacuum, in other words. It never comes as a bolt from the blue. Even the revelation of biblical times presupposed the experiences of the nation, and then the Church, which went before it. Revelation can have no meaning, then, apart from an experiential context. No one can understand the revelational language who has not become aware of its grounding in the experience of the people of the Bible and who, further, is not finding their experience to coincide with his own, at least at some outstanding points. Of

---

[106] Brownson cited disparagingly Thomas Paine's complaint that those who have not had the benefit of immediate inspiration by God, or at least are not aware of it, must regard all the claims of revelation as mere "heresay". But interestingly enough, this is the precise import of a passage from Augustine's writings quoted by Calvin. See *Institutes* III, ii, 35. The problem of why some people can lay claim to such an immediate revelation and others cannot posed for both Augustine and Calvin the mystery of election. Brownson's view only pushes the problem back one step farther, for it is a fact that there are some who do and some who do not accept the authority of the system of doctrine set forth by the Roman Catholic Church. Such acceptance, he would lead us to think, is purely a matter of the will. But this is hardly convincing, in view of the fact that the claims of Roman Catholicism represent only one possible choice among many for the will to make. On what basis it does decide that one system of thought is true and others false is the the real question. Here experience (of which one's upbringing is a part) becomes determinative.

the words of the biblical revelation it is perfectly true, therefore, that they

do not literally convey, or pass over a thought out of one mind another, as we commonly speak of doing. They are only hints, or images, held up before the mind of another, to put *him* on generating or reproducing the same thought; which he can do only as he has the same personal contents, or the regenerative power out of which to bring the thought required. Hence, there will be different measures of understanding or misunderstanding, according to the capacity or incapacity, the ingenuousness or moral obliquity of the receiving party — even if the communicating party offers only truth, in the best and freshest forms of expression the language provides.[107]

Despite these important elements of truth, however, Bushnell's theory of language does not escape an indictment implied by Brownson's criticism, namely, that there is something besides direct awareness involved in the functioning of language. There needs to be a distinction made between what Bertrand Russell has called "the knowledge of acquaintance" and "the knowledge of description".[108] Bushnell's theory of language, like that of A. B. Johnson, in connection with which the criticism has already been noted,[109] failed to distinguish between these two kinds of knowledge and to perceive that "Most of our knowledge of things is knowledge by description. If our knowledge were confined to acquaintance we could know very little."[110]

Had Bushnell been astute enough to draw this important distinction, however, he would no doubt have still gone on to point out that, in order to assign characteristics or properties to a thing (knowledge by description) we must know already what those characteristics are. While we may know some characteristics by description, it is obvious that somewhere along the line our knowledge of description must presuppose knowledge by acquaintance. The latter, then, is still prior and is the foundation for the whole superstructure of our descriptive knowledge. This fact makes the

---

[107] Bushnell, *God in Christ*, 46.
[108] See Chapter V of Russell's *The Problems of Philosophy* (London: Oxford University Press, 1912).
[109] See above, pp. 130-131.
[110] Stebbing, *A Modern Introduction to Logic*, 24.

claim for a literal, or absolutely unambiguous, language having reference to the interior data of our minds untenable. We do, of course, know our own minds directly. But since all names or categories of description which we use in talking about our minds are abstractions from the undifferentiated immediacy which is self-consciousness, and since some persons are without a doubt more self-analytical than others, there is bound to be a good deal of latitude for the specific meanings which individuals will assign to words. The knowledge of acquaintance to which our knowledge of description is ultimately referrable is variable from one person to another, therefore, and our words, as abstractions, are at best only approximations of what we "literally" mean. In fact, were there not some degree of ambiguity attaching to words in what Bushnell called the second department of language, we could not communicate at all.[111] The distinction between a knowledge by acquaintance and a knowledge by description does not detract, then, from the basic thrust of Bushnell's language theory, although it does show some of his statements about what goes on when verbal communication takes place to have been technically inaccurate and incomplete.

This concludes our treatment of the criticisms directed at the theory of language of Horace Bushnell in the middle of the nineteenth century. Despite the many misinterpretations, rhetorical caricatures, and unexamined assumptions in those criticisms, they did serve to throw the spotlight of public attention on the language views of Bushnell and to bring to the fore some fundamental questions regarding the nature of language and its religious uses. The bearing of language upon theology had been long perceived, as witness the approach taken by Norton and Taylor toward the doctrine of the Trinity. But the debatable character of many of the

[111] See above, p. 132, item (5) See also Stebbing, *Introduction*, 20. Stebbing prefers the word "vague", however, to "ambiguous". It is notable that not even modern symbolic logic can fulfil the dream of the Lockean, Common Sense theory of language, making reasoning entirely mechanical and eliminating all ambiguity, because it is merely formal. As soon as specific words are inserted in place of the variables in the formulas, ambiguity arises, and the specific formulas themselves are judged to be appropriate to given statements on the basis of inferences made from words.

root assumptions in the Lockean, Common Sense conception of language had been recognized only upon rare occasions prior to Bushnell. Whatever the quality of the criticisms, then, and there were some which were provocative and sound, the problem of the nature of language was at least discussed, and discussed on a level and scale and with an intensity that had no historical precedent in New England, at least outside of Boston. The theory of language set forth by Bushnell thus became an ingredient of some importance in that general ferment out of which a new liberalism in the Trinitarian theology of New England took its rise.

6. AFTERMATH: THEOLOGY IN NEW ENGLAND SUBSEQUENT TO BUSHNELL

There are at least four emphases in Bushnell's language theory which can be found to have played a significant part in the liberal theology of the latter half of the nineteenth century in New England. To point them out is to gain some estimate of the importance the theory has as a focal point for trends of the future. Of course, Bushnell also struck these same emphases in other ways, but nowhere were they made to bear so radically upon theology's entire method and approach as in his theory of language. It is true that the theory as a whole gained little following. But it contributed decisively, as Bushnell himself informs us in the opening pages of *God in Christ*, to the formation of his own theology. And that, in turn, as is well known, was widely influential in the generation which came after him. The theory was also a subtly disintegrating force within the strongholds of the old Calvinistic theology,[112] precisely because it called so many of its underlying methodological assumptions into question for the first time. It therefore made the eventual breaching of the walls by the new liberalism all the more inevitable.

The first important emphasis in the language theory is upon a new freedom and the need for fresh creativity in theological in-

---

[112]   Charles Dole, "Horace Bushnell and His Work for Theology", *The New World*, VIII (1899), 699.

quiry. By pointing to the symbolical character of so much of the traditional language of Christendom, and to the severe limitations of a purely logical method, it helped to pry open the jaws of the vise of rigid rationalism which held captive the spirit of even so original a thinker as Nathaniel W. Taylor, and which goes a long way toward explaining the dogmatic and vituperative atmosphere of the times. One of the best known of the later liberals, Washington Gladden, testified that Bushnell's "introductory essay, on Language, was, for me, a 'Novum Organon', giving me a new sense of the nature of the instrument I was trying to use, and making entirely clear the futility of the ordinary dogmatic method".[113] There must have been many young theologues, weary of the hair-splitting logomachy of their fathers and left cold by their elaborate doctrinal and apologetic defenses, who felt the same way. For them the language theory spelled the freedom to articulate their points of view in a more practical, down-to-earth way than had long been the fashion. It made the fear of heresy seem less important than the maintenance of integrity. It taught them to worry less about being shown deficient in dialectical skill than about foisting an over-intellectualized, academically irrelevant gospel on a people needing to be confronted afresh with the rudiments of the Faith.

A second emphasis in the theory of language is upon the error of interpreting the Bible in a wooden, literalistic fashion. Any significant change in theological method and approach must be marked by a change in attitude toward the Scriptures, and Bushnell's language theory helped immeasurably to bring this latter change about. For it made the Bible less a textbook of facts and arsenal of proofs and more a delight to the heart and imagination, a guide to the mind but not an absolute binder of thought. Its insights were flexible and could be accomodated to the changing times. The way was thus prepared for theologians to react positively, instead of in a hostile negative way, to such new currents of thought as Darwinian evolution and Biblical Criticism. The closer rapprochement between faith and cultural thinking that theological

---

[113] Washington Gladden *Reminiscences* (Boston and New York: Houghton Mifflin Company, 1909), 119.

liberalism was able to achieve in the late nineteenth century was fundamentally dependent, therefore, on the kind of attitude toward the Scriptures that Bushnell's language theory provided for.

A third emphasis in the theory of language is upon religious experience as being of more fundamental importance than detailed dogmatic systems. This stress is of course an unmistakable mark of the new liberalism.[114] For example, Newman Smyth was one of the influential thinkers of the later generation upon whom Bushnell made an impact. And in his plea for a more adequate psychology than that in terms of which the old "Orthodox Rationalism" had been operating, we can see reflected quite clearly this emphasis in the language theory.

We need for Christian theology a psychology which shall be true to the actual processes of man's life; which shall seek to understand consciousness, not by verbal dissection of it, but by following its living development; which shall have some account to give of the rise of ideas out of impressions; of the crystalizations of undefined and general elements of consciousness into conceptions; of the formation of intellectual feelings into rational beliefs. But the habit of regarding reason as the beginning and the end of mind, of reducing the rich manifold development of self-conscious personality to a bare process of thought, and substituting the logic of ideas for the logic of life — in one word, rationalistic narrowness and one-sidedness in mental philosophy, — has hampered theology, and prevented even the intuitionalists from following up their own advantage, and gaining through a better apprehension of the objective and divine significance of mental and moral feeling a complete victory over the skepticism of Kant.[115]

Another example which can be cited of a theologian of the later generation in whose thought the emphasis upon experience held a predominant place was George Harris. Harris took "the Christian consciousness" to be that which gives religious certainty, and lest it be confused with the old Common Sense, he had this to say by way

---

[114] See D. D. Williams, *The Andover Liberals*, 22. For a helpful discussion of the important role played by "experience" as a methodological category in the development of Protestant theology in America, see Williams' essay, "Tradition and Experience in American Theology", in *Religion in American Life: The Shaping of American Religion*, ed. James Ward Smith and A. Leland Jamison (Princeton, New Jersey: Princeton University Press, 1961), 443-495.
[115] Newman Smyth, "Orthodox Rationalism", *The Princeton Review* (Jan.-June, 1882), 299.

of describing it. "The 'consciousness' which grows out of experience has a meaning which is not reproduced by 'consensus' or 'testimony'. It suggests experience, immediateness, and certainty, even when used in its collective sense; and for these no other term yet proposed is an equivalent."[116] Harris was the successor of Edwards Park at Andover; and Park, as we have seen, tried hard to achieve a synthesis between the prevailing conception of language and the theory of Bushnell, insofar as these bore upon theology. The spirit of the attempt was strongly present in Harris, for he held that

Rationalism is as ineffective in defense as in attack. It requires the help of mysticism. The two, which have so often been enemies, should be allies. Either is powerless alone. Rationalism needs to be converted. Mysticism needs to go to school. There should be, not reason alone, nor feeling alone, but reason glowing with emotion, and feeling illuminated with knowledge. In theology as in oratory, the thought should be all feeling, and the feeling all thought.[117]

The connection of theology with oratory is expecially reminiscent of the language theory of Bushnell.

We should also not fail to make mention of Theodore Munger, one of Bushnell's most fervent admirers and the author of a biography of him which, until very recently, was one of only two in existence. In a sermon written just after news had come of Bushnell's death,[118] Munger declared that his wide and compelling influence upon the later theologians had been exerted in four main directions. One of these was Bushnell's opposition to the then prevailing forensic and juridical view of the Atonement, and in discussing it, Munger had this statement to make, bringing out forcibly what we have called the third emphasis in the theory of language.

Bushnell took everything to the test of life and reality. Language for him was the servant, not the master of thought; and even canonized thought, to win acceptance, must prove its applicability to life. Thus the doctrine

---

[116] "The Christian Consciousness — Criticism and Comment", *Andover Review* II (1884), 594. Cited D. D. Williams, *The Andover Liberals*, 88.
[117] "The Function of the Religious Consciousness", *Andover Review* II (1884); 351. Cited D. D. Williams, *The Andover Liberals*, 88.
[118] Bushnell died on February 17, 1876.

of the Atonement became again what it had been in its first formulation, an attempt to explain the function of unmerited suffering. Bushnell's answer laid hold of its observed effect in the moral realm; a return from logic to reality, from deductive theory to induction from fact.[119]

The fourth emphasis in the language theory was upon a generous comprehension of religious differences, the necessity of taking into account all attempted expressions of Christian truth, and not just those of one's own denomination or theological persuasion. Only in this way, so the theory maintained, could one even begin to apprehend the many-sided truth of the Christian symbolism. This too, as Daniel Day Williams has pointed out, is nineteenth-century American liberalism in theology; indeed, it is perhaps its very essence. For "liberalism is not primarily a system of doctrine, but rather an attitude toward doctrine. It is the position that truth can be attained only through a never-ending process of criticism and experiment. It is the willingness to understand many points of view."[120]

The spirit, then, if not the whole content of the theory of language lived on. Perhaps the time has now arrived, in a century so acutely aware of the problem of "the nature, capacities and incapacities of language, as a vehicle of truth", when the content as well can command new respect and even provoke fresh insights. For we have not so far outgrown Horace Bushnell, eloquent spokesman for the needs of his own age and prophet of a coming day.

---

[119]   B. W. Bacon, *Theodore Thornton Munger*, 209-210.

[120]   D. D. Williams, *The Andover Liberals*, 64. H. Shelton Smith cites the theme of "Christian Comprehensiveness" as one of the three basic elements in Bushnell's theological method (along with his conception of religious knowledge and his view of the nature and limitations of theological language), and he notes that none of his three biographers has given any attention to the bearing of this theme upon his thought. Smith attributes this theme to the influence of Victor Cousin upon Bushnell. Cousin espoused an eclectic method of doing philosophy and viewing intellectual history. See H. S. Smith, ed., *Horace Bushnell* (New York: Oxford University Press, 1965), 106-108; 26.

BIBLIOGRAPHY

Adams, Frederic A., "The Collocation of Words in the Greek and Latin Languages, Examined in Relation to the Laws of Thought", *Bibliotheca Sacra*, I (1844).

Bacon, Benjamin W., *Theodore Thornton Munger* (New Haven: Yale University Press, 1913).

Bacon, Leonard, "Review of *God in Christ*", *New Englander*, VII (1849).

——, "Some of the Causes of the Corruption of Pulpit Eloquence", *Biblical Repository*, 2nd s. I (1839).

Bainton, Roland, *Yale and the Ministry* (New York: Harper and Brothers,1957).

Baird, Robert, "Horace Bushnell: A Romantic Approach to the Nature of Theology", *The Journal of Bible and Religion*, XXXIII (July 1965), 229-240.

Barfield, Owen, *Saving the Appearances: A Study in Idolatry* (New York: Harcourt, Brace and World, Inc., A Harbinger Book, n.d.).

Beach, Joseph W., *The Concept of Nature in Nineteenth Century English Poetry* (New York: Macmillan Company, 1936).

Bergson, Henri, *An Introduction to Metaphysics* (trans. T. E. Hulme; New York: The Liberal Arts Press, 1950).

Blair, Hugh, *Lectures on Rhetoric and Belles Lettres* (Philadelphia: James Kay, Jr., and Brother, n.d.).

Blau, Joseph (ed.), *American Philosophic Addresses* (New York: Columbia University Press, 1946).

Bloomfield, Leonard, *Language* (London: George Allen and Unwin, 1935).

Brown, Thomas, *Inquiry into the Relation of Cause and Effect* (Edinburgh: Archibald Constable and Company, 1818).

Brownson, Orestes, Review of *God in Christ*, *Brownson's Quarterly Review*, n.s. III (1849).

Bunsen, Christian C. J., *Christianity and Mankind, Their Beginnings and Prospects* (7 vols.; London: Longman, Brown, Green, and Longmans, 1854).

Burggraaff, Winfield, *The Rise and Development of Liberal Theology in America* (New York: Board of Publication and Bible Work of the Reformed Church in America, n.d.).

Bushnell Centenary (Minutes of the General Association of Connecticut at the One-Hundred and Ninety-Third Annual Meeting, Hartford: Hartford Press, 1902).

Bushnell, Horace, *Building Eras in Religion* (New York: Charles Scribner's Sons, 1903).

——, *Christ in Theology* (Hartford: Brown and Parsons, 1851).

——, *God in Christ* (New York: Charles Scribner's Sons, 1903).

——, *Nature and the Supernatural* (New York: Charles Scribner's Sons, 1903).

——, *Sermons on Living Subjects* (New York: Charles Scribner's Sons, 1903).

——, *The Spirit in Man* (New York: Charles Scribner's Sons, 1903).

Calvin, John, *Institutes of the Christian Religion* (2 vols, trans. Henry Beveridge; Grand Rapids, Michigan: William B. Eerdman's Publishing Company, 1953).

Cardell, William S., *Essay on Language* (New York: Charles Wiley, 1825).

Cheney, Mary B., *Life and Letters of Horace Bushnell* (New York: Charles Scribner's Sons, 1903).

Cherry, Conrad, "The Structure of Organic Thinking: Horace Bushnell's Approach to Language, Nature and Nation", *Journal of the American Academy of Religion* XL, 1 (March, 1972), 3-20.

Christian, William A., *Meaning and Truth in Religion* (Princeton, New Jersey: Princeton University Press, 1964).

Coleridge, Samuel Taylor, *Aids to Reflection* (ed. James Marsh; Burlington, Vermont: Chauncey Goodrich, printer, 1829).

Cross, Barbara, *Horace Bushnell: Minister to a Changing America* (Chicago: University of Chicago Press, 1958).

Day, H. N., "Eloquence a Virtue", *Biblical Repository*, 2nd s. X (1849).

Dole, Charles, "Horace Bushnell and His Work for Theology", *The New World*, VIII (1899).

Durfee, Harold A., "Language and Religion: Horace Bushnell and Rowland G. Hazard", *American Quarterly*, V (1953).

Eckermann, John, *Conversations of Goethe* (trans. John Oxenford; London: George Bell and Sons, 1879).

Edwards, Jonathan, *Images and Shadows of Divine Things* (ed. Perry Miller; New Haven: Yale University Press, 1948).

Emerson, Ralph Waldo, *Works* (12 vols.; Boston: Houghton, Mifflin and Company, 1887).

Farrar, Frederic W., *The Origin of Language* (London: John Murray, 1860).

Faust, Clarence H. and Johnson, Thomas H., *Jonathan Edwards: Representative Selections* (New York: American Book Company, 1935).

Feidelson, Charles, *Symbolism and American Literature* (Chicago: University of Chicago Press, 1953).

Fosdick, David, "Language", *Biblical Repository*, 1st s. X (1873).

Foster, Frank H., *A Genetic History of the New England Theology* (Chicago: University of Chicago Press, 1907).

Gibbs, Josiah, "Historical and Critical View of Cases in the Indo-European Languages", *The Christian Spectator*, IX (1837).

——, "On the Natural Significancy of Articulate Sounds", *Biblical Repository*, 2nd s. II (1839).

——, *Philological Studies* (New Haven: Durrie and Peck, 1857).

Gladden, Washington, *Reminiscences* (Boston and New York: Houghton Mifflin Company, 1909).

Goodrich, C. A., "What Does Dr. Bushnell Mean?" (a series of three articles in the *New York Evangelist*, XX. 13-15, March 29-April 12, 1849).

Goodwin, Henry M., "Thoughts, Words, and Things", *Bibliotheca Sacra*, VI 1849).

Hammar, George, *Christian Realism in Contemporary American Theology* (Uppsala, Sweden, 1940).

Hastings, George H., "Lyrical Poetry of the Bible", *Biblical Repository*, 3rd s. III (1847).

Hazard, Rowland G., *Essay on Language and Other Papers* (ed. E. P. Peabody; Boston: Phillips, Sampson and Company, 1857).

Heininger, Harold R., *The Theological Technique of a Mediating Theologian — Horace Bushnell* (part of a doctoral dissertation distributed privately by the University of Chicago Libraries; Chicago: University of Chicago Libraries, 1935).

Hodge, Charles, Review of *God in Christ, Princeton Review*, n.s. XXI (1849).

Hubbard, F. M., "Study of the Works of Nature", *Biblical Repository*, 1st s. VI (1835).

"Illustrations of the Elementary Principles of the Structure of Language", *Princeton Review*, 1st s. III (1827). Author undesignated.

James, William, *Varieties of Religious Experience* (New York: The Modern Library, 1929).

Johnson, Alexander B., *A Treatise on Language, or The Relations of Words to Things* (ed. David Rynin; Berkeley and Los Angeles: University of California Press, 1959).

Kant, Immanuel, *Critique of Pure Reason* (trans. Norman Kemp Smith; London: Macmillan and Company Ltd., 1958).

Kirby, William, *On the Power, Wisdom and Goodness of God, as Manifested in the Creation of Animals and in Their History, Habits, and Instincts* (2 vols.; London: William Pickering, 1835).

Locke, John, *Essay Concerning Human Understanding* (2 vols, ed. Alexander Frazer; New York: Dover Publications, 1959).

Lord, David, "Review of Bushnell's 'Dissertation on Language'", *The Theological and Literary Journal*, II (1849-50).

Lowth, Robert, *Lectures on the Sacred Poetry of the Hebrews* (ed. Calvin E. Stowe, trans. G. Gregory; Andover: Flagg and Gould, 1829).

Mead, Sidney E., *Nathaniel W. Taylor* (Chicago: The University of Chicago Press, 1942).

Means, John O., "Recent Theories on the Origin of Language", *Bibliotheca Sacra*, XXVII (1870).

Miller, Perry, "Jonathan Edwards to Emerson", *New England Quarterly*, XIII (1940).

——, *The New England Mind: The Seventeenth Century* (New York: Macmillan Company, 1939).

Miller, Perry (ed.), *The Transcendentalists. An Anthology* (Cambridge: Harvard University Press, 1950).

Miller, Perry, and Johnson, Thomas H., *The Puritans* (New York: American Book Company, 1938).

Morell, J. D., *Philosophy of Religion* (New York: D. Appleton and Company, 1849).

——, *The Philosophical Tendencies of the Age* (London: Robert Theobald, n.d.).

Müller, Max, *The Science of Language* (2 vols; New York: Charles Scribner's Sons, 1891).

Munger, Theodore, *Horace Bushnell* (Boston: Houghton, Mifflin and Company, 1889).

Nash, Arnold S. (ed.), *Protestant Thought in the Twentieth Century* (New York: The Macmillan Company, 1951).

Neander, Augustus, *The Planting and Training of the Church* (trans. J. E. Ryland; Philadelphia: James M. Campbell and Company, 1844).

Niswonger, Donald, *Nature and the Supernatural as Reflected in the Theological Works and Sermons of Horace Bushnell* (New York: Union Theological Seminary S. T. M. Thesis, 1961).

Norton, Andrews, *A Statement of Reasons for Not Believing the Doctrines of Trinitarians Concerning the Nature of God and Person of Christ* (Boston: American Unitarian Association, 1875).

——, *Tracts Concerning Christianity* (Cambridge: John Bartlett, 1852).

Ong, Walter, *Ramus, Method, and the Decay of Dialogue* (Cambridge: Harvard University Press, 1958).

"The Origin of Language", *Princeton Review*, n.s. XXIV (1852). Author unindicated.

Park, Edwards, "Connection Between Theological Study and Pulpit Eloquence", *Biblical Repository*, 1st s. X (1837).

——, "The Proper Mode of Exhibiting Theological Truth", *Biblical Repository*, 1st s. X (1837).

——, "The Theology of the Intellect and That of the Feelings", *Bibliotheca Sacra*, VII (1850).

Paul, Sherman, "*Horace Bushnell Reconsidered*", *ETC*, VI (1948-49).

Pond, Enoch, *Review of Dr. Bushnell's 'God in Christ'* (Bangor, Maine: E. F. Duren, 1849).

Rauch, F. A., *Psychology* (New York: M. W. Dodd, 1844).

Reed, Sampson, "Observations on the Growth of the Mind" (Boston: Cummings, Hiliard and Company, 1826).

Review of *God in Christ*, *The Christian Observatory*, III (1849). Author unindicated.

Review of *God in Christ*, *The Princeton Review*, n.s. XXI (1849). Author unindicated.

Review of Matthew Harrison's *The Rise, Progress and Structure of the English Language*, *Princeton Review*, n.s. XXII (1850). Author unindicated.

Review of Rowland Hazard's *Essay on Language and Other Papers*, *The Christian Examiner*, LXIII (1857). Author unindicated.

Russell, Bertrand, *The Problems of Philosophy* (London: Oxford University Press, 1912).

Schlegel, Frederick von, *The Philosophy of Language in a Course of Lectures* (trans. A. J. W. Morrison; London: Henry G. Bohn. 1847).

Shedd, W. G. T., "The Relation of Language to Thought", *Bibliotheca Sacra*, V (1848).

Smith, George, *The Origin and Progress of Language* (New York: Lane and Scott, 1849).

Smith, H. Shelton, *Changing Conceptions of Original Sin* (New York: Charles Scribner's Sons, 1958).

Smith, H. Shelton, (ed.), *Horace Bushnell* (New York: Oxford University Press, 1965).

Smith, Timothy L., *Revivalism and Social Reform in Mid-Nineteenth Century America* (New York, 1957).

Smith, Wilfred Cantwell, "The Faith of Other Men" (a lecture series broadcast over WRVR, Riverside Radio in New York City, March 4-April 15, 1962).

Smyth, Newman, "Orthodox Rationalism", *The Princeton Review* (Jan.-June, 1882).

Stebbing, L. S., *A Modern Introduction to Logic* (London: Methuen and Company, Ltd., 1933).

Stewart, Dugald, *Elements of the Philosophy of the Human Mind* (Brattleborough, Vermont: William Fessenden, 1808).

Stuart, Moses, "F. Schleiermacher 'On the Discrepancy Between the Sabellian and Athanasian Method of Representing the Doctrine of the Trinity'", *Biblical Repository*, V (1835), VI (1835).

——, *Miscellanies* (Andover: Allen, Morrill, and Wardwell, 1846).

Sweet, William W., *The Story of Religion in America* (New York: Harper and Brothers, 1950).

Taylor, Benjamin F., *The Attractions of Language* (Hamilton, New York: Atwood and Griggs, 1843).

Taylor, Nathaniel W., *Essays, Lectures, Etc., Upon Select Topics in Revealed Theology* (New York: Clark, Austin and Smith, 1859).

"Theological Systems Modified by Mental Peculiarities", *Biblical Repository*, 3rd s. V (1849). Author unindicated.

Tice, Terrence N., *Schleiermacher's Theological Method* (Princeton Theological Seminary Th. D. dissertation, 1961).

Tillich, Paul, *Dynamics of Faith* (New York: Harper Torchbooks, 1958).

Thilly, Frank, and Ledger Wood, *A History of Philosophy* (New York: Henry Holt and Company, 1951).

Thompson, Ernest T., *Changing Emphases in American Preaching* (Philadelphia: The Westminster Press, 1943).

Toksvig, Signe, *Emanuel Swedenborg* (New Haven: Yale University Press, 1948).

Urmson, J. O., *Philosophical Analysis* (Oxford: Clarendon Press, 1958).

Walker, Williston, *Great Men of the Christian Church* (Chicago: University of Chicago Press, 1908).

Whatley, Richard, *Elements of Logic* (New York: William Jackson, 1834).

Whitehead, Alfred North, *Religion in the Making* (New York: Macmillan Co., 1926).

——, *Science and the Modern World* (New York: New American Library, 1948)

Whitney, William D., *Language and the Study of Language* (New York: Charles Scribner and Company, 1869).

Williams, Daniel D., *The Andover Liberals* (New York: Kings Crown Press, 1941).

——, "Tradition and Experience in American Theology", in *Religion in American Life: The Shaping of American Religion*, ed. James W. Smith and A. Leland Jamison (Princeton, New Jersey: Princeton University Press, 1961).

Williams, George H. (ed.), *The Harvard Divinity School* (Boston: The Beacon Press, 1954).

Wilson, John, *Language and Christian Belief* (London: Macmillan and Company, Ltd., 1958).

INDEX OF NAMES

SUBJECT INDEX

PHILOSOPHY PUBLICATIONS

BROWN, CECEL H., *Wittgensteinian Linguistics* (= Approaches to Semiotics, Paperback Series, 12). 1974. 136 pp. Paperbound
Dfl. 22,—

BRUZINA, RONALD, *Logos and Eidos: The Concept in Phenomenology* (= Janua Linguarum, Series Minor, 93). 1971. 184 pp. Paperbound
Dfl. 21,—

BUTRICK, RICHARD JR., *Carnap on Meaning and Analyticity* (= Janua Linguarum, Series Minor, 85). 1970. 77 pp. Paperbound
Dfl. 12,—

CHAMPIGNY, ROBERT, *Ontology of the Narrative: An Analysis* (= De Proprietatibus Litterarum, Series Minor, 12). 1972. 114 pp. Cloth-bound
Dfl. 18,—

CLARKE, BOWMAN, *Language and Natural Theology* (= Janua Linguarum, Series Minor, 47). 1966. 181 pp. Paperbound
Dfl. 30,—

COOK, DANIEL J., *Language in the Philosophy of Hegel* (= Janua Linguarum, Series Minor 135). 1973. 198 pp. Paperbound
Dfl. 28,—

DRANGE, THEODORE M., *Type Crossings: Sentential Meaninglessness in the Border Area of Linguistics and Philosophy* (= Janua Linguarum, Series Minor, 44). 1966. 218 pp. Paperbound
Dfl. 29,—

ERDE, EDMUND L., *Philosophy and Psycholinguistics* (= Janua Linguarum, Series Minor, 160). 1973. 239 pp. Paperbound
Dfl. 38,—

GIANNONI, CARLO B., *Conventionalism in Logic: A Study in the Linguistic Foundation of Logical Reasoning* (= Janua Linguarum, Series Maior, 46). 1971. 157 pp. Clothbound
Dfl. 32,—

GRAVA, ARNOLDS, *A Structural Inquiry into the Symbolic Representation of Ideas* (= Studies in Philosophy, 18) 1969. 176 pp. Paperbound
Dfl. 27,—

GREENLEE, DOUGLAS, *Peirce's Concept of Sign* (= Approaches to Semiotics, Paperback Series, 5). 1973. 148 pp. Paperbound
Dfl. 18,—

MOUTON · PUBLISHERS · THE HAGUE

HARDWICK, CHARLES S., *Language Learning in Wittgenstein's Later Philosophy* (= Janua Linguarum, Series Minor, 104). 1971. 152 pp. Paperbound   Dfl. 18,—

HARTNACK, JUSTUS, *Language and Philosophy* (= Janua Linguarum, Series Minor, 157). 1972. 140 pp. Paperbound   Dfl. 21,—

JULIARD, PIERRE, *Philosophies of Language in Eighteenth-Century France* (= Janua Linguarum, Series Minor, 18). 1970. 111 pp. Paperbound
                                                                Dfl. 16,—

LANIGAN, RICHARD L., *Speaking and Semiology: Maurice Merleau-Ponty's Phenomenological Theory of Existential Communication* (= Approaches to Semiotics, 22.). 1972. 257 pp. Clothbound
                                                                Dfl. 50,—

LARKIN, SISTER MIRIAM T., C. S. J., *Language in the Philosophy of Aristotle* (= Janua Linguarum, Series Minor, 87). 1971. 113 pp. Paperbound   Dfl. 15,—

MATILAL, BIMAL K., *Epistemology, Logic, and Grammar in Indian Philosophical Analysis* (= Janua Linguarum, Series Minor, 111). 1971. 183 pp. Paperbound   Dfl. 28,—

MCKINNON, ALASTAIR, *Falsification and Belief* (= Studies in Philosophy, 25). 1970. 106 pp. Paperbound   Dfl. 20,—

MILO, RONALD D., *Aristotle on Practical Knowledge and Weakness of Will* (= Studies in Philosophy, 6). 1966. 144 pp. Paperbound
                                                                Dfl. 20,—

MORAN, JOHN, *Toward the World and Wisdom of Wittgenstein's "Tractatus"* (= Studies in Philosophy, 26). 1973. 126 pp. Paperbound
                                                                Dfl. 24,—

REILLY, JOHN P., *Cajetan's Notion of Existence* (= Studies in Philosophy, 4). 1971. 131 pp. Paperbound   Dfl. 25,—

SHEIN, LOUIS J., (ED), *Readings in Russian Philosophical Thought: Logic and Aesthetics.* Translated from the Russian. 1973. 337 pp. Paperbound   Dfl. 30,—

THOMPSON, KENNETH F., *Whitehead's Philosophy of Religion* (= Studies in Philosophy, 20). 1971. 199 pp. Paperbound   Dfl. 30,—

TRACY, THEODORE J., *Physiological Theory and the Doctrine of the Mean in Plato and Aristotle* (= Studies in Philosophy, 17). 1969. 396 pp. Paperbound   Dfl. 52,—

MOUTON · PUBLISHERS · THE HAGUE